GULF CITY COOK BOOK

The Library of Alabama Classics,

reprint editions of works important

to the history, literature, and culture of

Alabama, is dedicated to the memory of

Rucker Agee

whose pioneering work in the fields

of Alabama history and historical geography

continues to be the standard of

scholarly achievement.

GULF CITY COOK BOOK

Compiled by
THE LADIES OF THE ST. FRANCIS STREET METHODIST EPISCOPAL CHURCH, SOUTH, MOBILE, ALABAMA, 1878

With an Introduction by
George H. Daniels

The University of Alabama Press
Tuscaloosa and London

Manufactured in the United States of America

This Library of Alabama Classics reprint edition is a
facsimile of the original 1878 edition.

∞

The paper on which this book is printed meets the minimum
requirements of American National Standard for Information
Science-Permanence of Paper for Printed Library Materials,
ANSI Z39.48-1984.

Library of Congress Cataloging-in-Publication Data

Gulf City cook book / compiled by the ladies of the St. Francis Street
Methodist Episcopal Church, South, Mobile, Alabama, 1878; with an
introduction by George H. Daniels.

p. cm. — (The Library of Alabama classics)

Reprint. Originally published: Dayton, Ohio : United Brethren Pub.
House, 1878.

Includes bibliographicl references and index.

ISBN 0-8173-0508-4

1. Cookery—Alabama—Mobile. 2. Mobile (Ala.)—History, I. St.
Francis Street Methodist Episcopal Church, South (Mobile, Ala.)
II. Series.

TX715.G937 1990 90-11048
641.59761'22—dc20 CIP

British Library Cataloguing-in-Publication Data available

CONTENTS

The St. Francis Street Methodist Church, 1905. Except for the poles and wires, this photograph shows the scene as it would have appeared in 1878. *(St. Francis Street Methodist Church)*

INTRODUCTION

George H. Daniels

In 1876 when the ladies of the St. Francis Street Methodist Church began compiling a cookbook from the recipes of eighty-two members, the liveliest topic of discussion in Mobile was the imminent departure of the last of the Federal troops who had been there to manage the process of Reconstruction since the end of the Civil War. The city, which ranked third in the nation in the value of its exports in 1860, had suffered badly during the war because of the long blockade followed by Farragut's naval bombardment and the explosion of an ordnance depot that devastated the warehouse area of twenty square blocks. After the war, Mobile had not recovered from the damage: by the late seventies, it was well into a twenty-five-year period of economic decline so severe that before the decade ended it would voluntarily give up its charter and go into a kind of receivership. The years of Civil War, Reconstruction with its special economic demands, and two subsequent depressions had combined to leave the town in a state bordering upon economic ruin. The railroad building boom of the postwar years, heralded as the salvation of Mobile because it would bring the goods of north Alabama to the port city for export, had in reality diverted trade to inland cities or to ports with better harbor facilities. The city wharves, purchased at "enormous expense," according to the city auditor, were a constant drain on resources.[1] Cotton was no longer to be relied upon, and the anticipated forest products, coal, and other goods from the interior had not taken its place. After the initial spurt in activity to satisfy the pent-up demand of the wartime years, overall shipping at Mobile had declined steadily since 1871 and would continue to do so until the early 1880s, when the harbor was deepened by a few feet and further work was done on the river system leading from northern Alabama into the city.

As depressed as the city's commerce was, the manufacturing picture was equally grim. In 1880, census takers counted a total of ninety-one manufacturing establishments in the county, but their combined capitalization was barely over half a million dollars—less than $5,500 each, and total value of their products for 1879 had been just $1,335,579. Worse yet, the failed economic "improvements" of the Reconstruction period had left the citizens, who had financed much of the building, with such personal indebtedness that in many cases they were unable to pay the taxes that had been levied to service the city's bonded debt. Interest due to bond holders could not be met in 1875. The result was that Mobile in 1878 entered into what was known locally as the "seven years depression," which reached bottom in 1884 with the collapse of the Bank of Mobile. Meanwhile, in 1879, the city charter was revoked and the state established and operated the Port of Mobile as part of a relief package. All that was left of city government was a three-member commission and a police board to perform minimal administrative functions. This remained the situation until 1886, when a new charter was granted.

Still, Mobile was the state's most populous city, and its prewar population of 29,258 (1860 census) had grown to 32,034 by 1870, but then began a decline that lasted through the next decade.[2] Social stagnation had accompanied the economic downturn. Palmer Pillans, born in Mobile two years before the cookbook's publication, was correct when he looked back nearly a hundred years later and generalized that there had been no material change in the structure of life during the Reconstruction period. "The same people lived in the same houses and in the same social groupings in which they had always lived," he concluded.[3]

Whatever impact Reconstruction had on rearranging the southern social structure, there is little evidence that it reached Alabama's Port City. While it may be a biased sample, a brief look at the social backgrounds of the women who compiled this book certainly confirms Palmer Pillans' conclusion. Of the eighty-two listed contributors, it was possible to identify sixty-eight as the wives of urban middle-class professionals—attorneys, cotton or timber factors, real estate brokers, bankers, commission merchants, or insurance executives. Included in the list were the wives of the pastor of the church, two former mayors, six corporation presidents, and the long-time president of the Board of Trade. These husbands for the most part had their offices within a few blocks of the St. Francis Street Church, which sat at the western edge of Mobile's business district. "Downtown" consisted of two cobblestone paved streets running parallel to the river and four others covered for about three blocks each with oyster shells and running down to the river. Most of the wholesale businesses were located on the cobblestone streets, which could bear the stream of heavy wagon traffic, and the retail business was conducted along the twelve- or fourteen-block area of the shell streets.

The picture had been practically the same in 1860; eighteen years of war, social shock, and economic panics had done little to disturb the situation. The same business offices were there and were occupied by many of the same people. The husbands of fifty-seven of the cookbook contributors had been in positions of the same social status in the last year before the war as they were in 1878. Only eight had been clearly upwardly mobile, and nine did not appear in the city directory until 1866 or later. The remaining eight could not be definitely identified. None is known to have suffered a decline in status during that time.

The Southern Market and other municipal buildings, about 1880, looking south on Royal Street. *(Local History and Genealogy Division, Mobile Public Library)*

While Mobile's economy was lagging, in the 1870s the forces of industrialization and urbanization were creating a major transition in the American style of life. Drawing upon the possibilities offered by new transportation networks and the development of mechanical refrigeration techniques, food processing and delivery systems changed more during that decade than in any previous one, and as much, perhaps, as in any since then. The railroad network had rapidly expanded since the end of the Civil War to tie together every section of the country. Carrying fruits and vegetables from southern farms to northern cities, it created important new industries in Florida, Georgia, and Alabama, while increasing the health and well-being of the urban Americans who were on their way toward becoming a majority of the nation's population.

In 1878, Gustavus Swift had just sent his first specially designed refrigerator cars to carry fresh beef from Chicago to the cities of the east, and it would be many more years before they reached the Gulf Coast. However, refrigerated shipments of fish, including walleyes, bass, and pike from the Great Lakes, salmon from California, cod from the Atlantic, and oysters from the Gulf were already common in more affluent households in every part of the country. Liquids, especially milk and lager beer, a variety introduced by German immigrants during the 1840s, were shipped in the same kind of ice pack cars that carried oysters. Lager beer, unlike other types, required storage in cool temperatures after fermentation, and it had become a favorite of Americans. With the production centered in Cincinnati, there were generally good supplies of natural ice for cooling and the facilities of a major railroad network for shipment. The first artificial ice plant in the United States, the Louisiana Ice Manufacturing Company, had not been established until 1865, and by 1870 it had been joined by only three others. By 1880, however, thirty-five could be counted, and the long dependence upon a natural ice supply was nearing its end.

Improvements in can-making and organizational techniques within the industry resulted in a three-fold increase in American canned food consumption and the beginning of a thriving export market during the decade. In the single year of 1877, 21,000,000 pounds of canned goods with a value of over one and a quarter million dollars, were exported. From a modest 97 establishments canning fruits and vegetables in 1870, the census charted the growth to 411 by 1880, and it showed a doubling during the next decade. The canning of oysters, lobster, and shrimp, begun before the war as a solution to the shipping problems of Atlantic Coast fishermen, had also grown into a substantial industry. Technology was thus laying the groundwork for the submergence of regional differences and culinary traditions, but at the same time Americans were being offered a wider choice of foods than they had ever had before, and the result may have been a healthier diet for many people.

Although the inflated wartime and immediate postwar conditions had at first led to major price increases for foodstuffs, technical innovations and transportation improvements had begun bringing the prices down by the early seventies—the decade witnessed major decreases in the prices for beef, flour, and many other foods including canned goods, poultry, rice, sugar, and cheese, which was just moving into factory production and becoming a regular part of the American diet.[4]

The making of bread, still the staff of life for all social classes, had been enormously simplified by the development of roller-processing techniques that created a product with standardized quality that traveled well and was not so perishable as earlier flour. While it is true that most of the nutrition was squeezed out of the grain by the new process, it should also be recognized that its first major effect was to boost home baking, for it took a great deal less talent and effort to bake with the new superfine flour than was required with older flours. Home baking became simpler yet when a commercially prepared baking powder came on the market just before the Civil War and when compressed yeast cakes came on the scene about 1870. Such innovations made the job of baking a great deal easier for the ordinary housewife and no doubt explains the great variety of bread and cake recipes in all of the cookbooks of the 1870s, for the technology that was to take most of the baking out of urban homes—the continuous oven—only began to become available in that decade. Mobile's first such oven, the Alabama Steam Bakery, with a capacity to use two barrels of flour per hour, was not opened until early in 1879, and it was near the century's end before power mixers and power dough breaks became common bakery equipment.[5]

Added to such important cooking aids was a simplification of menus and dining styles prompted in part by growing urbanization and made urgent by the increasing difficulty in America of finding skilled household help. Even company dinners, observed one writer in 1870, were "not so sumptuous now as they formerly were."[6] Although that observer attributed the change primarily to the increasing cost of food, declining food prices during the next few years did nothing to reverse the trend he described. From the longer perspective of history, there is nothing more obvious than the fact that the groaning sideboards, the elaborate entrees, and the multiple-course dinners of the early nineteenth century, however much admired by modern food writers, were incredibly labor intensive. A formal dinner for eight that met all the expectations of diners of the 1830s would have required at least three servants to tend the table in addition to two others in the kitchen, and in America such labor was becoming impossible to get, except for the very rich who were able to import trained staffs from Europe. It is probably true that so far as the higher economic strata were concerned, the number and quality of servants played a more important role than did the cost of ingredients in determining what could be served.[7]

By the 1870s, the already difficult "help" situation had been exacerbated by the new opportunities for women's employment opened up by the industrial revolution and growing urbanizaton. Employment opportunities in stores, shops, or factories were all preferred to housework, in part because such jobs carried higher status than being a "servant," and also because they at least offered limited hours with a good bit more freedom. The result, according to one observer, was that all "girls" who went out to service viewed the occupation as temporary until they married or found some more congenial work. The consequent need for the mistress of a household to manage a constantly changing—and not very well trained—staff imposed new and often unfamiliar requirements upon young middle-class housewives. As one early leader in the cookbook industry said, "The mistress ought always to be able to do everything better and quicker than any domestic ever dared think of doing it."[8] Southern women, because of the more or less permanent staff supplied by slavery, were late in feeling the "help problem," but it struck them with particular force when it did come. As a popular work written by a St. Louis lady in 1876 put it, the author had been motivated by her conviction that American women were terrible cooks and that southern women, because they had so long been accustomed to slaves doing the cooking, were somewhat worse than others.[9]

The proliferation beginning in the early seventies of cookbooks and, in larger urban centers, of cooking schools, was an early response to these changing circumstances. By the end of the decade, schools attracting women (and some men as well) of virtually every social level had been founded in Boston and New York, and in Philadelphia Sarah Rorer, who was to become the leading cooking instructress in the nation, was taking lessons at the forerunner of her famous Philadelphia Cooking School.[10] Although the publication boom began earlier, it was these schools that produced the best known of the late-nineteenth-century American cookbooks.

According to the author of one important compilation, cookbooks rank among the best of the historical and sociological sources for the study of any culture with a written record.[11] While there may well be other types of writings to vie with cookbooks for the designation of "best" source, there is no doubt that eating is such a basic human activity that works dealing with it do reveal a great deal about the society that produces them. This observation must especially be the case in the South, for that region has always had a distinctive food. Writers on the history of southern cuisine typically believe that the discovery of what has happened in southern kitchens and dining rooms will lead to deeper knowledge of such matters as physical health and economic conditions, as well as to a better understanding of regional mores.[12]

The very fact that a great many cookbooks were produced during a given period tells us something important about the society, and it is certainly true that all over the South cookbooks were designed especially for southern white women who, as a recent student of southern culture remarked, "found themselves quite literally help-less after the Civil War."[13] Some of the books, however, are much better than others in telling us about the way people actually lived, cooked, and ate. The didactic work, such as that produced by the cooking schools or even a compilation by a single author, is not especially useful for this kind of information, for it typically tends to select the "best" from a wide variety of sources in the hope that readers may be taught to improve themselves. One book that sold widely in the South, for example, *The Dixie Cookbook,* was published in 1879 by Estelle Woods Wilcox, a northerner who two years earlier had published *Buckeye Cookery and Practical*

Housekeeping for an entirely different audience and soon produced others for Colorado and for Minnesota readers. Of one popular Reconstruction era cookbook, *Mrs. Porter's New Southern Cookery,* the Chicago chef and cookbook collector Louis Szathmary cautioned that one should not expect to find "what is generally called Southern cooking"; on the contrary, her self-appointed mission seemed to be to help southern cooks change their style. One student has termed such works "reconciliation" cookbooks, pointing out that it is a Yankee fruitcake, not the Confederate one, that Mrs. Porter pronounces "unrivaled."[14] Similarly, Mrs. Henderson, who did live in St. Louis, after noting that American women were terrible cooks, included careful directions for service a la Russe and in the English mode, expressing a preference for the compromise plan attributed to the French. She included recipes taken directly from Careme and Brillat-Savarin, and she several times mentioned recipes learned in London.[15] Whatever its value for other purposes, her book does not describe the cuisine of St. Louis in the mid-1870s. Like others of its kind, it may indeed have described no cuisine on earth, although the publication of so many and especially the frequent reissues indicate a need for such works.

The *Gulf City Cook Book* had nothing in common with the books of either Mrs. Porter or Mrs. Henderson. It was a relatively new type of publication that seems to have been invented in the United States and still to my knowledge is found only here—the charitable compilation composed of recipes contributed by a large number of individuals, most commonly a ladies' group, privately printed, and sold on a local basis for the benefit of some organization. A great virtue of nineteenth-century examples of such committee work is that it really did represent the regional cuisine.[16] The apparent popularity of this particular work is one indication of its acceptability in its region—during the next thirty-one years it went through at least four separate printings and a second edition. The real scarcity of surviving copies, along with their dog-eared appearance, suggests that it saw a great deal of use.

It is clear that the authors were responding to some of the same conditions that produced the cooking schools. The generally carefully written recipes and the extremely elementary information on the basics of cookery are indications that the ladies looked upon themselves as filling a need by offering basic instruction for unskilled cooks. The novice, for example, was reminded to stir mushrooms with a silver spoon, which it was widely believed would turn dark if poisonous toadstools were present. She was told to test eggs by putting them in water; if the large end turned up, they were not fresh. But just in case, it was best to break eggs into a saucer before putting them in the frying pan, for only in this way could one be certain. Under "How to cook a beefsteak," the contributor began with a caution to wipe dry the cooking vessel and proceeded step by step in language that could be followed by one who had never seen a beefsteak.[17] And also in the interest of basic instruction, the book contains examples of typically southern dishes. There are recipes for grits, for greens, for hominy bread, for the basic skillet bread, and enough variations on sawmill gravy to clog many an artery. For example, it is served with fried liver, hash, and squirrel and with the favorite fowl of the time, canvassback duck. Clearly, the audience for whom this work was compiled was hardly composed of skilled cooks.

There are enough obviously economical dishes included in the book to suggest that the hard times were affecting even ladies of the professional classes. There is, for example, an extremely interesting "Jam Bolaya" that uses the giblets, neck, and feet of a chicken along with the very cheap local oysters to produce a dish that would probably have fed a family of four for a cash outlay of about eight or nine cents, if one had to buy the two dozen oysters, or two to three cents if the oysters came free.[18] The large number of recipes scattered throughout the book calling for leftovers or stale bread suggests the need to economize that has always been characteristic of southern cooking. Time and again, the suggestion "nice breakfast dish" or "delicious for breakfast" is noted in recipes using leftover fish, potatoes, ham, veal, or the general "meat." Of special interest under this heading are such dishes as fish pudding (p. 20), cod-fish balls (p. 21), ham and potato balls (p. 85), and veal patties (p. 43). They are all recommended both as good food and as good examples of a theme that has always been important in southern cooking.

Eggs were not cheap if one had to buy them, running up to thirty cents a dozen during the winter. However, the ownership of chickens, even by middle-class city residents, was so common that eggs could almost be regarded as a free good during much of the year. This no doubt explains their appearance more frequently than any other single item in the book. Not only is there an entire chapter of egg recipes, but also they are used as a garnish, a thickener, and an accompaniment for meat. They are boiled and chopped up in soups (even in an okra soup), and their yolks are rubbed with oil, vinegar, and flavorings to produce salad dressings. Their prevalence is also responsible for the large number of "light" breads, and they are used in great quantities in cakes—one dozen, for example, in a sponge cake.

Because of the authors' backgrounds, it is a reasonable assumption that the recipes represented fare that the typical Mobile insurance broker, commission broker, or attorney might expect to find on his table. The assumption gains added force because one can deduce both from their backgrounds and their writing style that most of the ladies, despite their relatively high social standing, did much of their own cooking, or at the very least, closely supervised the task.

By the seventies, partly as a response to the dearth of hired cooks and the low level of skill of some southern housewives, restaurants catering to entire families began to spring up in Mobile, as elsewhere in the urban South. Beginning in January 1877, the Diamond Restaurant offered to provide meals "to families at residences," and from time to time individual ads in the *Mobile Daily Register* offered to furnish "a few families" with meals. In general, despite the depression the restaurant business boomed, with six new restaurants reportedly being opened during October 1877, one of which advertised "lunch," composed of five hot dishes, "at all hours," for fifteen cents. There were also two private clubs, the Manassas Club and the still-existing Athlestan Club, the latter having been organized in the 1870s as a businessmen's club serving lunch daily and dinners on special occasions.[19]

While the "correct" time for the main meal of the day was still some time between 2:00 and 4:00 P.M., the evidence indicates that Mobile like other urban areas was heading toward the more modern schedule, with a brief lunch break at noon and dinner being pushed later into the evening to accommodate urban working schedules. Special-occasion dinners might be held any time between 7:00 and 10:00 in the evening. Truly elaborate ones, such as that held at the Athlestan Club on March 12, 1879, might continue well into the morning hours. That dinner, in honor of Thomas H. Herndon, a member of the Club who had just been elected to Congress, began at 9:00 with several speeches. It continued with a spectacular meal featuring opossum and turkey and then concluded with more speeches after the dinner. The exact time of adjournment is not recorded. The following year, when former President U. S. Grant came to town, the banquet prepared for him at the Battle House Hotel began at 8:30 and did not conclude until after midnight. Perhaps in honor of the cosmopolitan visitor, that dinner featured French haute cuisine and was served in the French style.[20]

It was during this same time that some local readers began urging an unwilling newspaper editor to provide "interesting" recipes as a regular feature. In January 1877 and a year later in response to the same request, the editor said that he had been burned so badly in the past that he had determined to have nothing to do with cooking. The more experienced cooks, so it seemed, had their own ideas on the subject and had not welcomed his amateur efforts. Despite his doubtlessly prudent refusal, the *Register* did publish a pickle recipe (with instructions for growing cucumbers), a recipe for cooking Irish potatoes, and recipes for making such popular drinks as shrub and syllabub. Subsequent articles also offered instruction on canning fruit and tomatoes, constructing a cheap smokehouse, making bacon, and pickling beef.[21]

That *Gulf City Cook Book* involved a certain amount of practical expertise is suggested by the fact that several of the ladies who worked on the book displayed their culinary skills at the Gulf States Fair each year; some even won first and second prizes. In the year of this book's publication, Mrs. Voss, for example, won second prize for her butter and also for her homemade bread; Miss Fanny Wilson won second place for honey; and Mrs. Robert H. Smith had the best display of homemade pickles.[22] Although individual recipes are not signed by contributors, it is likely that the prize-winning pickles and the bread found their way into this book, for they are two of the most characteristic of southern foods. Cucumber pickles and a variety of pickled, sweetened, and spiced fruits and vegetables were served with practically all meals. The "mangoes," several of which are included in this book, were more elaborate stuffed pickles that were a favorite in Mobile and other parts of the South.[23] The well-known southern taste for sweetness is certainly evident in this section; dill was not in use at all at that time, and sugar is featured in practically all of the recipes.

References to store-bought items, despite their general availability, are scarce in this cookbook, reinforcing the perception that it was prepared by people who were accustomed to cooking. Many types of canned vegetables and meats were being sold in Mobile by 1878, but beyond an occasional can of tomatoes for soup or stew, or a can of shrimp, lobster, or salmon, there would be no reason to mention them in a cookbook.

Since there were no processing plants in Alabama, there was not much local impact from the huge increase nationally in the export of canned goods that was taking place in the 1870s. On the other hand, Lea and Perrin's Worcestershire sauce appears to have replaced the traditional walnut catsup in middle-class Mobile kitchens, and there is frequent use of such commercial ingredients as bitters, prepared gelatin, vanilla extract, cornstarch, and Coleman's mustard. A few of the bread recipes call for compressed yeast cakes, only available since the beginning of the decade, but most call for a stock yeast using the traditional hops or potatoes.

On the whole, it is clear not only that the cooking of meals was still a job done "from scratch" but also that even in urban homes most of the basic food preparation was the responsibility of the individual household. Cranberries, the book explains, are kept under water in a cellar, with the water being changed monthly; herbs should be gathered when beginning to blossom and kept in paper sacks. There is a recipe for homemade yeast powder (baking powder) even though the difficulty of maintaining standard proportions at home had led to good sales for several commercial varieties by that time. Two different ways are suggested for keeping eggs fresh for up to a year.

In common with other cookbooks of the period, there is a section for medicines and for general household products. In addition to listing several soap recipes, the book includes a recipe for a solution for taking grease out of clothing and yet another for removing mildew. There are even directions for making a mixture of tallow and rosin, which when applied hot to shoe soles was guaranteed to extend their life. One could also receive advice about curing wounds in cattle, perking up droopy chickens, curing sick turkeys, increasing the yield of milk from cows, or cleaning oil paintings.[24]

There is no evidence at all in the cookbook that any of the incredible number of kitchen gadgets patented during the late nineteenth century were available in Mobile—except, of course, for the ubiquitous eggbeater. In this respect, however, the region may have been little different from other parts of the country. According to Susan Strasser, author of a recent book on the history of American housework, food preparation looked at the end of the century just as it had at the beginning—except for the addition of an eggbeater and the replacement of the open fireplace by a stove or kitchen range. In both respects, Mobile kitchens conformed.[25] By the mid-1870s, even in the impoverished South, open-hearth cookery had all but disappeared from middle-class urban homes, although it was still common in the countryside. In Mobile wood-burning stoves and ranges were the most commonly used types.

Recipes in this book assumed without question that the reader would have one of the better quality stoves with an oven, perhaps Rathbone's Acorn Cook Stove, which was popular in Mobile in the late seventies, or its rival for top quality, Buck's Brilliant Cooking Stove, which began to be sold by Deegan and Conley early in 1877. It was equipped with a chilled iron fireplace lining, hot and cold flues, and a broad smooth top surface for broiling. Both stoves offered the prospect of relatively even heat and an advanced degree of oven control, although oven thermometers were still unknown. Oil stoves, complete with ovens, were also available, as were gas stoves and ranges. The latter, however, were probably not commonly used because of problems with gas pressure in the city's lines.[26]

In any region of nineteenth-century America one would find the food heavy, rich, sweet, and served in much larger portions than we would expect today. Southern cuisine, as this book attests, was probably extreme in all of these characteristics. Fried foods were the most important in the diet, and large quantities of butter and cream were regularly added to roasted or boiled dishes. Bacon fat, lard, and butter were commonly used seasonings for a wide range of vegetable dishes. For example, a representative recipe for new potatoes (p. 84) directs the cook to simmer them in butter, then serve in a sauce made with fresh butter. Although some cookbook writers had long been campaigning against the use of animal fats in cooking, the advice was probably ignored all over the country as it certainly was in the South.[27]

Salt, pepper, thyme (by all odds, the most used herb), mace, claret, catsup, and sugar took care of flavoring needs not met by the reliance on fats; otherwise, spice cabinets in Mobile kitchens were sparsely stocked. Many cooks would have liked a few bonus items for specialty dishes—filé, molasses, Worcestershire sauce, sherry, whiskey, and brandy.

Alcoholic beverages, especially claret, were in such heavy use that it is obvious the prohibition movement had not touched the Port City—even in a book produced by Methodists. For many soups, a healthy dose of alcohol was added just before serving. Gopher soup, for example, called for the addition of a pint of Madeira and a quart of claret to about a gallon of soup; a similar quantity of redfish soup called for a quart of claret. Whiskey, used in cooking a variety of meat dishes, was also the basis for the powerful and popular Prince Regent punch—which in this cookbook calls for a gallon of whiskey and a quart of curacao to seven quarts of less potent liquids.

The frank use of alcohol is all the more striking if one compares it with the 1893 publication in Anniston by the First Presbyterian Church of *Housekeeping in Alabama*. Treading cautiously, the editor of that work noted that the objection to the use of alcoholic beverages in sauces did not hold against using them in baking, because the cooking process converted the alcohol into vapor. But in case anyone should object, the writer suggested that "molasses will be found an excellent substitute."[28] Even the 1911 edition of *Gulf City Cook Book* contained no such compromise. The difference is undoubtedly rooted in the culture of the city, which according to a very recent analysis "responded to the challenges and reversals of the New South with drink and festivity." A contemporary put it more colorfully, perhaps, and certainly more charitably, when he noted that "the whole people are amusement lovers and the Creole blood touches everything with brightness and beauty."[29]

Sugar is properly listed as an essential because the already developing taste for sweetness had been further encouraged since the mid-century by dramatically declining sugar prices—so much so that Americans along with their British cousins had notoriously become the world's greatest sugar lovers. Refined "loaf" sugar, available at relatively low cost from nearby Louisiana, was the favorite for Mobile desserts. However, locally produced honey, at about ten cents a pound, and brown sugar and molasses, also available at low cost from Louisiana or the Caribbean, seemed to be available in all kitchens.[30] Well over a third of this book is devoted to an incredible array of recipes for desserts, candies, and preserves, and sugar also figures prominently in pickles, savory dishes, and the much-used catsup. As a preservative for fruit, the common formula was a pound of sugar to a pound of fruit. The Mason jar, patented in 1858, made it possible safely to reduce the proportion of sugar by about 25 percent, but the change was not yet evident in Mobile kitchens.[31]

Demonstrating the availability of commercially prepared gelatin and the popularity of molded desserts, there are six variations given on charlotte russe, which is basically an egg-and-cream-rich boiled custard flavored with vanilla extract and mixed with gelatin before being placed in a mold lined with lady fingers or cake. Twenty-five frozen desserts testify to their general popularity in the South and also to the widespread availability of ice at an affordable cost. Even these, however, illustrate the love of rich, sweet foods. The ice creams, for example, frequently call for as many as a dozen eggs and a quart of rich cream to produce a gallon of the finished product. Even for family dinners in nineteenth-century America, some sweet dishes were invariably included—the custards, puddings, and pies in this book would have been likely choices, while the charlottes were probably reserved for company.

As in much southern cooking today, long simmering to merge flavors was a common feature. Soups were regularly boiled for three or four hours—even a redfish soup calls for this much time—and a veal stew is said to require 2½ to 3 hours. A taste for green vegetables, a part of the French influence that included ice cream and cold drinks, had been growing since the 1830s, and in the Mobile area one could find cauliflower, savoy cabbage, and celery in cold cellars along with the expected squash, pumpkins, potatoes, and carrots. Lettuce was much favored during the short period that it was available, before the development of the hardier and longer-keeping iceberg variety. Those vegetables not consumed raw as salads, however, were also subjected to lengthy periods of cooking, most often with a small quantity of bacon or other fat. Cabbage, for example, was to be cooked for an hour or more, preferably with two or more changes of waters. One stuffed cabbage dish required two hours, and cauliflower took an hour.

The simplicity of most meat and vegetable recipes is characteristic of southern cuisine, which has always relied more upon the merging of a few natural flavors and plenty of condiments and sides than upon the complexity of the recipes themselves. Some of the dishes need no improvement; the recipe for oyster stew (here called oyster soup, #2, p. 11) is classic, as is the recipe for fried chicken (p. 53). Others rely upon simple preparation and are served with a sauce to add interest. Poached fish, for example, could be glorified by having "sauce with oysters for fish" (p. 71) poured over it just before serving; another sauce, said to be excellent with fried fish, is a mixture of boiled egg yolks, oil, vinegar, mustard, walnut catsup, Worcestershire sauce, salt, pepper, and sometimes chopped pickles. A celery sauce is recommended for boiled fowls, and there is a tomato sauce and a horseradish sauce for boiled meats. By far the most common, however, is "drawn butter," basically a thin white sauce composed of flour, water, and butter, for which a recipe is given (p. 75). The simplicity of the sauces, which is in marked contrast to other cookbooks of the time, such as

Mrs. Henderson's or even *Housekeeping in Old Virginia*, suggests once again that we are dealing with the authentic cooking of a real group of people. Haute cuisine was served in the Battle House; there is little evidence of its influence upon these Methodist women.

Because of Mobile's position as a port and as a railroad terminus, cooks there probably had available a wider variety of foods over a longer portion of the year than would have been the case in most other southern cities. Before the war, the food industry there as elsewhere in the South had been centered on small, independent producers who grew and processed their own wares and marketed them for themselves. Since the only market had been a small local one, there had been little incentive for supplying it on a regular basis, and no opportunity for the appearance of middle men to handle the flow of country produce. City dwellers dealt directly with producers who came irregularly to the Southern Market or to the two very small markets, the Dauphin Market and the Western Market.

The rapid transportation and relatively low rates for shipping offered by the Mobile and Ohio Railroad beginning in the mid-seventies had set important changes in motion by stimulating the development of a ring of market gardens and small farms surrounding the city to take advantage of the sudden expansion of demand. Local residents received a kind of unearned increment from this development, for even though much of the produce was shipped out, the growth of food crops for export inevitably meant the enrichment of the local food supply as well. The same development also brought a growing number of middlemen by the late seventies. In 1877, there were eight dealers within the city bringing "country produce" to local housewives, whereas there had been none at all just before the Civil War. Their appearance on the scene led finally to the reno-

Loading vegetables for shipment to the North from the market gardens near Mobile (1895). This was a new industry that seemed to offer great promise after Reconstruction. *(T. E. Armitstead/Museum City of Mobile Collection, University of South Alabama Archives)*

vation of the Southern Market by the commitment of major sums of money to its upkeep beginning in the early eighties.[32] From such established dealers or from street vendors, one could buy collards, turnips, cowpeas, cabbage, tomatoes, salad greens, okra, sweet or white potatoes, sweet peppers, muskmelons, and often other fruits or vegetables. When faster freight trains were introduced in 1878 to carry fruit to the North, a great many more growers and dealers were induced to enter that market, and their presence meant even more variety and lower prices for the local market. By June 1879, the Mobile and Ohio and the Mobile and Montgomery railroads in a single week shipped out 3,754 boxes of tomatoes and 967 of watermelons. During that season they had shipped out 10,577 crates of cabbages, 6,536 boxes of beans, and 4,737 boxes of cucumbers.[33]

The same transport facility that took the vegetables out was bringing carloads of Weber's lager beer on ice to provide two different kinds of merchandise for several enterprising Mobilians. The first of these was George W. Lyons, "Dealer in Ice and Weber's Lager Beer from Cincinnati."[34] The ice, which Lyons sold separately, no doubt helped feed the Mobile appetite for ice cream and iced drinks, and it supplied the iceboxes that were assumed to be in every home by the contributors to the cookbook. By 1879, several vendors were handling Cincinnati lager beer "which comes to them in refrigerator cars," according to one ad. In the same year, when the Louisiana Ice Manufacturing Company established an office to sell its product in Mobile, ice for the first time became regularly available at a price that could stimulate a growth of trade in fresh fish and fresh meats.[35]

The year of publication of the cookbook, 1878, was also a bit too early for Mobile cooks to have realized the full benefit of their proximity to the Gulf. By far the most common seafood was salt mackerel or salt cod brought in from the New England fisheries. Although this situation may seem bizarre, a moment's reflection will suggest the reason: fresh fish is so perishable that it could not be handled in commercial quantities in the absence of reliable refrigeration or at least a cheap and continuous source of ice. In fact, there was practically no development of the Gulf Coast fishing industry until very late in the seventies. The census of 1870 lists only two people in Alabama employed in a fishery; the corresponding number for 1880 is 635. Snapper, redfish, and sheepshead figure in the recipes, but only in the most basic of dishes; they were available only rarely, usually in such hot weather that they had to be consumed immediately. Oysters were plentiful at twenty-five cents a hundred or they could be had for the taking from the apparently

The oyster fleet at the foot of Government Street, 1895. *(T. E. Armitstead/Museum City of Mobile Collection, University of South Alabama Archives)*

inexhaustible beds in the shallow waters at the south end of the bay. Because it was simple to keep them alive with only minimal cooling, they could be shipped so easily that they sold for very little, even in inland cities. The highly perishable shrimps, on the other hand, were rarely available fresh; they were most commonly used canned for salads or garnishes. This difference helps explain why there is an entire chapter containing twenty-two oyster recipes in the book, but only three for shrimp, one of which asks specifically for the canned variety. Shrimp, in fact, was not common anywhere along the Gulf except for the relatively small ones from Lake Pontchartrain and the even smaller river shrimp. Not until after 1912, when the invention of the

Cartmen with a load of fish, Mobile, 1895. Most of the fish are red snappers, for which a commercial trade began in the 1870s. *(T. E. Armitstead/Museum City of Mobile Collection, University of South Alabama Archives)*

trawl net and the development of higher-powered shrimp boats made deep dredging feasible, did shrimp begin to take an important place in Gulf Coast cuisine.[36]

When the Louisiana Ice Manufacturing Company opened a branch in Mobile early in 1879, the new opportunity was seized by F. W. Miller who acquired some large ice vaults from a failed beer vendor. He immediately began an ambitious program of export in refrigerated cars and local retail delivery of a large variety of fresh Gulf fish. For six cents a pound at his store on the waterfront or for eight cents a pound delivered anywhere in the city, customers could for the first time obtain strictly fresh fish along with enough free ice to preserve their purchase for the day. Saturday purchasers were given double quantities of ice in order to carry the fish over for Sunday dinner. Shortly he opened a branch near the Spring Hill streetcar line, offered delivery within the city three times a day (at *no* advance in price), and began shipping so many oysters on ice to the Northwest that he had to place a continuing ad for containers of all kinds. He claimed that his stock was always fresh, because of the constant shipments to the Northwest.[37] Since Miller was the first his business thrived for a while, but locally, his business seems to have declined after December 1879, when a competitor, J. T. Maybury, began offering to fill orders for oysters and fish by telephone.[38]

As a port city with direct access to the trade of Europe and the Caribbean, Mobile could offer its residents a great deal more diversity than could cities farther inland. By the

Sorting and counting bananas as they are being loaded on refrigerator cars. An important banana trade began in Mobile in the late 1870s, though this picture is from about 1905. *(Erik Overbey Collection, University of South Alabama Archives)*

1870s, despite the depression affecting the entire nation, importers were offering an array of fine wines, liquors, and specialty foods. W. B. Vail and Company, for example, as direct agents of Crosse & Blackwell of London, regularly advertised herring paste, oriental pickles, preserved ginger, lobster in olive oil, and similar delicacies. Meanwhile, Vail's neighbor on Dauphin Street, John O'Reilly & Company, was offering French patés, tinned Lyons sausage, French asparagus, and boneless sardines—the last named being a local favorite. Vail's advertisement for May 6, 1878, offered "Something new and nice—Boston Baked Beans in cans," but there is no way to determine how well they stood up to the competition of the simpler version that appears on page 77 of this book.[39] Fresh fruit arriving regularly from Florida and the West Indies could be purchased at the docks or at the shop of Cady & Vuscovich, who termed themselves: "wholesale and retail dealers in native and West Indian fruit." In November 1877, the firm was offering coconuts at a nickel each, oranges at three cents, and bananas beginning at $1.50 a bunch. A few weeks later, with much excitement, the suppliers announced that a shipment of cranberries had arrived from Cape Cod.[40] Plantain was encountered commonly enough to appear in one recipe in this book (p. 83).

Pork, long central to the southern diet, was obviously surviving the onslaught then being made upon it, primarily by northern writers. In the year before *Gulf City Cook Book* was published, *Godey's Ladies Book* had called pork "difficult to digest," and it had been banished from many tables in the North; in the same year, Mrs. Henderson of St. Louis was confessing to "a decided prejudice against this meat [pork]" and suggesting that it be used only in very small quantities for flavoring. Bowing to her environment, however, she did offer a recipe for curing bacon and a few pork recipes, including roast baby pig. The last named was obviously included under protest, for she tartly commented that "Anyone who fancies can cook a little pig, not I."

That beef had already become the preferred middle-class meat before 1880 is demonstrated by the fact that Maria Parloa's suggested menus contain neither pork nor ham; soon Mrs. Rorer of Philadelphia was campaigning against pork, flatly proclaiming that "no product of the hog is fit to eat."[41] Locally, the *Register* was touting the superior efficiency and economy of mutton and pointing to "the gaunt spectre of cholera that so persistently stalks the swine yards." But even though there are a number of beef and mutton recipes in the Mobile book, the meat section starts with the traditional boiled ham and is followed by fourteen ham and pork recipes. Incoming shipments of cured and pickled pork from Cincinnati and the large number of dealers advertising it confirm the widespread popularity of the traditional meat. On one day in October 1877, for example, a single dealer received two hundred barrels of pork and two carloads of bacon. Beef, on the other hand, did not come into the city in sufficient quantities to be listed among the Board of Trade's "Receipts of Leading Articles" until 1878, when only 125 barrels were recorded. During the same year, the Board counted 585 barrels of pork and 3,462 casks of bacon. In the case of both pork and bacon, the figures were down substantially from the previous year, no doubt owing to a combination of decreased meat consumption and increased local production stimulated by the depression then raging. In 1877, the figures had been 1,072 for pork, and 4,150 for bacon.[42]

Because fresh pork was available only briefly at the beginning of winter, and fresh beef only during the few cool months, cooks relied primarily upon the smoked, salted, or pickled varieties. Beef tongue, which reacted well to the pickle, was a particular favorite. Most of the other beef sold in Mobile was "spiced round," which traveled well and had good keeping qualities, although it did not pickle so well as did pork, which was commonly thought to be improved by the process. The dramatic developments in the handling of meat that were occurring in the seventies and that were to revolutionize the food industry did not appear to affect Mobile and its cooks.

The city had started to develop a livestock market based upon Texas steers before the Civil War, but in 1877 nothing remained. In fact, the Census of 1870 had listed no names under the heading of "meat packers, curers, and picklers," for the state of Alabama or for its Gulf Coast neighbors—Florida, Mississippi, and Louisiana. While choice western beef was offered at from 4¼ to 4½ cents a pound in early 1879, it does not appear that there was a commercial slaughterhouse in Mobile at that time; there may have been none until the Armour Packing Company opened a branch in 1891. A stockyard, opened in December 1878 near the railroad depot and downtown Mobile, offered commission sales, services, feeding lots, and a water supply. It promised special attention to stock being shipped through to New Orleans (from Florida), but there is no indication that it served as a slaughterhouse.[43]

The beef and pork were supplemented by poultry from the country—again, only in the cool weather—or at other times, from one's own chicken yard. During the winter months, dressed turkeys were available for as little as seventy-five cents each, while domestic ducks brought thirty-five cents and broilers fifteen cents. Game was also popular in season—venison, small birds, rabbits, squirrels, wild turkeys, pigeons, opossum, and ducks were enjoyed by city residents. Although most game must have been sold from time to time by street vendors, only wild ducks, flocks of which then came to Mobile Bay each winter, are known to have been regularly hunted on an organized basis. There was, in fact, an important industry based upon the duck flight, which was then being threatened by a new game law (outlawing hunting from blinds with decoys) passed in 1877.[44] Typical recipes for all of these wild delicacies expect for opossum are found in the book. For most game, the Mobile taste stressed simplicity—pan or gridiron broiling being a favorite technique—but the recipe for bird pie on page 51 is a splendid example of a somewhat more complicated dish using the locally available doves and oysters.

Taken as a whole, this particular cookbook reflects the diet, economic situation, and some of the traditions of Mobile's upper-middle class at the end of the 1870s. Read carefully, it can help historians paint an accurate and human picture of a place and at least some of its people at a particular time. Mobile was then, as it perhaps always has been, a curious mixture of local peculiarity and national experience. The difference between the dinner at the exclusive Athlestan Club, honoring a local hero and featuring opossum and turkey, and the one a year later at the Battle House honoring a national hero and featuring French haute cuisine is symptomatic of this mixture. When "chicken a la mange" in this cookbook turns out to be broiled chicken with gravy surrounded on the platter by a dozen hard-fried eggs, it is likewise symptomatic.

As for the "southernness" of Mobile's cuisine in the 1870s, this book indicates that it was an authentic variant of that much-discussed style. The essence of southern cooking has always been a combination of plenty and simplicity, with the plenty being achieved largely by skillful use of locally available ingredients that could be obtained without great expense. A 1990 edition of *Gulf City Cook Book* would not contain gopher soup or canvassback duck, for both varieties of game have practically disappeared. It would not have an entire chapter on oysters, for one ecological disaster after another has turned them from being the most affordable food on the Gulf Coast to being one of the most expensive, and of increasingly questionable health value as well. Neither would it rely to such an obvious extent upon eggs, for the conventional chicken coops are no longer found in middle-class neighborhoods. On the other hand, it would have a wide range of recipes for varieties of fish not even known in the 1870s, and it would still rely heavily upon what the rest of the world regards as an unconscionably long time in cooking in order to blend properly the natural flavors of the raw materials. Through all of this, the principles are the same.

Notes

1. Auditor's Report, City of Mobile, 1876. Radical city officials in 1870 had paid $360,000 for the wharves, financed by city bonds. See Don H. Doyle, *New Men, New Cities, New South: Atlanta, Nashville, Charleston, Mobile, 1860–1910* (Chapel Hill and London: University of North Carolina Press, 1990).

2. Doyle, *New Men, New Cities*, p. 79; Alma E. Berkstresser, "Mobile, Alabama in the 1880's" (M.A. thesis, University of Alabama, 1951), pp. 207–8. Figures on Mobile population and some of the information about the economic conditions are taken from Berkstresser, pp. 1–11, 61. In the 1880 census, 2,123 persons were excluded because of a change in the boundary lines through the legislative act of 1879. Had the boundary lines remained the same, however, the loss would have still been 779 for the decade (4.2 percent).

3. Palmer Pillans, "Mobile in Two Centuries," typescript, n.d., in University of South Alabama Library. Quote is from unnumbered page preceding p. 1. My student, Elizabeth Oaks-Colley,

spent several days with city directories and the manuscript census to track down information that appears below about the husbands of the contributors.

4. The factory system of cheesemaking began to be developed in the 1850s and continued at a rapid rate during the 1860s. The census found ten cheese factories in the entire United States in 1860 and over 1,300 in 1870. For an interesting account of this development, see Mark H. Wilde, "The Industrialization of Food Processing in the United States, 1860–1960" (Ph.D. diss., University of Delaware, 1988), p. 23.

5. William G. Panschar, *Baking in America*, vol. 1 (Evanston, Ill.: Northwestern University Press, 1956), pp. 56–60.

6. W. A. Henderson, *Common Sense in the Kitchen* (New York: Hurst & Co., 1870), p. 7.

7. While critics of American cooking had long blamed abundance for what they considered the poor cooking they encountered, I think that Harvey Levenstein is correct in focusing upon the importance of the number and quality of servants. See his *Revolution at the Table: The Transformation of the American Diet* (New York and Oxford: Oxford University Press, 1988), p. 18.

8. [Estelle Woods Wilcox], *Buckeye Cookery and Practical Housekeeping* (Maryville, Ohio: Buckeye Publishing Co., 1877), pp. 367–68.

9. Mrs. Mary F. Henderson, *Practical Cooking and Dinner Giving* (New York: Harper and Brothers, 1878), p. 31.

10. Emma Seifrit Weigley, *Sarah Tyson Rorer: The Nation's Instructress in Dietetics and Cookery* (Philadelphia: American Philosophical Society, 1977), p. 16.

11. Lavonne B. Axford, *English Language Cookbooks, 1600–1973* (Detroit: Gale Research Co., 1976), p. vii.

12. Alan Grubb, "House and Home in the Victorian South: The Cookbook as Guide" in Carol Bleser, ed., *In Joy and In Sorrow: Women, Family and Marriage in the Victorian South, 1830–1900* (forthcoming, Oxford University Press). I am indebted to Professor Grubb for supplying me with an advance copy of his paper, in which he makes this point on p. 2.

13. John Egerton, *Southern Food* (New York: Knopf, 1987), p. 16.

14. Grubb, "House and Home"; Louis Szathmary, "Preface" to *Mrs. Porter's New Southern Cookery Book* (facsimile reprint of 1867 edition, New York: Promontory Press, 1974). On Estelle Woods Wilcox, about whom very little else is known, see John Egerton, *Southern Food* (New York: Knopf, 1987), p. 25.

15. Mrs. Mary F. Henderson, *Practical Cooking and Dinner Giving* (New York: Harper and Brothers, 1878), pp. 31, 221, 228, 216, 214.

16. Alan Grubb, who has studied southern cookbooks as well as British cookbooks of the nineteenth century, has also concluded that the charitable cookbook is a "uniquely American phenomenon." See his forthcoming article "House and Home." John Egerton is correct in pointing out that the later Junior League cookbooks, becoming important in the 1940s, did ignore more common dishes (*Southern Food*, p. 32). This is probably because the element of basic instruction for new cooks, important for the early ones, has disappeared as a motive.

17. *Gulf City Cook Book*, pp. 81, 64, 62, 40.

18. Ibid., p. 57. Incidentally, it is a very tasty dish, although the contributor forgot to mention that about a quart of water would be needed in addition to the other ingredients. This type of omission is unfortunately common in books of the period.

19. Mobile *Register*, January 7, December 9, November 9, 1877.

20. Mobile *Register*, March 13, 1879. William Warren Rogers, Jr., "The Past is Gone: Ulysses S. Grant Visits Mobile," *Gulf Coast Historical Review*, V (Fall 1989), 15. By 1893, the modern schedule of a light lunch and the main meal in the evening was assumed without special comment by the editors of *Housekeeping in Alabama*; see, for example, the sample menus on pp. 236–38.

21. *Mobile Daily Register*, January 7, 1877, January 20, 1878, June 24, July 25, November 9, 16, 1877, May 26, August 29, September 1, 1878.

22. Mobile *Register*, May 13, 1877.

23. The recipe for oil mangoes (p. 194) is particularly noteworthy. The "melons" referred to would most likely have been small muskmelons. On mangoes, see the Glossary. The green tomato sauce (p. 199) is also highly recommended.

24. *Gulf City Cook Book*, pp. 231–43. According to Grubb, references to storebought items became more common in cookbooks of the 1890s (p. 26).

25. Susan Strasser, *Never Done: A History of American Housework* (New York: Pantheon Books, 1982).

26. Mobile *Register*, January 3, February 11, March 3, 1877.

27. *Miss Beecher's Domestic Recipe Book* (1846) proclaimed that "The most injurious food of any in common use is the *animal* oils and articles cooked with them." As quoted in Waverly Root and Richard de Rochemont, *Eating in America: A History* (New York: William Morrow & Co., 1976), p. 164.

28. *Housekeeping in Alabama* (Anniston: for the First Presbyterian Church, 1893), p. 116.

29. Thomas C. DeLeon, "Mobile—The Gulf City," *Harper's Weekly*, XXVIII (February 2, 1884); Doyle, *New Men, New Cities*, p. 247.

30. Levenstein, *Revolution at the Table*, p. 6.

31. *Housekeeping in Alabama* makes a point of the reduction in sugar made possible by the air-tight jar (p. 181).

32. The Southern Market had fallen into such a state of disrepair that many ladies were refusing to patronize it. Despite an allocation of more than $16,000 to the upkeep of the market between 1872 and 1876, it remained "one great eye-sore," according to one correspondent to the Mobile *Register* (January 11, 1880). A much larger commitment during 1883 and 1884 made it possible to renovate it thoroughly and restore it to the status of a major market. See DeLeon, "Mobile—The Gulf City," p. 78.

33. Mobile *Register*, June 28, 1879.

34. Mobile *Register*, September 30, 1877, March 23, 1879, December 2, 1877.

35. Mobile *Register*, April 20, 1879. The Louisiana Ice Manufacturing Company opened the first commercial ice plant in the United States in New Orleans in 1865; in 1868, it improved its

process and greatly enlarged its capacity. By the time it opened the branch office in Mobile, the supply was practically unlimited.

36. Even though shrimp was sometimes available in New Orleans, there is not a single recipe for it in Lafcadio Hearn's 1885 work *La Cuisine Creole*, and it has only a very minor place in the *Picayune*'s cookbook of 1901.

37. Mobile, *Register*, April 25, 30, May 9, 18, September 27, 1879.

38. Mobile *Register*, December 20, 1879. The connection between Miller's declining business and Maybury's expanding one is only a guess, but it appears reasonable enough. Miller's advertising in the *Register* and in the City Directories tapered off as Maybury's expanded. They were located next door to one another on South Commerce Street, and Maybury eventually took over one address previously occupied by Miller.

39. Mobile *Register*, October 27, 28, 1877, May 6, 1878.

40. Mobile *Register*, November 21, December 12, 1877.

41. *Godey's Ladies Book and Magazine*, vol. 95 (1877), p. 395; *Miss Parloa's New Cook Book and Marketing Guide* (Boston, 1880); Levenstein, *Revolution at the Table*, p. 21; Henderson, *Practical Cooking*, pp. 160, 161; Weigley, *Sarah Tyson Rorer*, p. 61.

42. Mobile *Register*, April 5, October 28, 1877, December 28, 1878.

43. Mobile *Register*, January 1, 18, 1879.

44. Mobile *Register*, February 18, 1877.

GLOSSARY

borage a salad herb of European origin, having a flavor resembling cucumber.

blanc-mange a sweetened, flavored and molded dessert made from either gelatinous or starchy substances and milk.

Boker's bitters one of the many flavoring agents sold as "bitters" and frequently used also as a mild tonic or stimulant. They are usually alcoholic liquors prepared by maceration or distillation of a bitter herb. Boker's was sold in Mobile to the trade by John O'Reilley.

celery vinegar a flavored vinegar in common use for salads and cooking vegetables. It was prepared from celery, celery seed, salt, and sugar and steeped in vinegar for two or more weeks before use.

clabber thickened or curdled sour milk, considered a delicacy especially in the rural South.

cochineal a red dye prepared from the dried bodies of a red-scale insect found in Mexico and Central America.

Coleman's mustard a commercially prepared powder of yellow mustard seeds; the brand is still available.

cracknel a hard, brittle cake or biscuit made in a variety of stylized shapes, such as stars, triangles, etc.

drawn butter a thin white sauce made with butter, flour, and water. It differs from a roux because the flour is not browned first in the butter. See recipe, p. 75.

essence of lemon a lemon extract, made at home with oil of lemon, lemon peel, and a small amount of the purest alcohol available.

felon a severe inflammation on a finger or toe, involving a bone.

filé a flavoring and thickening agent made from powdered sassafras leaves, adopted from the Choctaw Indians; widely used in Cajun or Creole cookery, and especially valuable for gumbos. See recipe, p. 13.

gopher a burrowing land tortoise attaining the length of a foot or so. It is native to the Gulf Coast, where its eggs and flesh were once widely regarded as food.

hartshorn the antler of a hart, finely shaved and used medicinally.

hominy dried, hulled corn, usually cooked by boiling. In the nineteenth-century South, the term *always* indicated a version that was ground into a coarse meal, now termed "grits."

Irish moss a dried and bleached preparation from red algae, used as a thickener or emulsifier.

isinglass a very pure form of gelatin prepared from the air bladders of sturgeons or other fishes, used in making jellies and glue.

loaf sugar refined sugar formed into a conical loaf, weighing about 9–10 pounds. Ordinary granulated sugar, which replaced it when a new vacuum-pan and centrifuge process was developed in the late nineteenth century, is an acceptable substitute if measurements are by weight.

mango a name primarily for sweet peppers or small melons prepared by stuffing (usually with shredded cabbage) and pickling. Other vegetables prepared in this manner were also termed "mangoes." See pp. 194–95.

rosewater a solution made by distilling fresh rose flowers with water or steam, used as a perfume and as a flavoring agent.

sago starch prepared from the pith of an East Indian palm, used in puddings and for stiffening textiles. A great many sago palms were planted in the Mobile area during the nineteenth century, and some still exist.

saleratus baking soda.

salmis a ragout made from leftover game.

sangaree a sweetened, cooling drink, prepared with wine, beer, or liquor, served over ice and usually garnished with nutmeg and served in a tall glass.

shrub a beverage of fruit juices, sugar, various spices, and usually containing alcohol.

sweet oil usually refers to olive oil; sometimes used for other mild oils, as rape oil.

syllabub a popular drink, originating in England, made by

curdling milk or cream with wine. Original recipes called for drawing milk directly from the cow into serving glasses containing the wine and spices.

tetter a term used for any number of vesicular skin diseases, ranging from pimples through ringworm and herpes.

Vichy water soda water.

walnut catsup a puree of green, immature walnuts pounded with anchovies and a variety of spices and flavorings, usually including black pepper, mace, ginger, and sometimes garlic or horseradish. It was used in cooking or as a table sauce for meats, much as Worcestershire sauce would now be used.

yeast powder ordinary baking powder, containing cream of tartar and carbonate of soda with some kind of vehicle, usually wheat flour. It was made at home (see recipe, p. 231) but was also sold packaged under a variety of labels. The commercial variety became popular because of the difficulty in maintaining exact proportions in the homemade version.

yelk an old spelling for "yolk," used consistently in this volume, but already out of use elsewhere.

A Note on Nineteenth-Century Weights and Measures

The absence of standardization in weights and measures is one of the great problems encountered by modern readers in attempting to use nineteenth-century recipes. The problem is two-fold. In the absence of any conventionally agreed-upon measuring instruments, cooks tended to use whatever they had on hand. Thus a kitchen cup, a coffee cup, a tumbler, two wineglassfuls, and two gills all signify the same amount, namely eight ounces. In addition, a great many spoons of different sizes were used, ranging from a saltspoon (about ⅛ of a modern teaspoon), to an ironspoon (somewhere between ⅓ and ½ cup). The teaspoon itself was changing in size at the end of the nineteenth century; a tablespoon holds three modern teaspoons, but four of the size that might have been made during the middle of the past century. A second problem is that before the 1890s, cooks commonly used rounded measurements, with consequences varying with the instrument and with the substance being measured. Thus, a tablespoonful of butter always indicates one ounce, not the half-ounce that would be intended today. On the other hand, it is difficult to heap a wineglassful of liquid; therefore a wineglassful of claret was just four ounces, as it is today, although it is quite likely that some cooks would have used the six-ounce glass. The designation of a wineglass as two ounces, which is found in some turn-of-the-century books, was apparently a short-lived effort at standardization—to find a measure between a tablespoon and a gill. The problem is that there never has been a wineglass in common use that held just two ounces and the attempt simply added to the confusion. At any rate, a wineglassful in this book should always be considered a four-ounce glass in which red wine would have been served. Sometimes in this book level measurements are called for, but unless otherwise indicated, it is best to assume that what is being called for in any recipe is all that the measuring instrument can conveniently hold. Standardization of measurements was an important achievement of the cooking school movement at the end of the century; in the Mobile of the 1870s the concept had not appeared.

With the above cautions in mind, the following list of measurements, derived from a number of nineteenth-century cookbooks, may be helpful.

pinch about 1/8 of a modern teaspoon
saltspoonful 1/8 of a modern teaspoon
dessert-spoonful a measure intermediate in size between a teaspoon and a tablespoon; about 2½ fluid drams
4 teaspoonfuls, fluid 1 tablespoonful
ironspoonful between 1/3 and ½ cup
wineglassful 4 fluid ounces (some cooks used 6-ounce glasses!)
1 gill ½ cup
kitchen cup, coffee cup, tumbler 8 fluid ounces
butter the size of a walnut 1 ounce
butter the size of an egg 2 ounces
1½ pints cornmeal (3 cups) 1 pound
4 cups flour 1 pound
10 eggs 1 pound
2 cups granulated sugar 1 pound
1 pint of butter (2 cups) 1 pound
1 pint of brown sugar 13 ounces

GULF CITY COOK BOOK

"We may live without poetry, music, and art;
We may live without conscience, and live without heart;
We may live without friends; we may live without books;
But civilized man *can not* live without *cooks*.
He may live without books,—what is knowledge but grieving?
He may live without hope,—what is hope but deceiving?
He may live without love,—what is passion but pining?
But where is the man that can live without dining?" —*Lucile*

CONTRIBUTORS.

Mrs. D. C. Anderson.
" Wm. L. Baker.
" Leslie E. Brooks.
" J. Curtis Bush.
" Henry Barnewall.
" R. C. Cunningham.
" Dr. Wm. P. Crawford.
" Wm. P. Carter.
" George Coster.
" J. C. Calhoun.
" Wm. Cox.
" James W. Campbell.
" Alexander Carr.
" George B. Clitherall.
" Jno. Douglas.
" A. DuMont.
Miss V. W. Dorman.
Mrs. Jonathan Emanuel.
" C. K. Foote.
" A. M. Fosdick.
" M. S. Foote.
" John Gaillard.
" S. Goodall.
" Henry Goldthwaite.
" H. N. Gould.
" J. R. Gates.
" H. Gets.
" Chas. W. Gazzam.
" J. D. Goodman.
" Peter Hamilton.
" T. A. Hamilton.
" Ann T. Hunter.
Miss Mary E. Hodges.
Mrs. F. R. Hill.
" Jefferson Hamilton.
" Alfred Irwin.
" Geo. A. Ketchum.
" Wm. Kelly, Sr.
" Thomas King.
" L. W. Lawler.
" T. T. A. Lyon.

Mrs. A. J. Leslie.
" James F. Lyon.
Miss Josephine Long.
Mrs. Wm. G. Little.
" Robert Middleton.
" James B. Malone.
" Chas. F. Moore.
" Alfred R. Murry.
" R. F. Manly.
" Daniel McNeil.
" A. M. Punch.
" Henry Pope.
" H. E. Pease.
" J. W. Phares.
" A. Proskauer.
" A. A. Payne.
" Geo. B. Preston.
" Thomas H. Price.
" A. M. Quigley.
Miss Fannie Quigley.
Mrs. F. A, Ross.
" John Reid.
" John K. Randall.
" Frank S. Stone.
" Wm. A. Smith.
" Joseph Seawell.
" Peter Stark.
" Henry A. Schroeder.
" C. C. Sherrard.
" Sidney Smith.
" Henry Sossaman.
" M. T. Sprague.
" Robert H. Smith.
" Douglas Vass.
" Wm. T. Webb.
" N. Weeks.
Miss S. B. Waring.
Mrs. L. M. Wilson.
" A. G. Ward.
" B. Ward.
" R. L. Watkins.

GULF CITY COOK-BOOK.

SOUPS.

In making good soup it is necessary to observe only a few points. Beef is the best meat for this purpose, but mutton or veal will answer. Cold water should always be used at first, and only in sufficient quantity to prevent burning, until the strength or juice of the meat is extracted. Allow one pound of meat to one quart of water. Three or four hours are required to cook soup well; generally three hours' simmering, and one hour boiling after the vegetables and seasoning are put in. Thickening, such as rice, vermicelli, macaroni, or dumpling, should be put in last. Vegetables should be nicely chopped.

OKRA SOUP.

Take a shank-bone, or about three pounds of beef, and boil in three quarts of water until tender, skimming when necessary. Add one quart of chopped okra, one pint of prepared tomatoes, one onion cut fine, and pepper and salt to taste. If desired, four hard-boiled eggs may be cut up and added before serving. This soup should boil three or four hours. Three or four ears of grated corn are an improvement.

CORN SOUP.

Cut and scrape about twelve ears of corn. Boil the cobs about half an hour in one quart, then remove, and add the corn. Boil half an hour, and add two quarts of sweet milk. Season with pepper, salt, and butter, and thicken with one table spoonful of flour that has been dissolved in a little of the milk. Let all boil about fifteen minutes, then pour over the yelks of three eggs, which have been well beaten in the tureen.

TOMATO SOUP.

To about two pounds of fresh beef or shank-bone, put three quarts of water, and season with pepper and salt. When boiled and skimmed, add one quart of ripe tomatoes that have been skinned and quartered, a large onion cut up fine, and a little thyme. Boil until the tomatoes are all dissolved. It may be thickened with rice, flour, or vermicelli.

TOMATO SOUP WITHOUT MEAT.

To one quart of prepared tomatoes, cooked and seasoned as for table use, add a salt-spoonful of soda, and one quart of milk, boiled and thickened to the consistency of drawn butter, with two table-spoonfuls of flour. Mix and strain into the tureen. Serve immediately.

GREEN-PEA SOUP.—NO. I.

Put two pounds of veal, lamb, or beef, and a quarter of a pound of fat salt pork sliced thin, into two quarts of water. Set it over a moderate fire, and when it boils skim it clear. Add a quart of shelled peas, and a dozen small new Irish potatoes, well scraped. Cover closely for an hour, or until the peas are tender; then add half a tea-cup of sweet butter with a heaping tea-spoonful of flour worked into it. Pepper and salt to taste.

GREEN-PEA SOUP.—NO. 2.

Take about four quarts of peas, shell and boil the pods in about as much water as you want soup. When the sweetness is extracted, strain the water, return to the kettle and add the peas. Boil three quarters of an hour; then add one tea-cup of milk, thickened with a tea-spoonful of flour and two or three young onions, cut fine and fried in butter. On serving, add the yelks of three eggs, beaten in a little cream or butter. Season with pepper and salt.

SPLIT-PEA SOUP.

Put one pint of split peas into two quarts of water. Boil until you can mash them, which will be in about two hours, then pass through a sieve. Pour the liquor and the peas back into the pot, and add boiling water to make it of proper consistency, one small spoonful of lard, or a small slice of bacon, and salt and cayenne pepper to taste. If not as thick as you desire, thicken with a little flour. Boil until done. Toast some bread, cut it in small pieces, put them in the tureen, and pour the soup over them.

VEGETABLE SOUP WITHOUT MEAT.

Slice a few onions and fry brown; add as much flour as is needed to thicken a pint of water. When nearly done add a dessert-spoonful of butter, stir quickly, and add one pint of water and one pint of milk. Toast to a very light brown a couple slices of bread, and crush into the soup. Cover up for a few minutes. Just before serving, add two hard-boiled eggs, chopped fine.

VEGETABLE SOUP FOR WINTER USE.

One bushel of skinned tomatoes, one peck of okra cut up, six red peppers without the seeds, two dessert-spoonfuls of ground black pepper, four table-spoonfuls of salt. Cook all together until it is a thick marmalade. Put up hot in close jars for winter use. When wanted for table, add beef-water in quantities to suit the family taste, adding seasoning or not, as you choose. Of course, some additional boiling will be needed to thoroughly incorporate the water.

SCOTCH BROTH.

On four pounds of good beef pour one gallon of cold water. When this boils add one half pint of coarse barley. Then prepare and add one fourth of a small cabbage, four carrots, two parsnips, four turnips, one and a half pints of Irish potatoes; these should all be chopped fine before adding. Three quarters of an hour before serving, add one good-sized onion, cut fine, a sprig of parsley, and pepper and salt to taste. This should cook at least four hours. A pint of green peas is a great improvement, to be added with the onion, parsley, etc.

OX-TAIL SOUP.

Cut up two or three ox-tails, separating them at the joints. Put them in a stew-pan with one and a half ounces of butter, two carrots cut in slices, one stalk of celery, two turnips, a quarter of a pound of lean ham cut in pieces, a tea-spoonful of whole pepper, a sprig of parsley and thyme, and half a pint of cold water. Stir over a quick fire to extract the flavor of the herbs, then pour on three quarts of water. Simmer four hours, or until the tails are tender, skimming well. Strain the soup, reserving the ox-tails. Stir in a little flour for thickening, a wine-glass of Madeira wine, one of catchup, and a half stalk of celery, previously boiled. Put the pieces of ox-tail into the strained soup, boil a few minutes, and serve.

CHICKEN SOUP.

Cut up one chicken and boil in three quarts of water till the strength is extracted. Then add two table-spoonfuls of rice, a sprig of parsley and thyme, and salt and pepper to taste. Before serving, add two hard-boiled eggs, chopped fine, and if the chicken is not fat, a table-spoonful of butter.

OYSTER SOUP.—NO. 1.

Take one hundred oysters, with two quarts of the liquor

strained. Boil until the oysters begin to curl; then add two table-spoonfuls of butter, mixed with one table-spoonful of flour. Season to taste with pepper, salt, and allspice. Serve with slices of toasted bread or broken crackers.

OYSTER SOUP.—NO. 2.

To two quarts of strained oyster-liquor, boiling, add one hundred oysters, with salt and pepper to taste. Let all boil together till the edges of the oysters curl, skimming constantly. Remove the oysters to the tureen, and thicken the soup with one table spoonful of flour, rubbed in two table-spoonfuls of melted butter. Boil in a separate vessel—to prevent curdling—one quart of sweet milk, and pour in the tureen, pouring in the soup last.

TURTLE SOUP.

Take a turtle weighing eight or ten pounds, cut its head off and let it drain. Take it from the shell, select the liver and other parts used, being careful to remove the gall. Quarter the turtle, lay it in a pan, pour boiling water over it. then scrape it clean and cut the claws off; then lay it in cold water, wash it thoroughly, and wipe dry. Put into a soup-kettle one large table-spoonful of lard, and four of flour. Let it fry until the flour is brown; add to it a medium-sized onion, chopped fine. Cut the meat into small pieces and fry, as you would chicken, in lard and flour, for a short time. Put all into the kettle, adding one gallon of water; boil slowly until reduced one half. When the meat is tender add spices as follows: One small table spoonful of cinnamon, one tea-spoonful of mace, and twelve or fifteen cloves, beaten fine; also, thyme, parsley, salt, and pepper, both cayenne and black. Then add one tumbler of Madeira, and one-half tumbler of claret. If the turtle has eggs, put them in about fifteen minutes before the soup is served. When ready to serve, add the juice and rind of one lemon. Gopher is an excellent substitute for turtle.

MOCK-TURTLE SOUP.

Take about two pounds of beef, lamb, fowl, pig's-head, or tongue; any of these kinds of meat will make good soup. Boil the meat well, take it out, cut it in small pieces, and put back into the soup. Season it with one tea-spoonful of mace, one of cloves, one of cinnamon, one dozen of whole black pepper, one small onion, chopped fine. Grind the spices before adding them. Brown one tea-cup of flour to thicken the soup; burn two table-spoonfuls of sugar, and add, with six hard-boiled eggs, the yelks being rubbed fine, and one tea-cup of tomato catchup. Boil all these ingredients until done, and just before serving add a glass of claret or other wine. Put the soup on as soon after breakfast as possible.

GRAVY SOUP.

Boil your soup-meat until tender, then chop it fine. (Beef-steak "left over" is better than meat, and does not require to be boiled.) Brown two table-spoonfuls of flour with a tea-spoonful of butter. Cut up two onions into it, add your meat, and enough of the pot-liquor to moisten it (if beef-steak is used, moisten with water); let it fry ten minutes, then return to the soup-pot. Cut up three carrots, three turnips, and one can of tomatoes, very fine, and put them into the soup. Boil two eggs hard, and add, a quarter of an hour before dishing, a salt-spoonful of ground mace and a tea-spoonful of ground cloves. Before sending to table add a tumbler and a half of claret. Serve with rice.

CLAM SOUP.

Open the clams by putting them in a pot with a little water, and steaming them until the shells begin to part.

when they can be taken out with ease. Boil them well, and when they have been chopped fine add enough of the liquor to make them taste well, a lump of butter rolled in flour, two crackers rolled fine, a tea-spoonful of mace, and half that quantity of cayenne pepper. When ready to be served, add a tea-cup of sweet cream.

EGG-BALLS FOR SOUP.

Take the yelks of eight eggs, boiled hard, and mash them smooth with a little flour, salt, and the yelks of two raw eggs. Mix well together, roll into balls, and drop into boiling water.

RED-FISH SOUP.

One large table-spoonful of lard, and the same of flour, put in a soup-pot to brown; two large onions, some thyme and parsley chopped up fine and put in with the gravy of lard and flour. Let them brown a little; add one can of tomatoes (or one quart of fresh ones). Pour on two quarts of water, and let it boil. For a four-o'clock dinner put this on at noon, and let it boil until half an hour before dinner; then have a small red-fish (or any coarse-grained fish) sliced in pieces, about half the size of your hand. Put in the fish with one large lemon, sliced, one table-spoonful of whole allspice, salt, red, and black pepper, and a little more than a pint of claret. Serve with rice.

CUBION.

Stir into two table-spoonfuls of hot lard sufficient flour to brown it, and red and black pepper to taste. Then add eight onions, sliced, a large bunch of parsley chopped fine, a little thyme, and one quart of tomatoes. Let these cook fifteen minutes, stirring all the time; then add two quarts of boiling water, and boil slowly for three hours. Three quarters of an hour before serving add one quart of claret, one table-spoonful of whole allspice, and one large lemon, sliced thin. Cut your red-fish in pieces about three or four inches square, bones and all, and half an hour before serving put it it in and let it boil until dinner. Serve with rice, as gumbo. Salt to taste.

DAUPHINE SOUP.

Place in a stew-pan half a pint of water, half a pint of lean ham, six apples, one onion, two cloves of garlic, one carrot, one turnip, and a knuckle of veal. Boil briskly over a quick fire, stirring occasionally. Let all cook until the bottom of the stew-pan is covered with a brownish glaze; then add three table-spoonfuls of curry-powder, one of curry-paste, and half a pound of flour. Mix well, and pour on a gallon of water; add a table-spoonful of salt, and half as much sugar. Let all boil up once; then remove to the back of the stove, and let simmer two and a half hours, skimming off the fat as it rises. Strain into the tureen and serve.

GUMBO.

Fry two fowls, old ones are best, with parsley, onions, pepper, salt, and lard or bacon. Put these into the pot with water sufficient for the soup, and boil until the flesh drops off the bone. Just before taking off the fire, add your oysters, and a few minutes after a table-spoonful of gumbo powder, or file′; scraps of ham or fried sausage are an improvement. The gumbo does not require boiling after the file′ is put in.

OKRA GUMBO.

Cut up one chicken, sprinkle with flour, and fry till brown; then add one onion and one quart of okra, both chopped fine, and fry with the chicken. Pour on three quarts of boiling water, and one pint of prepared tomatoes, and pepper and salt to taste. Boil three hours and serve with rice.

The chicken, okra, and onion should be fried in the vessel in which the soup is made, and in a porcelain or tin-lined vessel, as iron discolors the okra.

CRAB GUMBO.

Take one dozen large crabs, one cup of butter, and two or three onions. Wash the crabs, taking care to get them free from sand; take off the feelers and gills and divide the crabs into quarters; brown the onions in the butter with two table-spoonfuls of flour. Put in the crabs with about a handful of chopped ham. Fill up the pot with three quarts of cold water. Just before serving sift in about two table-spoonfuls of file′. Do not let it boil after the file is put in. Serve with rice.

OYSTER GUMBO.

Cut up a chicken, sprinkle with flour, and fry in the vessel in which the gumbo is made. When the chicken is nearly done, chop an onion and fry with it. Pour on this three quarts of boiling water and let it boil slowly till the flesh leaves the bones; then add the liquor from the oysters, salt and pepper to taste, two table-spoonfuls of tomato catchup; let this boil a short time, then add one hundred oysters, and allow them to boil only *five minutes.* When taken from the fire, and before pouring into the tureen, sprinkle in two table-spoonfuls of file′ or sassafras powder.

TO PREPARE FILE′ FOR GUMBO.

Gather sassafras leaves as late as possible in the season, before they turn red. Put them in the shade and open air to dry. When perfectly dry pound them, sift the powder, bottle it, and keep tightly corked.

GUMBO CHOU.

Boil the cabbage, take out and chop very fine, sprinkle with a little flour and put into hot lard with water enough to keep from burning. Add one pint of oysters and oyster-liquor, one tea-cup of tomatoes, salt and pepper to taste. Just before dishing add three table-spoonfuls of molasses. Serve with rice boiled dry.

GOPHER SOUP.

For a large gopher take two table-spoonfuls of lard, five of flour, and one onion, chopped fine. Put the lard in the pot in which the soup is made, and when it is boiling hot add the flour; when it is nicely browned add the onion and fry quite brown. Then put the meat in, fry fifteen minutes, then add three or four quarts of boiling water. About an hour and a half before serving, season with thyme, parsley, a little mace, cinnamon, cloves, allspice. The spices should be beaten and tied up in a bag, and the bag removed before serving. If there are gopher eggs put them in half an hour before dinner. Just before serving add one pint of Madeira, two of claret. This soup requires four hours' gentle boiling. Season with salt and pepper after adding the boiling water. The wine is a great improvement, but the soup is very nice without it.

FISH, CRABS, ETC.

BOILED COD-FISH AND BUTTER-SAUCE.

Put it in cold water, and boil gently fifteen minutes. Serve with drawn butter, and garnish with hard-boiled eggs.

BOILED RED-FISH.

Tie a large, solid fish in a domestic bag, and lay it in a long baking-pan on top of the stove, with enough water to cover it. Let it boil half an hour, turning it over carefully, that both sides may be well done. Serve with butter-sauce, for which take three table-spoonfuls of butter and one of sifted flour. Mix the flour and butter together, and have ready about a pint of boiling water. Stir the butter and flour in while boiling, being careful not to let lumps form. Boil four eggs hard; when cold, slice over the fish, seasoning well with black pepper and salt; then pour the sauce over the whole.

STEWED FISH, WITH OYSTERS

Cut the fish in pieces two inches thick. Put in a stew-pan a quarter of a pound of butter, a table-spoonful of flour, one onion minced fine, a little parsley and celery. Let this come to a boil; then add the fish, one pint of oyster liquor, the juice of a lemon, pepper and salt. Stew quickly, shaking the pan frequently. When nearly done, add two dozen oysters. Cook five minutes longer. Keep the pan well covered, to retain the flavor.

FISH "COURT BOUILLON."

Cut up a large fish and take out the bones; pour over it a cup of vinegar. Chop one onion and some parsley; fry these in *hot* lard, with red and black pepper, a table-spoonful of all-spice, a dozen pounded cloves, and three blades of mace. Pour into this a pint of tomatoes. Place the whole into a sauce-pan, and let it simmer slowly. Three quarters of an hour before dinner put the fish in, with a large spoonful of butter. Serve with crusts of toast around the dish.

BOILED FISH.

Having cleaned the fish thoroughly, wipe dry, and sprinkle with salt and pepper. Broil on a gridiron, over hot coals. When ready to serve, pour over the fish melted butter into which the juice of a lemon has been squeezed. Garnish the dish with sliced lemon Fish to be broiled must be opened down the back.

FRIED FISH WITH SAUCE.

Cut a red-fish or large trout in pieces four inches square. Season with salt and pepper, then roll each piece in corn-meal. Fry to a light brown in boiling-hot lard.

SAUCE FOR THE FISH.—Take the yelks of twelve hard-boiled eggs, creamed with a table-spoonful of sweet-oil, one of mustard, and a tea-spoonful of salt, half a cup of vinegar, and Worcestershire sauce or walnut catchup. Add three or four pickled cucumbers cut up fine. Place the fish around the edge of the dish, and the sauce, which must be quite stiff, in the middle.

FRIED RED SNAPPER.

Cut in thin slices from the bone. Brown four or five crackers, and roll them very fine. Beat well three or four eggs, and season them with salt and pepper. Have your lard ready, very hot. Dip the slices in the egg first, and then in the cracker. Have ready some parsley and butter, to make the gravy after the fish is taken out.

STEWED FISH.

Red fish or snapper is the best fish to cook in this way: Brown some flour in hot lard, and fry in it one onion sliced, one clove of garlic, and two table-spoonfuls of prepared tomatoes. Put in the fish cut in pieces, and half a pint of water, or just enough to cover the fish. Cook slowly for half an hour. Do not stir much, or it will break the fish. Season with pepper and salt. Just before taking up, add one half tumbler of claret wine.

MARY'S FISH—CUBION.

Cut a red-fish or red snapper in pieces and fry brown. In a separate vessel, cut up and fry one onion and two cloves of garlic; when brown, add two table-spoonfuls of flour, one pint of prepared tomatoes, a little pepper, salt to taste, one table-spoonful of Worcestershire sauce, and half a dozen whole cloves. Let this simmer for half an hour, then mix in half a pint of wine. Pour over the fried fish, and serve immediately.

BAKED FISH.—NO. 1.

Make a dressing of light bread, seasoned with butter, pepper, salt, and onion chopped fine. Fill the fish with this; then put in a pan, sprinkle with flour, and put on a little butter, pepper, and salt. Cover with tomatoes, and bake slowly. Pour half a pint of water into the pan, and baste occasionally.

BAKED FISH.—NO. 2.

Make a stuffing as you would for veal or poultry, with plenty of onions. Mix with it slices of fried salt pork, and pour on a pint of tomato catchup. Take part of the stuffing and put into the fish; pour the remainder over the fish.

Bake for one hour, if an ordinary sized fish; if larger, bake longer.

BAKED RED SNAPPER, OR SHEEP'S-HEAD.

Take two or three Irish potatoes, boil, then mash them with two table-spoonfuls of butter, a small onion cut very fine, black pepper, and salt to taste. Salt the fish, put it in a baking-pan, and stuff it with the potato-dressing; sprinkle a little flour over it. Put in the pan with the fish two table-spoonfuls of butter, two desert-spoonfuls of sweet-oil, a dozen tomatoes sliced (or half a can of prepared tomatoes), and a tea-cup of water. Bake in a moderate oven until done. When the fish is done, slice over it three hard-boiled eggs. Stir into the gravy a table-spoonful of tomato catchup, and one of Worcestershire sauce. Pour over the fish, and it is ready for the table.

FISH A LA CREME.—NO. 1.

Take any kind of fish boiled. Pick the fish to pieces, taking out all bones; place in a baking-dish. Beat together a spoonful of butter and a little flour; pour on this a pint of boiling cream, stir smooth, and season with salt and pepper, adding, if you choose, the yelks of two eggs, well beaten. Pour over the fish, grate a little cheese over the top, and bake twenty minutes.

FISH A LA CREME.—No. 2.

Boil a firm fish, pick it to pieces, removing the bones. Mix one pint of cream, or rich milk, with two table-spoonfuls of flour, a quarter of a pound of butter, salt, and one onion cut fine. Set it on the fire, and stir until it is the thickness of custard. Fill a baking-dish with alternate layers of fish, powdered cracker, and cream, using four crackers. Bake twenty minutes.

TURBOT A LA CREME.

Take four pounds of fish, for a large party; boil it with plenty of salt in the water. Take out all the bones, remove the skin, and flake the fish off. Boil a quart of cream; while boiling, stir in three large table-spoonfuls of flour perfectly smooth, add a bunch of parsley, three fourths of an onion, to flavor the cream; but when boiled take both out. Clarify a quarter of a pound of butter, and add to the cream after it is boiled, with a little cayenne pepper. Then butter a baking-dish, and put in first a layer of fish, then a layer of sauce, and repeat until the dish is full, making the sauce come on top. Strew over the top a thick layer of bread-crumbs. Bake half an hour. Garnish with egg and parsley.

SCALLOPED FISH.

Free the fish from the bones, and cut up in small pieces, with chopped onions, parsley, salt, and pepper. Beat two eggs well with one table-spoonful of catchup. Mix all together, and put in a baking-dish, with three slices of bacon over it. Bake a short time, and serve with melted butter.

CHOWDER.—NO. 1.

Boil half a pound of salt pork, cut it into slips, and cover the bottom of a pot with some of them; then strew in some sliced onions. Have ready a large fresh fish, cut it in large pieces, and lay part of them on the pork and onions, seasoning with pepper and salt. Then cover it with a layer of biscuit or cracker that has been soaked in milk or water; and on this put a layer of sliced potatoes. Then put a second layer of pork and onions, fish, cracker, etc., and continue this till the pot is nearly full, finishing with soaked crackers. Put in about one and a half pints of cold water, cover the pot closely, set it on the stove, and let it simmer about an hour. Then skim it, and turn it out in a deep dish. Leave the gravy in the pot until you have thickened it with a bit of butter rolled in flour, some chopped parsley, and a table-spoonful of Worcestershire sauce. Give it one boil up, and pour in the dish.

FISH CHOWDER.--NO. 2.

Take a red or any other firm fish, cut it in pieces about three inches square; one pound and a half of salt pork cut n thin slices; one dozen and a half of Irish potatoes, and the same of tomatoes, both sliced thin; half a dozen onions cut fine, and one dozen hard crackers broken in small pieces. Take a large pot, put a layer of pork on the bottom, then a layer each of fish, potatoes, tomatoes, onions, and crackers. Sprinkle each layer with a little salt, black pepper, and flour. Repeat the layers of pork, fish, potatoes, etc., until all are used. Fill with hot water until it covers the whole. Put the pot on the fire, and let it boil thirty minutes; then add a pint of claret and boil five minutes longer. The chowder will then be ready for the table.

FISH-PUDDING.

Take three pounds of fresh fish, boil in the evening, take out the bones, mince the fish quite fine. In the morning, make a sauce of one pint of milk, three eggs, three table-spoonfuls of flour, one table-spoonful of butter, a tea-spoonful of salt, the same of black pepper. Boil all together, and mix with the fish. Put all in a pudding-dish, and bake half an hour. Serve hot.

HOW SALT FISH SHOULD BE FRESHENED.

Mackerel, or any other salt fish, should be soaked in fresh water, with the flesh side down, as the salt falls to the bottom. If the skin is down, the fish comes out nearly as salty as when put in.

FRESH FISH-BALLS.

Pick clear of bones fish left from a dinner. Mix with this

as much bread-crumbs as fish, season nicely with pepper and salt, add one or two well-beaten eggs, and fry in hot lard. Eat with salad-dressing.

COD-FISH BALLS.—NO. 1.

Soak the cod in cold water in the morning, or over night. Change the water, and let it scald for an hour. Then boil five or six minutes. Chop very fine, and mix well with potatoes, using equal quantities of fish and potatoes, and adding butter, pepper, and milk, to soften. Make in small cakes and fry in lard.

COD-FISH BALLS.—NO. 2.

If intended for breakfast, soak the fish in cold water over night. *Do not boil.* In the morning take it from the water and place near the fire, where it may become warm while taking off the skin and picking the fish in small bits from the bone. Have boiled, meantime, some good Irish potatoes, —say about six or eight, for a good-sized fish. Take off the skins and mash while hot, with the fish adding a large table-spoonful of butter and one egg beaten. If too dry to make into balls, add a little sweet cream. Season with a little pepper. Make up into balls about the size of a biscuit. Roll them in flour, and fry in hot lard sufficient to swim the balls. When done, they will be a light brown.

FRIED EELS.

Cut the eels in pieces about four inches long. Beat some eggs, seasoning with pepper and salt to taste. Dip the pieces of eel in the egg, then in bread or cracker crumbs, and fry in hot lard.

STEWED CRABS.—NO. 1.

Scald the crabs, cut the bodies into four parts, pick the meat out of the claws. Take the *yelks* of two hard-boiled eggs, and rub them smooth in a desert-spoonful of vinegar. Roll some butter in flour; mince a small onion very fine. Put the crabs and these ingredients, with salt and pepper to taste, into a stew-pan. Cover them with about a pint of water, and let them cook slowly. When served, garnish the dish with sippets of toasted bread.

STEWED CRABS.—NO. 2.

Boil a dozen crabs, and pick them out, being careful not to leave a particle of shell with the crabs. Take a cup about three fourths full of butter, one large onion, one pod of red pepper. Fry the onion and pepper in the butter, with two table-spoonfuls of flour, browning them nicely. Put in the crab, stir up well, add half a pint of water, and black pepper and salt to taste. Let it stew gently ten or fifteen minutes. A couple of tomatoes chopped and added to this stew is an improvement.

STEWED CRABS.—NO. 3.

Take one dozen crabs well picked from the shell after being boiled. Boil one pint of fresh milk, with a tea-spoonful of finely-chopped onion, one table-spoonful of butter, salt, red and black pepper to taste, a pinch of mace, allspice, and one nutmeg grated, the whites of four hard-boiled eggs chopped fine, the yelks of the same rubbed smooth with a little milk. When this boils, add three or four table-spoonfuls of powdered crackers, and cook until the onions are quite done. Then put in half a pint of fresh cream and the crabs. Let all boil together a few minutes only. Serve with lemon-juice and sherry wine to your taste. It is necessary to stew quickly all the time. If too thick, add either milk or cream, whichever is most convenient.

FRICASSEED CRABS.

Boil and pick out the crabs; put them into a dish with black pepper, mustard, a small onion, thyme, and a large spoonful of butter with a tea-spoonful of flour rubbed into it. Add a tea-cup of water, grate bread-crumbs over them, and bake.

CRAB OMELET.

Take six or eight crabs. Prepare them by boiling and picking from the shell. Chop one onion fine, and fry it brown; then take it out of the pan. Then beat as if for cake six eggs; chop very fine one slice of ham and a small bunch of parsley. Put all together and stir well. Have the lard out of which you have taken the onion *hot*, and put in it the crab, egg, etc., stirring all until heated through. Just before taking off the fire, stir in a table-spoonful of butter. Roll it up as you would an egg omelet.

MOCK TERRAPIN.

Take half a calf's-liver, season and fry brown; hash it, but not too fine. Dash thickly with flour, and add one tea-spoonful of mixed mustard, a pinch of cayenne pepper, the same of cloves, two hard-boiled eggs chopped fine, a large table-spoonful of butter, one tea-cup of water. Let all boil two or three minutes, then add a wine-glass of wine. Cold veal may be used, if liver is not liked.

STEWED TERRAPIN.—NO. 1.

Boil six diamond-back terrapins whole, for about fifteen minutes; then take them out, pressing the liquor from them. Skim and strain the liquor. Cut the terrapins up, cleaning the entrails and removing the gall. Then put back into the liquor, and boil until done. Add the dressing, consisting of six wine-glasses of fine sherry, one pound of butter, one quart of cream, half a pound of flour well sifted, the yelks of six hard-boiled eggs, cayenne pepper and salt. Boil ten minutes, add lemon to taste, and serve.

STEWED TERRAPIN.—NO. 2.

Cut open your terrapin, take out the eggs, cut off the feet and legs; wash in pure water, then scald the legs and rub off the outer skin. Stew till tender, keeping the sauce-pan tightly covered; put in the eggs ten minutes before it is dished. Fry two onions and three spoonfuls of flour in one of lard. Pour the terrapin and gravy on this, seasoning with salt and pepper to taste. Before serving, add spices, two spoonfuls of whisky, four spoonfuls of wine. Garnisb the dish with lemon cut in slices.

TERRAPIN AU GRATIN.

Terrapin well cooked in a little water, with onion, salt, and pepper. Then put it in the upper shell, with a spoonful of butter, a little mace, grated cracker on top with an egg well beaten. Bake until brown. Serve with lemon.

SHRIMP STEWED WITH TOMATOES.

Take one can of shrimps, one can of tomatoes; add salt pepper, and butter to your taste, then stew twenty minutes

SHRIMP SALAD.

Boil the shrimps in salt-water, and remove the shells. Then make a dressing of the yelks of four hard-boiled eggs, creamed until smooth, one fourth of a tea-spoonful of cayenne pepper, one tea-spoonful of black pepper, two table-spoonfuls of mustard, and one of salt, one tea-cup of vinegar, two table-spoonfuls of olive oil. When thoroughly mixed, pour over the shrimp. This dressing will do for crabs also.

TO POT SHRIMPS.

Let the fish be freshly boiled, then shell them. Melt down with a gentle degree of heat some good butter; skim and pour it clear of sediment into a porcelain sauce-pan. Add a small quantity of salt, mace, nutmeg, and cayenne pepper.

When these have just simmered for three or four minutes, throw in the fish; toss them in the butter, that they may be well covered with it; let them heat through by the side of the fire, but by no means allow them to boil. Turn them into shallow dishes, and press them down into the butter. Should they not be well covered, pour a little more over them. Shrimps, one pint; butter, four or five ounces; mace, nutmeg, pepper, and salt to taste

For fish and turtle soup, and crab gumbo, see Soup Department.

OYSTERS.

FRIED OYSTERS.—No. 1.

Select large oysters, drain and spread on a cloth to absorb all moisture. Beat well two or three eggs, and season them with pepper and salt. Roll some crackers, and dip the oysters in the egg and then in the crumbs, then again in the egg and cracker crumbs. Drop into boiling lard, sufficient to cover them, and cook till of a light brown.

FRIED OYSTERS.—No. 2.

Drain large oysters and lay on a napkin. Beat well two eggs, and season with pepper and salt. Dip one oyster at a time first in the egg and then in corn-meal. Drop in boiling lard and fry a light brown.

OYSTER LOAVES.

Cut off carefully the end of a loaf of baker's bread, reserving the end; scoop out the crumb inside the loaf, leaving the crust entire. Fill the loaf with hot oysters, fried as in No. 1, leaving room for slices of pickle. Carefully replace the end cut off. If the oysters are hot, and the loaf well covered, they can be carried quite a distance, or eaten some time after being prepared, without getting cold. This is nice for a hasty lunch or a late supper. One dozen oysters will fill an ordinary sized loaf.

FRENCH STEWED OYSTERS.

Drain fifty large oysters, and strain the liquor into a stew-pan, seasoning with mace, half a pint of sherry wine, and the juice of two lemons. When this comes to a boil, stir well and skim; put in the oysters, not allowing them to boil as much as in an ordinary oyster stew.

FRANK'S STEWED OYSTERS.

For one hundred oysters take one pound of butter. Drain the oysters, put the butter in a sauce-pan, or chafing-dish, and when it is hot add the oysters, seasoning them highly with black pepper and salt. Let them stew gently until done. Break up about half a dozen crackers in small pieces, and sprinkle on top. Serve immediately.

STEWED OYSTERS.—No. 1.

Take fifty oysters, and all of the liquor; one pint of new milk, one tea-cup of sweet cream, two table-spoonfuls of flour with one of butter creamed with it, one dessert-spoonful of black pepper, and a very little cayenne. Salt to the taste just before dishing.

STEWED OYSTERS.—No. 2.

Take one hundred oysters and strain the liquor to remove any fragments of shell. Measure the liquor, and take an equal quantity of sweet milk; boil them in separate vessels. To the oyster liquor add a tea-cupful of cracker crumbs, salt and pepper to taste, and a large table-spoonful of butter. When this has boiled a few minutes add the oysters, which will require about five minutes to cook. Pour in a dish, and add the boiling milk last.

STEWED OYSTERS.—No. 3. (For a Pie.)

Put the oysters in their liquor on the fire. When they come to a scald take off and put in a sieve to drain. Strain some of the liquor; add butter, flour parsley, and mace; heat and put the oysters in it. For soup, use all the liquor, if needed, and boil a little milk in a separate vessel, and add after dishing.

OYSTER PATTIES.

Line a small patty-pan with puff-paste, and bake a light brown. When done, fill with oysters stewed as in No. 3. The patties should be served and eaten as soon as prepared, as the gravy soaking in the pastry will make it moist and heavy.

OYSTER PIE.

Butter a dish and spread rich pastry on the sides, but not on the bottom. Season the oysters with butter, pepper, and salt, and place them in the lined dish, with sufficient liquor to fill it. Over the top, sprinkle three hard-boiled eggs, chopped fine, and bread or cracker crumbs. Cover the whole with pastry, and bake in a quick oven.

OYSTER FRITTERS.—No. 1.

Take one pint of milk, two well-beaten eggs, and flour to make a smooth but rather thin batter. Season with pepper and salt. Stir in fifty large oysters; drop a spoonful of batter into boiling lard, having one or two oysters in each spoonful; cook brown, turning carefully to cook on both sides.

OYSTER FRITTERS.—No. 2.

Beat two eggs very light; stir in two table-spoonfuls of cream, three table-spoonfuls of flour, and pepper and salt to taste. Dip the oysters in this batter, and fry in boiling lard.

MINCED OYSTERS.

Take fifty oysters chopped fine; add one table-spoonful of chopped parsley, one of butter, one tea-spoonful of black pepper, six eggs well beaten, and enough crackers rubbed fine to make it the proper consistency to roll into balls. Fry quickly in boiling lard.

OYSTER SAUSAGE.

Take three or four dozen large oysters; cut them fine, and put in a colander to drain. Chop a small onion, and some thyme and parsley very fine. Melt a table-spoonful of butter, and pour it on the oysters, after taking them from the colander and putting them on a dish; season with salt and pepper. Roll eight large soda-crackers and mix with the other ingredients; beat two eggs and rub them in with the oysters and crackers. Add enough flour to roll into balls, and fry, like sausage, in very little lard or butter.

BROILED OYSTERS.

Drain and dry large oysters. Have ready an oyster broiler, hot and well-buttered, to prevent sticking. Season the oysters and broil well on both sides. Serve in a hot dish, with plenty of butter.

SCALLOPED OYSTERS.

Spread cracker crumbs on the bottom of a buttered baking-dish; place on these a layer of oysters, with pepper, salt, and bits of butter. Make alternate layers of crumbs and seasoned oysters till the dish is full, having a layer of crumbs on top. Make an incision in the center and pour in one well-beaten egg. Use butter only, and no oyster liquor. Brown nicely in a hot oven.

OYSTERS WITH FRICASSEED CHICKEN.

Fry the oysters in bread or cracker crumbs, and egg, a light brown. Lay them on the fricasseed chicken, and pour a thick-drawn butter-sauce over the whole.

A NICE WAY TO COOK OYSTERS.

Procure some nice, large, deep shells, cleanse thoroughly, and keep for the purpose. Open the oysters, place one in each shell, with a little of the water, a pinch of salt, and black pepper; grate a little Italian cheese over each. Cook in the oven of a stove.

MACARONI AND OYSTERS.

Boil a quarter of a pound of macaroni in salt-water until tender, then drain. Butter an earthen dish, and put in a layer of macaroni, then a layer of oysters, sprinkling on the oyster layer pepper, salt, and bits of butter, and on the macaroni layer bits of cheese. Make alternate layers of macaroni and oysters, till the dish is full, having a layer of oysters on top. Sprinkle cracker crumbs over the whole. Bake in a quick oven until brown. Fifty oysters will be sufficient for this quantity of macaroni.

STEAMED OYSTERS.

Turn the oysters into a steamer over a pot of boiling water; let them steam for half an hour, stirring occasionally. Serve in a hot dish with pepper, salt, and plenty of butter.

PICKLED OYSTERS.—No. 1.

Take one hundred fine, large oysters; drain the liquor from them and strain it, to remove all fragments of shell. Boil the liquor with one tea-spoonful of salt; when boiling drop in the oysters, allowing them to be only well scalded, not boiled. Remove the oysters, and add to the liquor one pint of strong vinegar, one tea-spoonful of black mace, two dozen whole cloves, two dozen whole black pepper, and two dozen allspice. Let the liquor, vinegar, and spices come to a boil, and when the oysters are cold pour it over them. These are for immediate use. If wanted to keep some time. allow the oysters to boil, and double the proportions of spices and vinegar.

PICKLED OYSTERS.—No. 2.

Boil the oysters slightly; then strain the liquor, and to one cup of vinegar put two cups of oyster liquor, cloves, allspice, mace, pepper, and salt to taste. Boil the liquor, spices, and vinegar, and pour over the oysters. When cold they are ready for use.

OYSTER SOUPS AND GUMBO.

See Soup Department.

MEATS, POULTRY, ETC.

TO BOIL A HAM.

Proceed inversely as with a soup-bone, since in the latter you wish to extract the juice, whereas in the ham you would preserve them. Hence the appropriateness of the directions given in chemical lectures to a class of embryo house-keepers, by Prof. Darby, of prophylactic notoriety. His directions are: "Have the pot of water boiling before putting in the ham with the skin on. The boiling water instantly coagulates the albumen, which prevents the escape of the juice." Keep the pot boiling constantly for four hours, if it is a ten-pound or twelve-pound ham, or longer for a larger ham. Do not allow the sight of a protruding bone to induce you to take it off too soon. When thoroughly done, remove from the pot and take off the skin. The essence which oozes out will be jellied when cold, and very nice, while the ham itself is tender and delicious, in every respect superior to the less boiled ham.

TO BOIL FRESH-PORK HAM.

Take sufficient boiling water to cover the ham. Put in this two quarts of salt, one half cup of dark molasses or brown sugar, a handful of whole black pepper, saltpeter the size of a large pea. Put the ham in this boiling mixture, and boil until thoroughly done, which will probably be when the meat leaves the knuckle-bone. Let this cool in the water in in which it is boiled, as all corned meats should.

BAKED STUFFED HAM.

Take a ham, wash well, put in a pot of hot water, and let it boil three hours. When nearly cold, take off the skin. Make a rich dressing of one loaf of baker's bread, three large onions chopped fine, one large table-spoonful of butter, one tea-spoonful of celery-seed, one of ground sage, and one of thyme; salt and pepper to your taste (a good deal of pepper); cook as you would dressing for a turkey. Make deep incisions in the ham, and fill them with the dressing in such a way that each slice may have some of the dressing in it. Two eggs well beaten and mixed with cracker crumbs, spread over the ham; and sprinkle brown sugar over this. Bake slowly for two and a half or three hours, basting *frequently* with the juice which runs from the ham.

BAKED HAM.

Soak the ham twenty-four hours, changing the water once or twice. Then skin and trim the ham. Take a quarter of a pound of fresh pork chopped very fine, two table-spoonfuls of pulverized sage, one table-spoonful of black pepper, one tea-spoonful of cloves, allspice, and cinamon combined, one onion chopped very fine. Moisten the mixture thoroughly with pepper-vinegar. Then, with a sharp knife make the incisions in the ham, starting toward the large end of the ham. Make one incision on the under side. Fill them with the stuffing. Put in the pan for baking. Sift well over with flour; and if the pan is deep, fill half full with water. Baste as you would a fowl. It will take from three to four hours to bake, according to the size.

ROAST PIG.—No. 1.

Take a pig of about eight or ten pounds; clean well, leaving on the head and feet. Make a stuffing of bread, two eggs, one table-spoonful of butter, sage, thyme, onion chopped, and pepper and salt. Stale bread is best. Soften with water, and put in a frying-pan, with a table-spoonful of lard to brown, mixing in the eggs, butter, and seasoning. When brown, stuff the pig and sew up the opening. Truss with the front legs bent backward and the back legs forward. Rub the pig with lard, and baste frequently. Cook till thoroughly done, and make the gravy (after removing the pig) by adding a little water thickened with flour, and the liver and heart of the pig (which have been cooked in the pan with it) chopped fine and mixed in. Serve in a gravy-dish.

ROAST PIG.—No. 2.

Shave off all the hairs, or burn them off with a white-hot poker, using it carefully and quickly enough not to burn the skin. Dress the pig, saving the heart, liver, and kidneys, which you must wash, slice, fry in a very little fat, and then chop fine. Wash the pig; dry it well with a clean cloth; stuff it with the following force-meat; sew it up; tie or skewer the legs in place; tie up the ears and tail in buttered papers, to prevent burning, and put it into a dripping-pan, with the following vegetables: Half a medium-sized carrot, one onion, a few sprigs of parsley, and a bay-leaf. Brush the pig thoroughly with salad-oil or melted butter. Put it into a hot oven until the crackling is set, basting it every fifteen minutes. A medium-sized pig will cook in from two to two and a half hours.

STUFFING FOR IT.—Fry together two ounces of sweet drippings or butter, half an ounce of chopped parsley, and about four ounces of chopped onion; season with one level table-spoonful each of powdered sage, thyme, and salt, and a level tea-spoonful of pepper. Soak half a pound of dry bread in tepid water for five minutes, then wring it dry in a towel. Add it to the onion and herbs, stir it until it is scalding hot, add the fried liver, the yelks of two eggs, and half a pint of boiling milk or water, and stuff the pig with it. Wash eight firm apples; cut them across the middle, but not down from the stem to the blossom; scoop out the cores, and bake only until tender, but not broken down. Peel and core eight more apples; stew them with a little sugar and the rind of a lemon. When perfectly tender, pass them through a sieve, and fill the halves of apple with this *pure'e.* Set them around the pig on a platter, and put a small lemon or sprig of holly in its mouth.

SAUSAGE.

In making sausage, allow one third fat to two thirds lean. Grind through a sausage-grinder, and season to taste with pepper, salt, and powdered sage-leaves. Make in small cakes, and fry without lard.

BAKED SAUSAGE-MEAT.

A medium-sized loaf of bread, eight pounds of beef, four pounds of fresh pork ground in a sausage-grinder, one table-spoonful of cloves, one large onion chopped fine, a small quantity of sage, one table-spoonful of whisky or brandy, pepper and salt to taste; cut up some red pepper; mix well before placing in pans; insert strips of fresh pork about two two inches long, and about an inch apart. Bake about four hours; do not take out until perfectly cold; slice crosswise. This will keep good some time.

FRENCH SAUSAGES.

Chop very fine, or pound in a mortar, equal parts of cold fowls, cream, dried bread-crumbs, and boiled onions; season them with salt, pepper, and nutmeg to taste; put them into the neck,—skins of poultry,—tying the ends, and fry them as you would fry sausages.

FRICADELS.

Mix well the following ingredients: Half a pound each of sausage-meat, dried bread-crumbs soaked in warm water and squeezed dry in a towel, one ounce of onion chopped fine, two eggs, one level dessert-spoonful of salt, and half a level tea-spoonful of pepper. Roll in the shape of corks, using a little flour to keep them from sticking to the hands, and fry brown in plenty of smoking-hot fat. Serve on toast. Any other minced meat may be substituted for the sausage-meat.

PAN HAMS.

Take hog's head and feet; boil them until the meat falls from the bones; withdraw them from the liquor, which strain and return to the vessel. Chop the meat very fine; season with pepper, salt, spice, onions chopped fine, thyme, sage, and parsley. Add all to the liquor, adding a sufficient quantity of corn-meal to make a stiff mush. Let it boil ten minutes, stirring all the time. Pour into a deep pan; when cold, cut in thin slices and fry.

PIG'S-FEET FRIED.

Have the feet well cleaned, and boiled until quite tender Split them, and lay in vinegar to pickle them. When ready to cook, have a batter made of an egg, flour, and water; pepper and salt to the consistency of pudding-batter. Fry in hot lard.

SMOKED MEAT ON TOAST.

Take a cold, smoked tongue or ham that has been well boiled; grate it on a coarse grater, or mince it fine. Mix it with cream and beaten yelk of an egg, a little pepper, and let it simmer over the fire. Prepare some nice slices of buttered toast; lay them in a dish that has been heated, and cover each slice with the meat mixture, which should be spread on hot. Place on the table in a covered dish. A nice dish for breakfast or tea.

DEVILED HAM.

Slice some ham very thin; sprinkle with cayenne and black pepper; broil until well down; place in a dish, and pour over it the following sauce, quite hot: Three table-spoonfuls of butter, one of vinegar, one of mustard, and one of Worcestershire sauce.

ROAST BEEF.

The surloin is the best piece of beef for roasting. Rub over the meat a little lard, and put in a baking-pan with the bone side down. When half done, sprinkle with pepper, salt, and flour, and baste frequently with the drippings. To make the gravy, remove the meat, and if there is not sufficient juice, add a little water and thicken with flour; season with pepper and salt to taste. Serve the gravy in a gravy-dish.

BOEUF 'A LA MODE.

Have a round of beef six inches thick. Take one and a half pounds of fresh *fat* bacon; cut in square pieces one fourth of an inch thick and four inches long. Then take one half ounce of allspice, one half ounce of cloves, and one ounce black pepper; grind together. To this add a small quantity of parsley, thyme, and three small pieces of garlic, all cut up fine. Roll the pieces of meat in the seasoning, and insert them in the round on both sides. Make incisions, and pour the remaining seasoning all over, adding a sufficient quantity of salt,—say two ounces. Let it stand eight hours before cooking. In cooking this, have a close vessel, with top to fit (an oven preferable); put in a spoonful of lard made hot. Place in the round, sprinkled with flour, two large onions cut up, and another spoonful of lard. Cover closely, and let it cook in its own juice four hours, turning it once.

HUNTER'S ROUND.

Rub well into a round of beef weighing forty pounds three ounces of saltpeter, and let it stand five or six hours. Pound three ounces of allspice, one of black pepper, and mix that with twenty pounds of salt and seven or eight pounds of brown sugar. Rub the beef well with this mixture, and pack it down to stay fourteen days. Scrape off the spices; place it in a deep pan, cover it with a common paste, and bake from eight to ten hours. When cool, wrap it in a linen cloth, and keep it in a cool place. Nothing nicer for lunch. This will keep well for several weeks.

SPICED BEEF.

Take a round of beef and rub it well with saltpeter; take out the bone in the middle, and fill the opening with salt. Bind the round in shape, or put it in a bucket or some vessel that fits rather close. Let it stand for three days; it will make its own brine. Then take one spoonful of powdered spice, one of black pepper, and one of brown sugar; rub the beef well with it. Then, after standing three days, rub it again with the spices, etc. After standing a week or ten days it will be ready for use.

TO COLLAR A FLANK OF BEEF.

Get a nice flank of beef, rub it well with a large portion of saltpeter and common salt. Let it remain ten days; then wash it clean, take off the outer and inner skin with the gristle; spread it on a board, and cover the inside with the following mixture: Parsley, sage, thyme chopped fine, pepper, salt, and pounded cloves. Roll it up; sew a cloth over it, and bandage that with tape; boil it gently five or six hours. When cold, lay it on a board without undoing it; put another board on the top with a heavy weight. Let it remain twenty-four hours; take off the bandages; cut thin slices from each end.

CORNED BEEF.

To six gallons of water add nine pounds of pure salt, three pounds of brown sugar, one quart of molasses, three ounces of saltpeter, and one ounce of pearlash. When the water is ready to receive the rest of the material, pour in the saltpeter *only*, and when dissolved, and the water *boiling*, dip your beef piece by piece into the boiling saltpeter water, *holding* it for a *few seconds only* in the hot bath. When the beef has all been immersed and become quite cool, pack it in the case where it is to remain. Then proceed with your pickle as first directed, and, when perfectly cold, pour it upon the meat, which should be kept down by a cover and stone.

BEEFSTEAK SMOTHERED.

Have the lard hot in the pan; put in the steak; season with pepper, salt, and sifted flour. Put a layer of onions and a layer of tomatoes; pour on a little water; then cover with another pan, and let it cook until nearly done. Take off the cover, and let it brown.

FRIED BEEFSTEAK.—No. 1

Surloin steaks are much the best for frying or broiling. Lay the steak in a frying-pan of hot lard or butter, after it has been dredged with flour and well sprinkled with pepper. Turn it frequently, until both sides are brown. When nearly done, sprinkle with salt. If onions are desired, slice enough of them to cover the steak, and fry with the meat. After taking the meat out, add a cup of boiling water, and thicken with brown flour for gravy.

FRIED BEEFSTEAK.—No. 2.

If the steak is not very young and tender, beat it slightly. Beat the yelks of two eggs, seasoned with salt and pepper; dip the steak in the egg, and then sprinkle over it cracker crumbs. Fry in hot lard.

STUFFED STEAKS BAKED.

Have a rich dressing as for turkey or sausage-meat, and take two steaks an inch thick each; place the dressing between them, and secure the dressing by serving them together. Have a wire frame rather smaller than the pan to be used; place the steaks on the frame, having previously prepared them with salt and pepper. Place a few bits of lard on the top of the steaks, a sufficient quantity of water in the pan, and bake; baste often; flour as usual for roasting or baking.

HOW TO COOK A BEEFSTEAK.

The vessel in which it is to be cooked must be wiped dry; place it on the stove, and let it become hot. Season your steak with salt and pepper; then lay it in the hot pan, and cover as tight as possible. When the raw meat touches the heated pan, of course it will adhere, but in a few seconds it will become loosened and juicy; turn the steak frequently, but be careful to keep covered. When nearly done, lay a piece of butter upon it; and if you want much gravy, add a table-spoonful of strong coffee. In three minutes the steak will be ready for the table.

Mutton-chops may be cooked the same way; but they require a little longer cooking. An excellent gravy can be made from them by adding a little cream, thickened with a small quantity of flour, into which, when off the fire and partly cool, stir the yelk of an egg well beaten.

BEEF-CAKES.

Pound some beef that is under-done with a little fat bacon or ham; season with pepper, salt, and onions. Make into small cakes, and fry them a little brown. Serve them in good gravy.

FORCE MEAT-BALLS

Mix with half a pound of veal chopped very fine, one half pound of pork chopped fine; season with salt, pepper, a little parsley minced, one table spoonful of curry-powder, the yelk of one egg, a tea cup of bread-crumbs, softened with cream or milk. They should be made in small balls, and fried in hot lard.

DRY HASH.

Take cold fresh meat of any kind that has been previously cooked; cut very very fine; mix with two boiled Irish potatoes well mashed, one egg, one onion minced fine. Season with pepper and salt. Put in a dish and bake.

HASH WITH GRAVY.

Cut up your cold meat in pieces half an inch thick; put it to stew with half a pint of water, one onion, one Irish potato chopped fine, one table-spoonful of lard, one table-spoonful of flour, pepper and salt to taste, and a little butter. Cook until the potato and onion are done. Serve with the gravy.

BEEF-HEELS.

Put the feet in hot water, with wood ashes sufficient to make a lye; let them stand in this until the hoof is softened, so as to pull off; put in cold water and boil until it leaves the bones. Take out and put in a bowl; season with pepper and salt, while warm. Take a large spoonful, roll in batter or in flour, and fry in hot lard.

BOILED MUTTON.

Put a leg of mutton into a boiler, with sufficient hot water to cover it; boil steadily; skim well, and keep covered by adding hot water. Allow fifteen minutes to every pound weight. Do not put in the salt until the meat is nearly done. Serve with egg-sauce, and a tea-cup of capers stirred in. If capers can not be obtained, cucumber pickles chopped fine is a good substitute.

ROAST MUTTON.

A roast of mutton should have lard or butter rubbed over it, and when half done a spoonful put in the pan; salt and pepper also. If it is a leg, it is improved by cutting gashes and filling them with a dressing made of bread-crumbs, pepper, salt, two eggs, butter or lard. When nearly done, dredge it with flour and baste frequently. Send to the table with its own gravy, slightly thickened with browned flour.

FRIED MUTTON-CHOPS.

Beat some eggs; season with pepper and salt; roll crackers fine. Dip the mutton-chops one by one in the egg, then in the cracker crumbs. Fry in hot lard.

Mutton-chops fried in bread-crumbs, laid on macaroni with slices of bread fried between, make a pretty dish.

HASHED MUTTON.

Cut thin slices of cold mutton, fat and lean; flour these; have ready an onion boiled in two or three spoonfuls of water; add a little gravy and the seasoned meat; let it get hot, but not enough to boil. Serve in a covered dish. Instead of onion, a clove, a spoonful of jelly, one half glass of port wine, will give venison flavor, if the mutton is good.

AN IRISH STEW.

Take mutton-chops; cover well with water; let them come to a boil; pour off the water; add more. Take a lump of butter the size of an egg, two table-spoonfuls of flour, a tea-cup of milk, with pepper and salt to taste; also a few Irish potatoes and one small onion. Boil until the potatoes are done.

VEAL LOAF.

Three and a half pounds of the finest part of lean and fat of a leg of veal chopped very fine, three soda-crackers rolled fine, two eggs, a piece of butter the size of an egg, a teaspoonful of salt, one of pepper, a thick slice of salt pork chopped fine. Mix all together; put bits of butter and grated bread-crumbs over it. Bake two hours. Put some water in another pan, and set in it the one containing the loaf. Bake two hours. To be eaten when cold. Cut in thin slices.

RICH AMELLA.

Mince your cold veal in a chopping-bowl, leaving out the stringy part. Put into a frying-pan a tea-cupful or more of milk or sweet cream, into which stir, when hot, a tablespoonful of butter and flour well mixed together; then add the chopped veal. Add a small piece of onion and thyme, or parsley chopped very fine; heat it well through; sprinkle over it a little mace. This is delicious for breakfast, and can be used for patties.

PRESSED VEAL OR BEEF.

Three pounds of veal knuckle well broken; boil in a little water until very tender; pick the meat to pieces, free from gristle and bone. Season the broth highly; add a little lemon-peel; butter in plenty; mix with the meat; add enough bread-crumbs to thicken; put into molds. Eat when cold.

VEAL OLIVES.

Slice as large pieccs as you can get from a leg of veal. Make a stuffing of grated bread, butter, a small onion cut very fine, a tea-spoonful of salt, a little black pepper, and spread over the slices of veal; beat an egg and put over the stuffing; roll each slice up tightly, and tie with a thread; stick a few cloves in them; grate bread-crumbs thickly over them, after they are put in the skillet with butter, and onions chopped fine. When done, lay them on a dish, make your gravy, and pour over them. Take the threads off, garnish with hard-boiled eggs, and serve. Cut the olives in slices.

CONFEDERATE VEAL.

Take two pounds of the round of white veal; beat a little; salt well; add plenty of red and black pepper; flour it well, and then lard it. Chop fine, parsley, thyme, carrot, and a little celery; spread these over as a paste; then grate the rind of a lemon over it. After squeezing the juice of a lemon over it, roll it up, tie it with a cord, sprinkle with flour, and fry until it is a light brown; then add one tea-cup of mushrooms. After pouring enough boiling water over it to make considerable gravy, let it simmer down; then add one table-spoonful of Worcestershire sauce.

VEAL CUTLETS.

1. BROILED.—When properly trimmed, they may be improved as directed for veal. Salt and pepper both sides; spread a little melted butter on both sides, also, by means of a brush; place them on before or under the fire; baste now and then with melted butter; turn over one, two, or three times, and when rather overdone, serve with a *maitre d' hotel* sauce spread all over. This way of serving them is sometimes called *au naturel.*

2. WITH CRUMBS.—When trimmed, dip them in egg beaten with salt, pepper, and chopped parsley; roll them in bread-crumbs, and then broil and serve them as the above, with a *maitre d' hotel.*

3. FINES HERBS.—Broil the chops as above, either with or without crumbs, and serve them with sauce *aux fines herbes.*

4. WITH MUSHROOMS.—When broiled and dished, surround them with a garniture of mushrooms, and serve warm. When there are several cutlets on the dish, and placed all around, overlapping, the garniture may be put in the middle of the chops.

FRIED VEAL-CUTLETS.

Pepper and salt two pounds of veal, sliced from the leg and cut in pieces half the size of your hand. Make a batter of two eggs and a little milk well beaten together. Have a tea-cupful of bread or cracker crumbs, and dip each piece of veal, first in the egg batter, and then in the crumbs, and fry quickly in boiling lard.

VEAL OMELET.

Three pounds of raw veal; four slices of salt pork chopped fine; three eggs; two table-spoonfuls of cream or milk; four powdered crackers. Season with thyme, one tea-spoonful of pepper, one of salt, half a nutmeg. Form into a loaf, and bake two or three hours in a slow oven. Baste with a little butter melted in hot water. Cut in thin slices for the table.

WELTON VEAL.

Boil four eggs hard; slice them, and line a dish. Then place a layer of raw veal cut thin. Mix chopped ham with one egg and sage for the next layer; then another of sliced veal, and so on, till the dish is full. Don't forget to salt and pepper to taste. Cover with a flat cover; put a weight on top to press; steam four hours. To be eaten cold, cut in thin slices.

VEAL BOUILLI.

Take about six pounds of fat veal, and cut in pieces about the size for stewing; sprinkle with flour, and fry brown. In the same vessel cut up and fry one onion and two pods of garlic; then add one pint of prepared tomatoes, one tea-spoonful of pepper, and the same of salt. When nearly done, cut up and add a sprig of parsley. This will require two and one half or three hours slow cooking.

STUFFED CALF'S-HEAD.

Put on your calf's-head to boil, with two sets of feet, either calf's-feet or hog's-feet. When perfectly tender, split the head on the under side, and carefully remove the bones, not breaking the skin; also, take the bones from the feet, and chop fine. Season to your taste with pepper, salt, a little onion, or any other seasoning you may fancy. Then stuff the skin and put it in nice shape in the baking-pan; then return it to the stove and let it remain until a light brown; then make a dressing of hard-boiled eggs, butter, and the brains of calf's-head. Serve with the head.

VEAL SWEET-BREAD.

Take two fresh sweet-breads; parboil them a few minutes; then lay them in cold water. Beat the yelks of two eggs; grate some cracker crumbs. When the sweet-breads are cold, wipe them dry; then dip them in the egg, and then in the crumbs; then cook them with a little butter, pepper, and salt, to a nice brown. Make a gravy by adding a little veal gravy to that in which they have been cooked, and the juice of a lemon. Toast thin slices of bread, and dip in this gravy and lay on the sweat-bread.

FRIED SWEET-BREADS.—No. 1.

Parboil them a few minutes, then drop them in cold water; skin them; roll them in a little flour, and fry moderately in boiling lard, seasoned with salt and pepper. Remove them from the fire, and stir into the gravy a little flour and hot water. When this boils, add a wine-glass of wine or catch-up.

FRIED SWEET-BREADS.—No. 2.

Scald them in salt and water; take out the stringy part; then put them in cold water for a few moments; dry them in a towel; roll some crackers or bread-crumbs; dip the sweet-bread in the yelk of an egg beaten; roll in the cracker, and fry brown in butter. When they are done, put them on a dish. Pour into a frying-pan a large cup of sweet cream, a little pepper and salt, and a little green parsley chopped fine; dust in a very little flour, and when it boils up, pour it over the sweet-breads and send to the table hot.

A PIE OF SWEET-BREAD AND OYSTERS.

Boil the sweet-breads tender; season with pepper and salt; make a gravy with the water in which they were boiled, adding half a cup of butter, the yelks of two eggs, and a tablespoonful of flour. Line the dish with puff-paste; have the same quantity of oysters as of sweet-breads; lay the oysters in first; cover with sweet-breads, and fill the dish with gravy; put on the top crust, and bake slowly until done.

STEWED SWEET-BREADS.

Prepare them by parboiling and letting them remain a few minutes in cold water, to whiten them. Stew in oyster-liquor until tender; then take them off and remove the gristle, and season with salt and pepper, a few oysters, and a large tablespoonful of butter. Pour on buttered toast.

Toast that is placed in the bottom of a dish upon which stews or gravies are to be poured, should be trimmed of the crust and dipped for a few minutes in hot water.

BAKED SWEET-BREAD.

Boil it half an hour; then throw it in cold water, to plump out; roll it in eggs and bread-crumbs, seasoned with salt and pepper. Lay them in the pan, put a lump of butter on each, and bake them.

FRIED LIVER.

Put in a frying-pan some slices of bacon, and fry out the grease, or a large spoonful of lard. Cut the liver in thin slices; season with pepper and salt; dredge with flower, and fry a good brown. It will require a longer time to cook than most meats. After taking up the liver, pour a little boiling water to the grease in which the liver has been fried, and sprinkle in a little flour to thicken the gravy. Let it boil up, and pour over the liver.

BEEF-KIDNEYS FRIED.

Remove all the fat and skin from the kidneys; cut in thin slices; mix with cayenne pepper, salt, parsley, and onion chopped fine; dredge with flour, and fry in hot lard. When the kidneys are taken out, add to the gravy a wine-glass of wine, a little lemon-juice, and a tablespoonful of butter.

KIDNEYS STEWED.

Take a set of kidneys and put in a stew-pan, with one half pint of water, two table-spoonfuls of butter, three onions sliced thin, pepper and salt, and a spoonful of flour.

TO BOIL SMOKED TONGUE.

Soak in cold water all night; put to boil in a pot of cold water. Boil gently for four or five hours. When done, peel and trim.

BAKED TONGUE WITH TOMATO-SAUCE.

Parboil a fresh tongue in salt-water until done enough to peel. Make a sauce of about one dozen ripe tomatoes, one large onion, black pepper, and salt; stew fifteen or twenty minutes. Put the tongue in a baking-pan, pour over it the sauce, and bake a nice brown.

STEWED BRAINS.

Scald a set of brains, to draw off the skin and blood. Put the brains in a stew-pan, with just enough water to keep them from burning. Season with a large table-spoonful of butter; pepper and salt to taste. When done, stir in one table-spoonful of cream or milk, with one table-spoonful of flour.

BRAINS FRIED.

Scald a set of brains, to take out the blood. Season with salt and pepper, and put in hot butter. When nearly done, break in a vessel six eggs, and turn in the frying-pan with the brains; cook a few minutes, stirring all the time.

FRIED TRIPE.

Cut in slices after being well boiled; dip each piece in thin batter, and fry in hot lard. It may be fried without batter; dredge with a little flour. Serve without gravy. In frying, lay the rough side down first.

STEWED TRIPE.

After the tripe is boiled tender, cut in small pieces an inch square. Make a dressing of cream or milk, one table-spoonful of butter, pepper, and salt; dredge a little flour in it; one small onion chopped. Stir these all together; put in the tripe one table-spoonful of curry-powder, and stew for twenty minutes.

ROAST TURKEY.

Cut three large-sized onions fine; take about half a loaf of bread, soak it in water, then squeeze the water from it. Put in a frying-pan two heaping table-spoonfuls of boiling lard; put the onion in, and when nearly done add the bread, and fry until perfectly brown. Season with two table-spoonfuls of butter; red and black pepper and salt to taste; a little sage may be used. Then put in about thirty or forty oysters, after the water has been drained off. Salt and pepper your turkey; put it in a baking-pan; then stuff it with the above mixture; sprinkle a little flour over it, two table-spoonfuls of lard, and the water that has been drained from the oysters, with about a pint of water. Baste the turkey often, and cook brown.

TO ROAST GOOSE.

Pick, draw, and singe the goose well. Cut off its head and neck. Take off the feet and legs at the first joint; also, take off the wings at the first joint. Stuff with a dressing made of bread-crumbs, seasoned highly with sage, onion, pepper, salt, and butter. Cover the breast with buttered paper, to preserve it from scorching, and roast to a fine brown. It will require from two hours to two hours and a half in roasting. Baste it well with butter, and a little while before it is done remove the paper and allow the breast to brown. Serve with apple-sauce.

WILD DUCKS

Prepare your dressing as you would for any other fowl, with the addition of more onion. Dry the ducks, sprinkle with salt and pepper, and roll in flour. Take three or four whole onions, put all in a pan with hot lard; turn frequently, until brown; add water enough to cover the fowls. Cook until there is just enough liquor left for the gravy.

CANVAS-BACK DUCKS.

Have the ducks wiped dry, and stuffed as any other fowl. Rub over them lard, pepper, and salt, and roast about an hour. Make a gravy by stirring slowly in a sauce-pan the giblets of the ducks rolled in butter, flour, and as little water as possible. Before sending to the table a little lemon-juice squeezed over them is an improvement.

MOCK DUCK.

Take a flank steak, make a dressing, the same as for ducks, spread it on the steak, then roll and tie tight with a string, to keep the roll in shape; lay it in a pan with a little water and lard, sprinkled with pepper and salt. Bake in the oven of the stove.

SALMIS OF COLD GAME, GOOSE, OR DUCK.

Put into a sauce-pan a piece of butter rolled in flour; let it melt, but not brown; add half a glass of broth, the same of red wine, two whole shallots, and a bunch of mixed herbs,—

to be taken out before serving,—pepper and a little salt; boil together for half an hour. Cut up the game or duck warm, but do not boil it in this sauce, and add the juice of half a lemon. Garnish the bottom of the dish with fried slices of bread, and put the game upon it. Pour the sauce over it and serve.

BIRD-PIE.

Take about eight doves, and make a stuffing of bread and onions. Stuff each bird, then put into a stew-pan about a table-spoonful of lard, and a dessert-spoonful of flour; let it brown perfectly; cut a small onion very fine, and fry it, adding the birds, which should fry awhile before putting a pint of water over them, and let them boil until done. Take them out; add about two dozen oysters, with a little of the oyster-water, to the gravy, a table-spoonful of butter, salt, black pepper, allspice, and nutmeg; then line a baking-dish with pastry, put the birds in with the gravy, and cover it over with pastry and bake.

SQUABS.

Squabs are in the best condition to eat when fully feathered. Broil on hot coals, seasoned with melted butter, pepper, and salt. Serve on toast. A pie made of squabs, as you would make chicken-pie, is an excellent dish.

BOILED CHICKEN.

For boiling, choose a fat fowl. Fill the breast with forcemeat or stuffing, and tie carefully round the body, or secure by sewing, which should be removed before sending to the table. Put it in hot water, and boil gently till done. Serve with drawn butter-sauce, in which three or four hard-boiled eggs have been chopped. This sauce can be made ornamental by chopping one boiled beet fine, and mixing with it. Pour part of the sauce over the chicken, to garnish it, and put the remainder in a sauce-boat, to be served out as dished.

CHICKEN POT-PIE.

Cut up a chicken at the joints,—as for frying. Make a rich dough or crust; place in the bottom of a pot, or large sauce-pan, a layer of the chicken, pepper, salt, bits of butter, and strips or squares of the dough; then place another layer of chicken, and over all put a crust of the dough in which an opening is left to pour a little water as the pie becomes too dry. Cover the pot closely, and cook about an hour and three quarters.

CHICKEN-PIE WITH EGGS.

To one chicken, six hard-boiled eggs, and one cup of butter. Cut the chicken as for frying; parboil in sufficient water,—in which you put a little salt,—to cook it tender. Line a baking-pan with puff-paste; put in a layer of chicken, then a layer of the eggs, with bits of the butter; sprinkle well with black pepper and salt to your taste, then another layer of chicken, eggs, butter, and pepper, until all are in the pan; cover the whole with the water in which the chicken was boiled; add a top crust and bake.

BROILED CHICKEN.

Cut the chicken open in the back, and lay it in salt-water for an hour, to extract all the blood; then wipe quite dry with a napkin or towel, and lay on a hot gridiron, over clear coals. Have in a pan some melted butter and pepper, with which to baste while broiling. Brown the chicken on both sides, and when dished pour over it the remainder of the melted butter. Only young and tender chickens should be used for broiling.

TO COOK AN OLD CHICKEN.

Wash carefully and fill with buttered bread-crumbs, seasoned with pepper, salt, and thyme; put in a pot with a tight-fitting cover, with about a pint of water; turn often, and cook two hours, or until tender.

TO FRY CHICKEN.

Beat two eggs, to which add a little milk; pepper and salt your chicken, dip it in the eggs and milk; then roll in powdered crackers, and fry in lard or butter until brown.

CHICKEN 'A LA MANGE.

Cut a raw chicken into two parts. Put half a tea-cup of sweet-oil in a sauce-pan; let it get hot; put your chicken in, and fry it brown on both sides; add a small onion, or a quarter of garlic, chopped with parsley, to suit the taste; dredge with flour, and fill the sauce-pan with water, so as to cover the chicken. Cover it very close, and stew inside the stove until done. Fry a dozen eggs on both sides, and serve with the chicken.

CHICKEN FRICASSEE.

Prepare a chicken; cut it into small pieces, put them into a sauce-pan, with half an onion, a small piece of mace, salt and pepper to taste, root celery; let all boil slowly until the chicken is tender and cooked, without falling to pieces, the water simmered away. Just before serving, beat up the yelks of two eggs; pour to them the broth of the chicken, hot, and stirring well; pour it back upon the chicken, but do not let it boil, or it will curdle.

FRICASSEE CHICKEN WITH APPLE.

Dress and disjoint a fowl. Place it in a deep kettle, with sufficient water to cover it, and a little salt. When quite tender pour off the liquor and brown nicely in salt-pork fat. Thicken the gravy and season with pepper. To one good-sized chicken take eight tart apples, wipe, halve, and take out the cores. Set them over the chicken, skin side down, then pour on the gravy, cover tightly, and let them cook ten minutes, or till tender. Serve the apple upon a separate dish, and eat as sauce. If the gravy needs butter, add it after the apple is taken out. Young turkeys are nice prepared in this way.

POUL'ET 'A LA MARANGE.

Fry the chicken in lard, brown as for gumbo, with onion. Of course, the chicken must be cut. When well done put it in a stew-pan and cover it with water. Let it simmer slowly; season with pepper, salt, butter, and a box of mushrooms. Garnish the dish with toast and eggs fried on both sides; or if you prefer, you may use pastry-cakes. A little wine, red or white, a few olives, with seed taken out. Some pickle and parsley is nice to garnish the dish. Very nice made of cold turkey.

A NICE WAY TO COOK CHICKEN.

Prepare a nice frying-size chicken; season with salt and pepper; fry in batter a nice brown. Lay on a dish in which you are going to serve. Make a sauce of five or six large tomatoes, chopped, a small onion, a little cream, pepper and salt, stewed for five or ten minutes. Pour over the chicken, and serve hot.

CHICKEN 'A LA BRUNSWICK.

Take two fat young chickens; cut them up, not too fine. Put into a good-sized sauce-pan one table-spoonful of lard, one of butter; brown two table-spoonfuls of sifted flour into the lard and butter, with an onion chopped fine. Salt and pepper your chicken to taste. Slice three or four pieces of salt pork or fat from a ham; fry it with the lard, butter, flour, and onion. Have ready, peeled and cut fine, one quart of new Irish potatoes, one quart of tomatoes, one of Lima beans, one of green peas, one of green corn, and a glass of good claret wine. First, brown the flour, then add the onion, then the chicken, then the vegetables, with just enough boiling water to cover the ingredients; let it boil until done. Just before taking up add the wine: let it stay about ten minutes. Stir well, and serve hot.

JELLIED CHICKEN.

Take one large chicken, or two small ones; boil them in a quart of water until tender. Cut off the meat, put the skin and bones back into the liquor and boil it down to a pint of jelly—about three quarters of an hour. Chop up the meat of the chicken and pound it fine; add to it a tea-spoonful of powdered mustard, one of salt, one of butter, a little pepper, and half a tea-cupful of the liquid jelly, from which you must strain the bones and skin; the remainder of the liquid jelly pour into the bottom and let it cool. Put the pounded chicken in a sauce-pan, and warm it, so that all the ingredients may be thoroughly mixed; then let it cool, and spread it on the top of the jelly, in the mold. Set the mold in a cool place. When wanted to use, set the mold, for an instant, in hot water, and turn out like *blanc-mange'*.

TURKEY GELATINE.

Chop fine and separately the meat of a cold turkey, some sliced ham, four hard-boiled eggs, and some mustard pickles, and put them in a mold in alternate layers. Place the remnants and bones in a stew-pan, with some thyme, mace, pepper, half an ounce of isinglass, and enough water to cover, and allow it to boil gently and thoroughly. When done, strain it through a sieve and pour on the chicken in the mold. Turn out when cold. Chicken may be used instead of turkey, if desired.

BRUNSWICK STEW.

At ten o'clock put on two slices of fat bacon, and one onion cut fine, and boil one hour. Then put on two quarts of tomatoes, skimmed, or mashed well, and boil one hour; then put in a large pod of red pepper, and two chickens, cut as for frying, and stew until two o'clock; then put in one cup of butter, and stale bread-crumbs for gravy. Add two ears of corn, first boiled and cut from the cobs, some Irish potatoes, mashed; salt to taste, and serve hot. A squirrel could be used instead of chicken.

"TO COOK A CHICKEN LIKE TARRAPIN."

Boil a fine, fat, young chicken; when done and warm, cut all the meat from the bones, in small pieces, as for chicken-salad. Put into a stew-pan with one gill of boiling water; then stir together, until perfectly smooth, one quarter of a pound of butter, one tea-spoonful of flour, and the yelk of a hard-boiled egg. Add to the chicken half the mixture at a time; pepper and salt to taste. After letting it simmer ten minutes, add a wine-glass of sherry or Madeira. Add spice and mushroom; catchup to taste.

PILLAU.

Boil one pint of rice in as much water as will cover it. When boiled, put in a chicken with one onion, a blade of mace, some whole pepper, and salt. When it is boiled sufficiently put the fowl in a dish, and pour the rice in it. A small piece of bacon boiled with the rice, and then taken out, adds to the flavor. Boil several eggs hard, and slice over the chicken.

CHICKEN CROQUETTES.

The lean of chicken, free from skin, minced finely with a little ham and stale bread-crumbs. The proportions will be six table-spoonfuls of meat, two of bread-crumbs, very fine, a shade of nutmeg, pepper, half a tea-spoonful of onions, a tea-spoonful of minced parsley; put all on with half a pint of stock—your soup for dinner will answer. When it comes to a boil mix a couple of eggs, well beaten, and some cream, and stew until it thickens. Spread it out on a dish to cool;

shape like an egg. Roll in crumbs, and throw them into very hot lard, and fry quickly. Serve on a napkin with parsley. Brains stewed with the above is a great improvement. Veal croquettes are made in the same way.

TO MAKE CROQUETTES.

Take cold chicken or veal, with slices of ham, fat and lean; chop them together very fine, and add a set of brains, mashed very fine also. Mix with stale bread, grated and seasoned to your taste; knead all well together, until it resembles sausage-meat. Make up in little balls; dip them in the yelks of eggs beaten; cover them quickly with grated bread, and fry them a light brown.

JAM BOLAYA.

Have the lard hot, put in flour, cook to a light brown, with a medium-sized onion. Take the giblets, neck, small part of the wings and feet of your chicken, and put in the lard; add half a tea-cup of prepared tomatoes, two dozen oysters, with their liquor, pepper and salt to taste; put in nearly a pint of rice, one table-spoonful of butter; stir frequently when nearly done; set back on the stove and let steam.

VENISON 'A LA MODE.

Remove the bone from the haunch, and make a large quantity of force-meat, or stuffing of bread-crumbs, bits of pork, an onion minced fine, a small piece of celery, or celery-seed, parsley, and sage. Season with pepper and salt to taste. Press in the stuffing till the hole left by the bone is filled. Sew up the opening and spread over it nice lard; pepper and salt to taste. Cook well done; take out the meat, stir in a dessert-spoonful of flour, a wine-glass of wine; let it boil up once, and serve in a sauce-bowl.

HAUNCH OF VENISON.

A good haunch of venison will take three or four hours to

roast. It being a dry meat it would be well to cover it with a paste made of flour and water, until nearly done; cover this with a thick piece of paper, tied on. Baste the paper well with butter, to keep it from catching on fire. When this is removed baste well with the drippings seasoned with salt, pepper, and a little browned flour sprinkled over. Butter or lard may be necessary to afford sufficient gravy. This meat should be accompanied with a tart jelly.

VENISON STEAKS.

Cut the steaks about an inch thick, sprinkle with flour, fry in hot lard or butter. Season with salt and pepper when half done; turn frequently. Take out the steak when done, stir a little flour in the pan, and pour enough hot water on to make sufficient gravy. Let it boil up; then pour in a wine-glassful of wine, and pour over the steak.

ANOTHER WAY TO COOK BEEF OR VENISON STEAKS.

Put it in a well-covered pan, and heat it thoroughly without water. Take it out, and when cool enough to handle press it, so as to extract all the juice. Mix with the juice a table-spoonful of butter, pepper, salt, a little mustard, vinegar, and walnut catchup, and put on the stove until they are well mixed. Return the steak to the covered pan, and pour the gravy over it and cook gently till done. It will not take much time, as the meat is partially cooked. This method is equally good for beefsteak.

BARBECUE.

To barbecue any kind of meat is simply to broil it. When you wish to cook a whole mutton, or any other animal, have a large pit dug in the ground, and several hours before cooking make a good fire of oak-wood, and let it burn to a bed of coals. Place over the top of this pit strips of dry wood, upon which you place your meat. Make a sauce of butter, vine gar, mustard, salt, pepper, catchup, and baste the meat frequently; use a stick with a piece of cloth tied on the end, to baste with. To cook meat in this way requires constant attention. Turn the meat often. A smaller piece of meat can be cooked in the same manner, on a gridiron, over hot coals.

SQUIRREL STEWED.

Skin them very carefully, so as not to allow the hair to touch the flesh; this can be done by cutting a slit under the throat, and as you pull it off, turn the skin over, so as to inclose the hair. Cut the squirrel in pieces (discard the head), and lay them in cold water; put a large table-spoonful of lard in a stew-pan, with an onion sliced, and a table-spoonful of flour; let fry until the flour is brown, then put in a pint of water, the squirrel seasoned with salt and pepper, and cook until tender. When half done put in some strips of nice puff-paste and a little butter.

SQUIRREL BROILED.

Broil over hot coals, and baste frequently with melted butter, pepper, salt, and a little vinegar. Rabbits should be prepared in the same manner as squirrels.

TO COOK FROGS.

Put the hind legs in salt and water over night. Wipe them dry with a cloth; sprinkle a little flour over them, and fry in hot lard to a light brown; or, they can be rolled in egg and cracker-dust before frying.

FROGS STEWED.

Skin, boil five minutes, throw into cold water, and drain as above. Put in a stew-pan two ounces of butter, for two dozen frogs; set it on the fire, and when melted lay the legs in; fry two minutes, tossing now and then; then sprinkle on them a tea-spoonful of flour; stir with a wooden spoon; add two sprigs of parsley, one of thyme, a bay-leaf, two cloves, one of garlic, salt, white pepper, and half a pint of white wine; boil gently till done, dish the legs, reduce the sauce on the fire, strain it, mix in it the yelks of two eggs; pour on the legs and serve them.

EGGS.

BOILED EGGS.

Put eggs into boiling water. If you wish the whites set, boil two minutes; if you wish the yelks set, boil three minutes; if for a salad it will require ten minutes.

TO POACH EGGS.

Break into a vessel of boiling water as many eggs as will cover the bottom; best not to touch. Let them cook until the whites are set. Take up with a perforated skimmer, pour melted butter over them, and dust with pepper and salt. They are nice served on toast.

TO SCRAMBLE EGGS.

Break the eggs into a bowl, and stir in salt and pepper. Put a good piece of butter in a frying-pan, and when it is hot pour in the eggs, stirring all the time; a few minutes will be sufficient. Grated ham is an improvement.

EGG-TOAST.

Boil one tea-cup of milk, thickened with a little flour or corn-starch, and one table-spoonful of butter; stir in your eggs that have been seasoned with salt and pepper, cook until the whites are set. Pour over buttered toast while hot.

OMELET.

Beat six eggs very light—the whites to a stiff froth, the yelks to a smooth batter. Add to the yelks a small cup of milk, pepper, and salt; lastly, stir in the whites lightly. Have ready in a hot frying-pan a good lump of butter; when it hisses pour in the mixture gently and set over a clear fire. It should cook in ten minutes. To be eaten as soon as cooked, as it will fall.

SHIRRED EGGS.

Take as many saucers or small earthen plates as are required for each person. Break into each two eggs, being careful not to break the yelks, and place in a well-heated stove to bake, the whites only to be done, the yelks half done. They are to be eaten out of the saucers, and seasoned to taste at the table.

FRIED EGGS.

Break the eggs in hot lard with a little salt and pepper. It is best to break the eggs in a saucer before putting in the frying-pan, as some may not be good. Do not turn them over. Serve with fried ham.

BAKED EGGS.

Boil one dozen eggs until perfectly hard, then put in cold water; shell, and divide the egg in half, remove the yelk and mash up smooth, add a few bread-crumbs, season with butter, pepper, and salt. Fill the whites of eggs with this dressing; grate a cracker over the top, and bake to a light brown.

STUFFED EGGS.

Boil the eggs hard; put in cold water. Cut out the small end of the eggs, take out the yelks, put in a bowl, and mash well, with a small onion and a little celery chopped fine, four spoonfuls of cream, black pepper and salt to taste, and one table-spoonful of butter; stuff the whites with the mixture and bake in a quick oven.

OMELET SOUFFLE'.

Half a cup of sugar, half a cup of butter, one cup of flour, one pint of milk; mix well together, set it on the fire and stir until it thickens, then add the yelks of five eggs, well beaten, and set aside to cool. Beat the whites of the eggs to a stiff froth, mix well in the above. Put in a pudding-dish well buttered, and bake in a tolerably hot oven. Eat warm, with or without sauce.

OMELET WITH HAM.

Six eggs beaten separately, season with pepper and salt; add grated ham, and fry in small cakes in boiling butter.

PICKLED EGGS.

Scald one quart of vinegar, with a half dozen cloves, one dozen allspice, one tea-spoonful of pepper, one table-spoonful of flour of mustard. Pour this over one dozen hard-boiled eggs that have been shelled and placed in a jar. When eggs are boiled hard and are intended to be used when cold, they should be thrown immediately into cold water, to keep them from becoming discolored.

EGG-BALLS FOR SOUP.

Rub the yelks of three or four hard-boiled eggs to a smooth paste, with a very little butter and salt; add to these two raw ones, beaten light, and enough flour to hold the paste together. Make into balls, with floured hands, and set in a cool place until just before your soup is taken off, when put in carefully and boil one minute.

EGGS A LA CR'EME

Hard-boil twelve eggs; slice them in thin rings; have ready a plateful of grated bread-crumbs. In the bottom of a large baking-dish place a layer of the crumbs, then one of the eggs; cover with bits of butter, and sprinkle with pepper and salt. Continue thus to blend these ingredients until the dish is full, having the crumbs on the top. Over the whole pour a large tea-cupful of cream, and brown nicely in a moderately heated oven.

TO TEST EGGS.

Put them in water; if the large end turns up they are not fresh. You can depend on any egg that will lay on the side in water and not float.

FRIED EGG-TOAST, OR DUTCH TOAST.

Slice bread, and butter it; beat five or six eggs very light, and dip into them each slice of bread, and fry in hot butter; pepper and salt to the taste just as you take from the fire. Serve hot.

SALADS.

CHICKEN SALAD.—No. 1.

DRESSING.—Twelve hard-boiled eggs; rub the yelks in one tea-cupful of olive-oil, two table-spoonfuls of ground mustard, one tea-spoonful of ground pepper, one table-spoonful of Worcestershire sauce, one half tea-cupful of tomato catchup, one half tea-cupful of vinegar, three good-sized pickles, chopped fine, and salt to taste; two stalks of celery chopped, and if this can not be obtained use a small head of cabbage, well chopped, and celery-seed as a substitute. The above will answer for one chicken, which should be well boiled, freed from bones, and chopped; mix all together and cut up the whites of the eggs fine; mix a part with the salad, and strew a portion over the top.

CHICKEN SALAD.—No. 2.

For about one pound of chicken, after it is minced, use six or eight eggs, boiled hard; separate the yelks and whites; mash the yelks to a smooth paste, in five or six table-spoonfuls of sweet olive-oil, or the same of melted butter if preferred; add to this a tea spoonful of pepper, and the same of salt, two even table-spoonfuls of dry mustard, a half tumblerful of good vinegar, one table-spoonful of sugar. Stir these all together; mince half as much white lettuce as there is chicken, and the same of white, tender celery. If celery can not be obtained, use a little extract of celery and more lettuce. Mix these well with the meat, using a wooden or silver fork. The whites of the eggs may be minced and mixed with it, or reserved to garnish the salad-dish, by cutting them in rings; add the sauce just before serving. A few small white lettuce-leaves, trim very nicely.

CHICKEN SALAD.—No. 3.

To each chicken allow ten eggs; chop the whites very fine; mix thoroughly with the chicken, rub to a smooth paste the yelks and allow half a tea-spoonful each of mustard, black pepper and salt, a sufficient quantity of vinegar to make it palatable; also one table-spoonful of oil, or the same quantity of melted butter. Celery to be used according to taste.

DRESSING FOR CHICKEN SALAD.

Yelks of four eggs, beaten well, one tea-spoonful of sugar, one salt-spoonful of cayenne pepper, two tea-spoonfuls made mustard, six table-spoonfuls salad-oil, five of celery-vinegar; stir all well and put in a sauce-pan, boil three minutes, stirring all the time; when cold pour over chicken salad.

LOBSTER SALAD.

To a can of lobsters make a dressing of one tea-spoonful of salt, one tea-spoonful of pepper, one table-spoonful of mixed mustard, four table-spoonfuls of olive-oil, four table-spoonfuls of good vinegar, the yelks of three hard-boiled eggs, rubbed smooth. Garnish with lettuce.

POTATO SALAD.

Peel and slice four boiled potatoes; chop fine half small onion, one bunch celery, and the whites of three hard-boiled eggs. The yelks mix with salt, pepper, mustard, oil, and vinegar to taste.

IRISH-POTATO SALAD.

Take a couple of cold potatoes, cut fine, with half a raw onion; put sweet-oil, pepper, salt, and vinegar upon them.

TOMATO AND POTATO SALAD.

Slice four tomatoes, four Irish potatoes, cold, and one onion. Make a layer of potatoes, then onions and tomatoes, alternating, until all are used; pour over this a dressing as for potato salad, and when ready to use place on top a lump of ice.

ITALIAN SALAD.

Soak in water six herrings for one hour; skin and bone them; cut up six boiled Irish potatoes, six onions, six apples, six hard-boiled eggs, half pound of cold veal or fowl, half pound salt anchovies; chop fine and mix together with four table spoonfuls of capers, and half dozen pickles, and one dozen olives; add three table-spoonfuls of olive-oil, pepper, and vinegar to suit. Place on a dish and ornament with olives, the yelks and whites of eggs, parsley, capers, and red beets.

SOLFERINO.

Equal quantities of grated ham, mashed boiled Irish potatoes, peeled raw tomatoes, chopped fine, and a little chopped onion. Then make a sauce of drawn butter, mustard, and vinegar; pour over immediately.

SALAD DRESSING.

One tea-cupful of vinegar, one dessert-spoonful of butter two table-spoonfuls of sugar, one dessert-spoonful of mustard, half tea-spoonful of salt, one egg, half tea-cupful of milk. The vinegar, butter, and sugar put on and let come to a boil, the other ingredients beat together; add to the vinegar after it cools a little, then put on the fire and boil to the thickness of cream. Add table-oil, according to taste.

SALAD DRESSING.

Take half a tumbler of vinegar, one table-spoonful of butter, one tea-spoonful of sugar, one tea-spoonful of salt, one tea-spoonful of mustard. Put it all on the fire and let it come to a boil; then stir in quickly two eggs, beaten well, the whites and yelks beaten separately, and very light; take off immediately. Serve when cold.

SALMON SALAD.

If the salmon salad is made of the fish preserved in cans, drain it from the oil, and mince the meat fine; cut up one third as much lettuce or celery. For one box of salmon boil four eggs hard, lay them in cold water a few minutes, shell and separate the whites and yelks, and lay the whites aside. Mash the yelks smooth with two table-spoonfuls of sweet olive-oil or one tea-cupful of sweet milk or cream; add one tea-cupful of vinegar, one table-spoonful of sugar, one tea-spoonful of salt, two or more tea-spoonfuls of fine mustard, pepper to the taste, and toss lightly over the meat with a silver fork. Ornament with the leaves of the celery, or with curled parsley, and the whites of eggs, cut in rings.

OYSTER SALAD.

Take half a gallon of fresh oysters, the yelks of four hard-boiled eggs, one raw egg, well whipped, two spoonfuls salad-oil, or melted butter, two tea-spoonfuls of salt, two tea-spoonfuls of black pepper, two tea-spoonfuls made mustard, one tea-cupful of good vinegar, nearly as much celery as oysters; cut up very fine, drain the liquor from the oysters and throw them into hot vinegar, on the fire; let them remain until they are plump, but not cooked. Then put them at once into clear cold water. This gives them a nice, plump look; and they will not then shrink and look small. Drain the water from them and set them in a cool place; mash the yelks very fine, rub into it the salt, pepper, and mustard, then the oil, a few drops at a time. When smooth add the beaten eggs and then the vinegar, a spoonful at a time. Mix oysters, celery, and pickle; sprinkle in salt to taste; then pour dressing over all.

SALAD CREAM.

Take the yelks of three fresh eggs, and whisk them well up with ten grains of cayenne pepper; then take one ounce of mustard, salt one dram and a half, salad-oil half an ounce; mix well with half a pint of the best vinegar, and then add the two lots together; shake them well and you will have an excellent mixture, which will keep for twelve months.

COLD SLAW.

Two eggs, one table-spoonful of butter, or olive-oil, one table-spoonful of sugar, one cupful of vinegar, one table-spoonful of mixed mustard and pepper; put into a tin bucket, and cook in a kettle of hot water. Be careful not to let it curdle. Cut cabbage very fine; salt it, and pour on the dressing when cold.

WARM SLAW.

Pour boiling water over the cabbage, and cut up very fine; melt butter with cream or milk; mix pepper, salt, mustard, and vinegar; pour over hot

HOT SLAW.

Cut the cabbage very fine, and lay in cold water; prepare a dressing of one tumbler of vinegar, one table-spoonful of mustard, one tea-spoonful of black pepper, one table-spoonful of olive-oil, or a large table-spoonful of butter, and one tea-spoonful of salt. Put the mixture on the fire, and when hot stir in the cabbage; cook a few minutes. Serve hot.

CELERY SLAW.—No. I. (Fine.)

Take half a head of cabbage and three bunches of celery, chopped fine. Mix well one cup of vinegar, lump of butter the size of an egg, yelks of three eggs, tea-spoonful of mustard, one of salt, one of pepper, and two of sugar; heat this mixture on the stove till it thickens, stirring constantly;

when cold add two table-spoonfuls of sweet cream, and pour over the cabbage and celery.

CELERY SLAW.—No. 2.

Take half a head of cabbage, two bunches of celery, and three hard-boiled eggs; chop cabbage, celery, and whites of eggs fine. *Dressing.*—Mix the yelks of eggs with two tea-spoonfuls of sugar, two of mustard, one of pepper, one of salt, and vinegar sufficient to moisten.

DRESSING FOR SLAW.

Beat lightly two eggs; then take half a pint of vinegar, one table-spoonful of butter, half a table-spoonful of flour; boil all together until as thick as custard, stirring constantly. Add pepper, salt, and vinegar to taste; pour, when cold, over the cabbage.

HAM SANDWICHES.

Cut bread into thin slices, and butter nicely; spread on a little mustard, very thin; lay a slice of boiled ham between two of bread; or, if you choose, cold tongue, grated.

SANDWICHES.

Chop old ham very fine, or grate it; beat an egg thoroughly, mix some ground mustard, let half a pint of vinegar come to a boil, stir in the egg and mustard, and mix with the ham. After buttering thin slices of bread spread on this mixture.

HAM TOAST.

Take a quarter of a pound of lean ham chopped fine, the yelks of three eggs well beaten, half a pound of butter, two table-spoonfuls of cream, and a little red pepper; stir this over the fire until it thickens, and then spread on hot toast.

DEVILED TURKEY.

Take half a cup of tomatoes, one table-spoonful of catchup,

one tea-spoonful of dry mustard, one table-spoonful of butter, and a little red pepper; pour this hot over the turkey after it is broiled.

SAUCES FOR FISH AND MEATS.

SAUCE WITH OYSTERS FOR FISH

To one pint of strained oyster-liquor add one goblet of claret, the juice of half a lemon, a blade of mace, and one table-spoonful of butter thickened with a table spoonful of flour; when this is scalding hot add half a pound of butter, stirring all till it melts; then add twenty oysters, let scald, not boil, and serve.

FISH-SAUCE.

Cream the yelks of four eggs in a table-spoonful of vinegar; salt and pepper to taste. Add half a pound of butter, and place on the fire till it thickens; do not let it get too hot, or it will curdle.

SAUCE FOR FISH.

Take the yelks of six hard-boiled eggs and cream them with sweet-oil, mustard, walnut catchup, Worcestershire sauce, salt, pepper, and vinegar to taste. Pickle chopped fine improves it.

TARTAR-SAUCE. (FOR BOILED OR BAKED FISH.)

Put into a small sauce-pan the yelks of two eggs, a des sert-spoonful of vinegar, and a pinch of salt; whip up this mixture as quick as possible; when the whole forms a sort of cream add two dessert-spoonfuls of oil and a tea-spoonful of mustard, which must be well mixed previously, a pinch of parsley minced fine, and a little cayenne pepper. The oil should be put in drop by drop, to mix perfectly. Heat thoroughly, not boil.

SAUCE PIQUANT. (For Fried Fish.)

Take three table-spoonfuls of sweet-oil, one of vinegar, one tea-spoonful of mixed mustard, some fine salt, some onion minced fine, chopped parsley, bright red pepper-pods cut up into small pieces. All these ingredients should be beaten well together and poured over the fish as it comes hot out of the frying-pan.

MAYONNAISE.

Place in the bottom of a salad-bowl the yelk of one raw egg, a tea-spoonful of salt, the same of dry mustard, a salt-spoonful of white pepper, as much red pepper as can be taken on the point of a pen-knife, and the juice of half a lemon; mix these ingredients with a wooden salad-spoon, until they assume a creamy-white appearance; then add, drop by drop, three gills of salad-oil, stirring the mayonnaise constantly; if it thickens too rapidly, thin with the juice from the second half of the lemon. Add gradually four table-spoonfuls of tarragon vinegar. Two spoonfuls of cream is an improvement. Keep cool until wanted for use.

VENISON-SAUCE.

One pint of currant jelly, three fourths of a pound of butter, four table-spoonfuls of brown sugar, one table-spoonful of ground mace and allspice, and one pint of wine. Boil till it thickens.

MINT-SAUCE FOR LAMB.

Three table-spoonfuls of chopped mint, three table-spoonfuls of brown sugar, half pint of vinegar, and a salt-spoonful of salt; stir well until the sugar is dissolved. Do not heat.

CRANBERRY-SAUCE.

To a quart of ripe cranberries add half a pint of water,

stirring frequently; when soft, mash well; when done, stir in a pound of sugar; let it boil up once, as much cooking after the sugar is put in will cause the sauce to be dark; pass through a sieve. Makes a beautiful jelly when cold.

MUSHROOM-SAUCE.

Take a pint of mushrooms; remove the outside skins if fresh, if canned they are ready for use; stew them slowly in milk or cream, seasoning with pepper, salt, and a spoonful of butter rolled in flour; stew them until they are tender, stirring them with a silver spoon. This sauce served with beefsteak or chicken boiled is very good.

CAPER-SAUCE.

Melt a quarter of a pound of butter with a table-spoonful of flour; add a pint of sweet milk, let it come to a boil; season with salt and pepper, then add a tea-cup of capers, and four eggs boiled hard and minced fine. Cucumber pickles, well minced, make a nice substitute. This is a nice sauce for boiled meats.

ONION-SAUCE.—No. 1.

Put six sliced onions in a sauce-pan, with three table-spoonfuls of butter, one tea-spoonful of salt, same of sugar, and half a tea-spoonful of ground pepper; cook slowly till it thickens to a pulp, stirring constantly; then add one pint of milk, thickened with one table-spoonful of flour. Boil till about as thick as drawn butter. Strain through a coarse sieve and serve.

ONION-SAUCE.—No. 2.

Slice one onion, fry slightly in two table-spoonfuls of butter, in which one tea-spoonful of flour has been stirred; pour into this one tea-cupful of sweet milk and a little chopped parsley; cook a few minutes; pour over three hard-boiled eggs, minced fine. A very nice sauce for fish or boiled meats.

CELERY-SAUCE.

Cut two heads of celery into small pieces; put them into a pint of water, boil until tender, then add one half tumbler of cream, salt, pepper, and a small lump of butter rolled in flour; let the whole stew gently five minutes. To be eaten with boiled fowls.

TOMATO-SAUCE.

Remove the skin by pouring boiling water over them, chop them up and put them in a stew-pan, cook thoroughly, strain through a sieve, add a heaping table-spoonful of butter, pepper, and salt to taste, and half a tea-spoonful of allspice; put it in the stew-pan and let cook slowly till it thickens. Use sugar instead of pepper, if preferred.

HORSE-RADISH SAUCE.

Mix together one dessert-spoonful of mustard, two table-spoonfuls of vinegar, and three table-spoonfuls of cream; season with salt and grated horse-radish to suit the taste.

CURRY-POWDER.

Pound fine and mix three ounces of coriander seeds, three of turmeric, one of vinegar, one of black pepper, one of mustard, one quarter of an ounce of cinnamon, the same of cayenne pepper, and cumin-seed. Keep this powder in a bottle with a glass stopper.

TO MELT BUTTER.

Take four ounces of good butter; rub into it one table-spoonful of flour, one table-spoonful of water, a little salt; set the vessel in another of boiling water; shake it until the butter begins to boil. Do not place the pan containing the butter on the fire, as it is easily reduced to oil, and will be much impaired. This may be seasoned with any kind of herbs; a litttle more water is needed when herbs are used. Take parsley, boil for a few minutes, drain off the water, mince fine, and stir in the butter when it begins to draw. This sauce is fine for all boiled meats and fowl.

DRAWN BUTTER.

Take half a pint of boiling water, two tea-spoonfuls of flour, two ounces of butter; mix flour and butter till smooth; stir into the hot water and salt to taste.

EGG-SAUCE.

Make like drawn butter, with the addition of three eggs, boiled hard and chopped fine. Serve this with fish.

BROWNING SUGAR.—(For Soups and Sauces.)

Take half a pound of sugar, and put just water enough to wet it; pour in a vessel and simmer slowly, stirring all the time, until it is a light-brown color; add one ounce of salt and water to the consistency of sirup, boil a few minutes, taking off the scum. Keep in a bottle. Before putting in the soup or sauce stir in the quantity you intend using in a cup of the broth.

VEGETABLES.

ASPARAGUS.

Tie in bunches of about twenty-five each, and evenly as possible; throw in warm, salted water, and boil quickly for twenty minutes. When done, take up with a skimmer and lay on buttered toast. Serve with drawn butter or cream sauce.

BURR ARTICHOKES.

The burr should be boiled in hot water, with a little salt, until tender, which you can ascertain by pulling out a leaf; if it leaves the burr easily, it is done. To be eaten with melted butter or oil, pepper, and vinegar

STRING BEANS.

String the beans by breaking off the ends and pulling the fibrous thread on each side. If old, it is best to break them in two, besides stringing. As they are strung, throw them into cold water until ready to be cooked. Put them in boiling water, with a little salt, and cook till tender, which will take about an hour. Drain them, and season with butter, pepper, and cream; return to the sauce-pan and cook a minute.

Another way to cook beans is to boil with a small piece of salt pork. The meat should be half done before putting in the beans, and also skim while cooking.

LIMA OR BUTTER BEANS.

Shell and wash them in cold water; put in enough boiling water to cover them, with a little salt; boil for half an hour; pour off the water, and season with butter and pepper. If they are a little old, add a small pinch of bi-carbonate of soda.

TO BAKE DRY BEANS.

Soak them over night in cold water; put them to boil in enough of cold water to cover them well; let them boil two hours. Drain off the water, season with salt and pepper, and put in a dish to bake; place in the center of the beans a small piece of salt pork that has been boiled in another vessel, and bake half an hour.

BRUSSELS SPROUTS.

Soak in water a short time, and wash it clean; boil in salt-water. When done, strain and fry in a table-spoonful of butter, in which has been browned a table-spoonful of flour, and a small onion cut fine; add pepper and salt to taste.

BEETS.

Wash them well; be careful not to cut the top too close to the beet, or break off the ends, as this will allow both the color and sweetness to escape; boil one hour. When done, drop in cold water and rub off the skin, and slice very thin. Dress with melted butter or salad-oil, pepper, and salt; serve hot. They are more commonly dressed in vinegar, salt, and pepper, when cold. Old beets will take two hours to boil.

CABBAGE.

This vegetable, when properly cooked, will not disagree with the most delicate stomach. An eminent physician taught me how to have it prepared. It is simply to change the water two or three times while cooking; but be sure to have the water well drained each time, and a kettle of boiling water at hand to replace that which has been thrown off. Change the first water about half an hour after boiling, and so on as many times as you wish. Put the meat into the last water.

ANOTHER WAY.

Quarter a large cabbage, and lay in enough cold water to cover it for two or three hours; then have enough boiling water to well cover the cabbage, and plunge it in. One hour's cooking is sufficient. Put in a little salt before taking up, and serve with drawn butter.

CABBAGE `ETOUFE'.

Take a white-head cabbage; make two incisions across the head deep enough to cleanse it; wash it clean; then shake the water from it; strew between each leaf nice sausage-meat, and tie up with strips of white cloth, to keep it in shape. Have ready a very large spoonful of lard in a pot large enough to contain the cabbage; brown some flour, and when boiling put in the cabbage; cover closely. After twenty minutes withdraw the pot to a more gentle heat; simmer for two hours; salt and pepper to taste; serve whole.

STUFFED CABBAGE.

Take a good-sized, very hard head of cabbage, lay back half a dozen of the outside leaves, and cut a square out of the center of the cabbage; put back this square, and tie the leaves firmly around it; then plunge the cabbage in boiling, salted water; let it boil till quite done, and remove from the water. Make a stuffing as for turkey; take out the square from the cabbage, and chop with this dressing. Fill the cabbage and place in a pot, with one pint of cream or rich milk and two table-spoonfuls of butter. Let all simmer till most of the milk is absorbed.

HOT DRESSING FOR CABBAGE COOKED WITHOUT MEAT.

Beat together the yelks of two eggs, two table-spoonfuls of brown sugar, four table-spoonfuls of vinegar, a large table-spoonful of butter, and pepper and salt to taste. Stir well in a sauce-pan till it boils; then add a cup of milk or cream. Pour hot over the cabbage, and serve.

CORN-PATTIES.

Take six ears of boiled corn; cut off from the cob by dividing the grains and scraping after cutting; season with pepper and salt. Mix with the yelks of four eggs well beaten, two table-spoonfuls of flour; whisk the whites to a stiff froth, and stir in lastly. Drop one table-spoonful at a time in hot lard, and fry a light brown on both sides.

FRIED CORN.

Cut the corn from the cobs, and put in a frying-pan with one half tumbler of water to a quart; let it stew a short time, as it will be more tender; then stir in pepper and salt and a table-spoonful of lard, and fry a very light brown.

GREEN-CORN PUDDING.

Take twelve ears of green corn and grate it; add a quart of sweet milk, a quarter of a pound of fresh butter, four eggs well beaten, pepper and salt to the taste. Stir all well together and bake one hour in a buttered dish.

SUCCOTASH.

Boil the corn and beans in separate pots until done; then cut and scrape the corn from the cob, and to every measure of beans allow two of corn; mix them; season with milk, butter, pepper, and salt. Boil up once, and serve

GREEN-CORN PUDDING, WITH CHICKEN.

Boil six large ears of corn; slice the grains off, commencing with a very thin coat of the outer grains. Boil a spring chicken until quite tender; salt, pepper, and flour each piece of the chicken. Beat four eggs with a small cup of butter, a spoonful of pepper and salt; add to the corn, making a thick batter with the top of the chicken-water; place the batter in a large, buttered baking-dish; lay the floured pieces of chicken carefully down into the batter; sift a little flour over the top of the batter, but not on the sides of the dish. Bake it until the bottom, sides, and top are a light brown.

CARROTS.

Carrots should be boiled in salt-water until they can be pierced by a straw. The water should then be poured off, and the carrots stewed a few minutes in melted butter and cream.

CAULIFLOWER.

Wash it clean; peel the stem, wrap it in muslin, and boil in salt-water one hour; make butter or egg sauce. *Egg Sauce.*—Beat two table-spoonfuls of butter until it foams; stir with it the yelks of four eggs; add half a table-spoonful of flour, and stir it while boiling in some of the liquor of the cauliflower.

CAULIFLOWER OMELET.

Take the white part of a boiled cauliflower, after it is cold, and chop it very small; mix with a sufficient quantity of well-beaten egg, to make a very thick batter; then fry it in fresh butter, and serve hot.

EGG-PLANT FRIED.

Boil in water until perfectly done, first peeling it; mash well, and stir into it when cool one egg, one table-spoonful of butter, one table-spoonful of flour to one plant; season with salt, pepper, and onion cut fine, if desired; fry in cakes. The batter should be soft enough to drop with a spoon

ANOTHER WAY.

Peel the egg-plant; parboil ten minutes; cut in slices crosswise; season with salt and pepper. Beat up one egg; dip the slices in the egg, then in cracker crumbs. Fry a light brown in boiling lard. Egg-plants prepared in this way, and fried in batter, are equally nice.

BAKED EGG-PLANT.

Cut the egg-plant lengthwise; take out the inside, and mix it with nearly as much bread-crumbs, one egg, pepper, and salt; fry the mixture in hot butter; return to the shells, and bake half an hour.

GRITS.

Pick over and wash nicely; allow twice as much water as grits; season with salt, and boil till done. Cold grits can be nicely utilized by slicing, and dipping the slices in a beaten egg in which there is mixed a little flour, and fry in hot lard.

ANOTHER.—Soften the cold grits with warm water. Mix with eggs, a little butter, salt, and milk, and bake in a buttered dish.

HOMINY.

Wash thoroughly through two or three waters, and boil three or four hours, allowing twice the quantity of water to that of hominy. Just before it is done, season with salt. Place a small lump of butter in a deep dish, and pour the hominy over it.

MUSHROOMS.

Cut off the stems, peel off the skins, and put in a stew-pan, with a little salt and water; cook about half an hour; add butter, pepper, and thicken with a little flour. Boil five minutes, and serve on toast or over steak. It is safest to stir with a silver spoon, as any toad-stools, which are poisonous, will turn the spoon dark.

BROILED MUSHROOMS.

Wash, stem, and peel off the skins of the mushrooms; put them on the gridiron over hot coals, with the hollow side up; sprinkle a little pepper, salt, and butter on each one; cook a few minutes, but do not turn.

STEWED OKRA.

Wash the okra in cold water, and cut it in thin slices crosswise. To one pint of cut okra cut up one small onion, one table spoonful of flour, and fry in a frying-pan in which some slices of pork have been fried, or a large table-spoonful of lard. Scald and peel six tomatoes, and stir in the mixture. Cook until all are done.

TO BOIL OKRA.

Okra should be young and tender. Cut off the stems and the tip of the small end; boil till tender, but not long enough to cause it to fall to pieces; pour over melted butter, seasoned with salt and pepper.

FRIED OKRA.

Boil the okra in salt-water until tender; mash it up, and stir in one egg, pepper, salt, and flour enough to hold together. Take up a large spoonful, and fry in hot lard.

ONIONS.

Onions boiled in milk, instead of water, are rendered more delicate and improved in flavor. Let the milk boil; add a little salt. Peel the onions, and put them in the boiling milk, and let them boil half an hour, or until well done. Drain them in a colander; put them in a warm dish, and pour a little melted butter over them; sprinkle with black pepper.

STEWED ONIONS.

Slice your onions; have ready in your frying-pan a table-spoonful of lard. When it is hot, put in the onions; let them fry a few minutes; pour in about half a cup of hot water or milk; sift over the top about a tablespoonful of flour; cover closely, and let it stew gently until the onions are done. Season with pepper and salt.

ONION OMELET.

Six large onions boiled quite done; mash, and season with pepper, salt, one table-spoonful of butter, one half cup of sweet milk, and one egg. Bake five minutes.

FRIED ONIONS.

Peel and slice the onions; season with pepper and salt to taste; fry in boiling lard to a light brown.

ONION PUDDING.

One and a half cups of chopped onions, one cup of sweet milk, one slice of light bread, two eggs, one large spoonful of butter, pepper and salt to taste. Bake in a pudding-dish. Cabbage pudding in the same proportions, substituting cabbage for onions.

PARSNIPS.

Wash and scrape them; cut in halves or quarters, according to the size; boil them until tender,—about half an hour. Season with butter, salt, and pepper.

PARSNIP FRITTERS.

Boil the parsnips until tender; mash and pass them through a colander; stir in one well-beaten egg and enough flour to make it hold together. Season, and fry in hot lard.

FRIED PARSNIPS.

Boil until tender; slice them lengthwise; dip in batter, and fry brown in hot lard.

PLANTAINS.

Cut your plantains lengthwise, and put them in a pan;

cover with sugar, and let them stand for several hours, so that they will absorb the sugar. Fry in a spoonful of butter.

POTATOES.

The best way to cook Irish potatoes is to put them in just enough boiling water to cover them, leaving the skins on. Let them boil steadily till done. When nearly done, put in a little salt; remove the skins while hot, and just as you áre going to send to the table, pour over melted butter. A very poor potato cooked in this way, and pressed, while hot, in a coarse cloth, will be mealy; and if mashed with a little butter, cream, or milk, you can not tell it from the best. Potatoes should not be served in a covered dish, as the condensing of the steam makes them clammy.

ANOTHER WAY.

Pare the potatoes very thin, as the best of the potato is near the skin; put in sufficient boiling water, salted, to cover them. When done, pour off the water, allowing them a little hard, and set back on the stove to dry, with the cover of the vessel removed, to aid evaporation, or a towel over the top, to absorb vapor. Boil half an hour.

NEW POTATOES.

Rub off the skins with a coarse towel in cold water; put them in boiling water; cook twenty minutes; drain off the water, sprinkle with a little pepper and salt, and pour over melted butter or cream.

ANOTHER WAY.

Skin, wash, and dry some new potatoes; melt some butter in a stew-pan; when it is quite hot, put the potatoes in it; simmer them slowly, turning them occasionally. When done, take them up and place them in another stew-pan, with sufficient fresh butter to form a sauce; shake them over the fire merely till the butter is melted. Put them in a dish and pour the butter over them, and sprinkle with a little salt.

POTATOES A LA CRE'ME.

Put into a sauce-pan about two ounces of butter, a small table-spoonful of flour, some parsley chopped fine, salt, and pepper; stir these together; add a wine-glass of cream, and set it on the fire, stirring continually until it boils. Cut some boiled potatoes into slices, and put them into the sauce-pan with the mixture; boil up once, and serve hot.

POTATO BALLS.—No. 1.

Two cups of mashed potatoes, one cup of grated ham, two well-beaten eggs, two table-spoonfuls of cream or milk, one table-spoonful of butter; salt and pepper to taste. Make into balls, roll in flour, and fry in boiling lard. This is a good way to utilize cold potatoes; and it is a nice breakfast-dish.

POTATO BALLS.—No. 2.

Boil the potatoes; peel, and mash smooth, with one egg and a little flour, to keep it in form; add a little salt, pepper, and butter, and fry in boiling lard.

BAKED POTATO.

Boil the potatoes, and mash, with one egg, one table-spoonful of butter, and two table-spoonfuls of cream or milk. Bake quickly.

Potatoes roasted in a very hot oven are both healthy and palatable.

POTATOES MASHED WITH ONIONS.

Prepare some boiled onions by putting them through a sieve, and mix them with potatoes. Regulate according to taste, seasoning with butter, pepper, and salt.

MASHED POTATOES AND TURNIPS.

Boil Irish potatoes as in No. 2; mash, and season. Boil

turnips; mash, and season. Allow two thirds potatoes and one third turnips; mix well, and add cream or milk to taste. This is an excellent dish, if nicely prepared.

TO FRY SARATOGA POTATOES.

Pare and cut Irish potatoes very thin; put them in cold water to soak over night. When ready, take them out of the water and wipe them dry, as they will not brown if they are not well dried. Have your lard about as you would for frying doughnuts, dropping in about two handfuls at a time, stirring all the time, so that they will brown evenly. The quicker they are cooked,—so that they do not burn,—the better they are. Add a little salt when you take them out of the fat

GREEN PEAS.

Shell and wash the peas; cook in hot water enough to cover them for twenty minutes. When nearly done, add salt; take them up clear of water. Season with butter, and, if desired, add a little cream.

GREEN PEAS WITH MINT.

Put the peas in cold water to boil, with a little salt. Add one sprig of mint, one dessert-spoonful of sugar. When done, take out the mint, drain off the water, and season with butter and pepper.

This is an English method of cooking peas.

FRIED FIGS.

Have large, ripe figs; peel, and cut in half the long way of the fruit; fry in a pan of hot butter, leaving the flat side of the fig up. Fry a light brown, and after dishing sprinkle with brown sugar. These are almost, if not quite, equal to fried plantains.

TO BAKE LARGE, YELLOW CUCUMBERS.

Cut off each end, carefully scrape out the inside, and peel them. Make a force-meat of beef or veal, onions, a part of a clove of garlic, pepper, and salt; roll in flour, and fry in hot lard; add a little water, and let it cook over a slow fire. By cooking slowly, it will make its own gravy.

TO BOIL RICE

Wash one pint of rice, and put in one and one half pints of boiling water, with one tea-spoonful of salt. When this boils up two or three times, set back where it will boil gently. Do not stir after setting back.

RICE CROQUETTES.

Half a cup of rice, one pint of milk, two table-spoonfuls of sugar, three eggs, one table-spoonful of melted butter, grated peel of a lemon, and a little salt. Soak the rice one or two hours in enough warm water to cover it; drain it almost dry; put in the milk; steam until tender; add the sugar, butter, and salt; beat the eggs to a stiff froth and add to the mixture; cook five minutes; add the lemon-peel, and turn all on a buttered dish. When cold, flour your hands and roll in oval-shaped balls; dip them in well-beaten eggs and cracker crumbs, and fry in boiling lard.

BOILED SWEET-POTATOES.

Wash and boil as Irish potatoes, but without peeling. When done sufficiently to pierce with a straw, take up and peel; if large, cut in two the long way; put in a covered dish, and pour over them melted butter. Very new sweet-potatoes should always be boiled, as they are not sufficiently juicy or sweet to bake.

BAKED SWEET-POTATOES.

Wash, and bake in the oven with the skins on. When

done, serve without peeling. When roasting beef or pork, peeled sweet-potatoes laid in the same pan around the meat, and allowed to cook in the gravy, are very nice. When cooked in this way, the potatoes, if large, should be cut through the length, so as to get thoroughly done.

SLICED AND BAKED POTATOES.

Boil sweet-potatoes nearly done, peel, and cut in slices; put a layer of potatoes, bits of butter dotted over them, and sprinkle them well with sugar; add another layer of potatoes, butter, and sugar, until the dish is full enough. Add very little water, and bake.

TO FRY SWEET-POTATOES.

Parboil the potatoes, peel, cut in slices, and fry to a nice brown in boiling lard. They can be fried without boiling, though it will require a longer time, and more lard or butter.

TO STEW SALSIFY, OR VEGETABLE OYSTERS.

Wash the roots nicely, parboil, and scrape off the outer skin; cut in thick slices, and put into a stew-pan, with water enough to cover it well; add a little salt and pepper; cook until quite tender. Then pour off the water; put in a large table-spoonful of butter; thicken with a little flour. A table-spoonful of cream improves it very much. A table-spoonful of vinegar added gives a pleasant flavor. Serve hot. Carrots and parsnips may be prepared in the same way, leaving out the vinegar.

SALSIFY PATTIES.

Wash and scrape the roots; boil until quite tender; mash well; make a batter of one egg, a tea-cupful of flour, half a table-spoonful of butter, a little salt and pepper, and a little milk. Stir this into the salsify, and drop a large spoonful into boiling lard. Fry brown.

SPINACH.

Wash thoroughly through two or three waters; boil in salted water for fifteen or twenty minutes; then drain in a sieve. Put in a sauce-pan, with butter and pepper to taste; warm through, and serve with hard-boiled eggs sliced.

BOILED SQUASH.

Peel, cut, and boil the squash in salted water till tender. Drain and mash smoothly, seasoning with pepper and butter.

ANOTHER WAY.

Peel, and cut the squash in small squares of about an inch. Put a table-spoonful of butter in a stew-pan; when heated, throw in the squash and cover tight; stir occasionally, and when nearly done add pepper and salt to taste.

SQUASH-FRITTERS.

Boil the squash; mash smooth, with butter and pepper, adding a little flour and a well-beaten egg. Make in little cakes, and fry in hot lard.

FRIED SQUASH.

Peel and slice thin and evenly. Dip each slice in egg which has been seasoned with pepper and salt; then dip in bread or cracker crumbs, and fry in hot lard.

ANOTHER WAY.

The slices of squash may be dipped in batter, and fried in hot lard. When prepared in either of the above ways, it is almost impossible to distinguish it from egg-plant.

MASHED TURNIPS.

Peel, and boil in boiling water, with a little salt, until tender; drain them carefully from the water, mash smooth, and season with butter, pepper, and salt to taste.

WHOLE TURNIPS.

Peel, and boil in salted water till tender; drain off the water, and add cream, butter, pepper, and salt to taste.

TOMATOES.

Pour scalding water over them, and let them remain in it a few minutes, or until the skins will come off easily. When peeled, put them in a stew-pan, with a little salt and butter, and stew them half an hour; add a little bread-crumbs or grated cracker. If sugar is not used, add a little black pepper.

SCALLOPED TOMATOES.

Peel them; cover the bottom of a deep dish with them; put salt, pepper, and butter on them; then add a layer of bread-crumbs or rolled cracker; then another layer of tomatoes, and a layer of crumbs, until the dish is filled; cover the top with crumbs. If sugar is desired, leave out pepper. Bake half an hour. If canned tomatoes are used, drain off the fluid before using.

STUFFED TOMATOES.

Select large and firm tomatoes; cut a very thin slice off the end opposite the stem; carefully take out the seeds and juice, so as not to break the tomato. Mix with the seeds and juice stale bread-crumbs or rolled cracker, salt, pepper, or sugar if preferred, two table-spoonfuls of butter. Then fill each tomato with the stuffing, place them in a deep baking-dish, and cover them with a thin layer of the above mixture, and sprinkle dry crumbs on top. Bake from one half to three quarters of an hour, according to the size of tomato.

BROILED TOMATOES.

Cut them in thick slices; place them on a well-buttered broiling-iron, over a clear fire, having previously sprinkled with salt and pepper. Have ready a warm dish, place them in it, and pour melted butter on them. Serve them quite hot.

BAKED TOMATOES.

Wash and cut the tomatoes in halves; take out the seeds. To six large tomatoes take half a pint of bread-crumbs, one onion chopped fine, one ounce of butter; pepper and salt to taste. Fill the cells with the dressing; tie the halves together; bake in a pan with an ounce of butter and one gill of water; when soft, cut the thread and serve.

FRIED TOMATOES.

Wash and cut in halves; take out the seeds; season with pepper and salt, and fry slowly until soft.

SPANISH WAY TO COOK TOMATOES.

Peel a dozen ripe tomatoes, and fry them in butter, with two or three sliced green peppers; sprinkle on a little salt; add an onion, and cook well together.

EGGS AND TOMATOES.

Peel the skins from twelve large tomatoes. Put four spoonfuls of butter in a frying-pan; when hot, add one large onion chopped fine; let it fry for a few minutes, add the tomatoes, and when nearly done, six eggs well beaten.

MACARONI AND TOMATOES.

Boil one half pound of macaroni in milk or water, and in a separate vessel stew one quart of tomatoes. Chop the tomatoes, and beat them up with two eggs, a table-spoonful of butter, and salt and pepper to taste. Mix all with the macaroni, and bake.

BAKED MACARONI.

Boil one half pound of macaroni till tender; strain off the water, and put in a deep dish,—buttered to prevent its sticking,—with layers of grated or finely-cut cheese, butter, pepper, and salt, alternating with layers of the macaroni. Finish with the cheese layer on top. Bake till a nice brown—about twenty minutes or half an hour.

MACARONI WITH EGGS.

Boil till tender one half pound of macaroni; drain off the water; beat well two eggs, and mix in the macaroni. Butter a dish, and put in alternate layers of macaroni and eggs, and grated cheese, pepper, and salt. Pour over all about half a tea-cup of milk. Bake till a good brown.

BREAD, BISCUIT, ETC.

MILK YEAST FOR BREAD.

Boil one pint of milk and half a tea-spoonful of salt. When the milk is cool, stir in enough flour to make a batter as thin as cream; keep it in a warm place; it will require about six hours to rise. To make up in bread, add flour until it is a soft dough; then mix one table-spoonful of lard, and let rise again for half an hour. Bake in a moderate oven.

TO MAKE HOP YEAST.

Pour a pint of cold water on a table-spoonful of hops; let it boil a short while; strain the tea from the hops; make a batter of flour and water, and mix with the tea; let it boil again. When cool, stir in meal as long as you can do so. with a spoon; add two yeast cakes or a cup of yeast; let it rise Then work in flour until it is stiff enough to roll; cut out in cakes, lay on a dish, and dry in the shade.

TO MAKE STOCK YEAST.

Put one ounce of hops into a quart of boiling water; boil *two* minutes; strain enough of the tea on a half pound of flour to make a stiff paste. When well mixed, put in the balance of the hop tea; let this cool, and add half a pint of stock yeast. This will keep three days in warm weather, and a week in winter.

TO MAKE THE FERMENT FOR BREAD.

Wash three Irish potatoes, and boil (with skins on) in a

quart of water until soft; use half a pound of flour; mash the potatoes, and rub them well into the flour. Make a paste the same as for stock yeast; then, with the potato tea and cold water, make this cool enough to bear the hand in it. Now add one half pint of stock yeast, and let it stand six or eight hours to rise. When this has risen and fallen, make the sponge for bread. Strain one pint of this ferment through a colander; add to this one pint of water, and make a soft batter of flour. Let this sponge rise four hours; add salt to make your bread; mold, and let it rise, and bake.

ROLLS AND LIGHT BREAD.

Take three pints of unsifted flour, and at noon have boiled a large Irish potato; while the potato is boiling, dissolve the half of a gem yeast-cake in a coffee-cup of lukewarm water. Take *one* of the three pints of flour, and *sift* it into a bowl; mash the potato *quickly* and very smoothly, and while HOT; put it into the pint of flour, and mix potato and flour well together with the hand; add a tea-spoonful of sugar and a small tea-spoonful of salt. Now pour onto this the cup of dissolved yeast; beat this batter well with a spoon; cover this bowl of batter, and place it where it will keep moderately warm. About eight o'clock at night, sift the other two pints of flour on the biscuit-board, leaving out a very little to knead the dough in the morning. Then take a table-spoonful of lard (not very heaping); mix it into the flour, adding another tea-spoonful of sugar and a tea-spoonful of salt. Now pour the batter into this flour, and knead the dough well; put this dough into a jar or bowl that has a cover. Early next morning knead this dough over; make into rolls, and set to rise for breakfast. If this recipe is exactly followed it *can not* fail.

POTATO YEAST.

Grate four Irish potatoes; scald well in a quart of boiling

water half a tea-cup of sugar, and the same quantity of salt; put the mixture in a glass or stone jar, with a little yeast to make it rise; cork well, and keep it in a warm place the first day, or until it ferments. For two quarts of flour, use half a tea-cup of this yeast. It will keep for two weeks.

LIGHT ROLLS.

One quart of flour, a large spoonful of yeast, the same quantity of lard; mix with warm water to a soft dough; cover well, and let it rise all night in a warm place. Make out in rolls in the morning. They will rise in twenty minutes. Bake in a moderate oven.

PARKER-HOUSE ROLLS.

Two quarts of sifted flour, one pint of cold boiled milk, one table-spoonful of white sugar, one tea-spoonful of salt, half a pint of baker's yeast, and one large table-spoonful of lard. Make up sponge about three o'clock in the afternoon; if quite light, about ten o'clock it will be ready to make into a dough. Knead well and let stand all night. It will be ready in the morning to mold into rolls. They rise and bake in a very little time.

POTATO YEAST.

Peel and boil one dozen good-sized Irish potatoes in one gallon of water till soft; mash them through a seive. Boil one handful of hops in the same water the potatoes were boiled in, and strain them into the mashed potatoes. Beat it well together; then add half a tea-cup of salt, half a tea-cup of sugar, and stir it well. After it becomes perfectly cold, add one yeast-cake, dissolved in a little of the hop-water. In two days it will be ready for use. Always stir it well before using.

BREAD.

Make the bread with the above yeast as follows: Use three

pints of flour; into one quart rub a table-spoonful of lard, with a little salt. To one tea-cup of yeast add one egg, if you have it, and one table-spoonful of sugar; stir well together, and pour into the quart of flour. Work it up with lukewarm water, adding by degrees the other pint of flour. Knead it till the dough is perfectly smooth, but not too stiff. In the morning, make out rolls. If the dough should be too soft, add a little more flour.

SWISS ROLLS.

Make a batter of one pint of flour, one cake of yeast dissolved in lukewarm water, a large Irish potato, if convenient; when risen, two quarts of flour, one table-spoonful of lard and one of sugar, two eggs, and half a table-spoonful of salt. Pour in the yeast, rub the dough smooth, and set it to rise again. When well risen, make it into splits as follows: Roll out the dough half an inch thick; baste top with butter; cut out the size of a biscuit; lay one on the top of the other, and set it to rise. Just before baking, beat an egg and baste the top of each.

POCKET-BOOKS.

Beat the yelks of four eggs with two dessert-spoonfuls of sugar; then add one tea-cup of sweet milk, with one large yeast-cake dissolved in it; flour enough to make a stiff batter. Lastly, add the whites, after beating them to a stiff froth; let rise. When very light, add one table-spoonful of butter; also one of lard. Sift the flour, and make a soft dough; let it rise again, then make your pocket-books in the following manner: Work out the dough with a little more flour; roll in pieces about five inches long and three wide; spread very little butter on one end; sprinkle with flour; fold like a pocket-book, put them to rise, and when risen bake.

LIGHT BREAD.

One quart of flour, one pint of boiled fresh milk, one table-spoonful of lard, one table-spoonful of sugar, tea-spoonful of salt, three table-spoonfuls of yeast dissolved in a little water; put the sugar and salt in the water. As soon as the milk boils, put it in a bowl to cool, and put in the lard. When quite cool, mix all and set it away to rise over night. Next morning work in a pint or more of flour, into which put one tea-spoonful of soda; make into rolls or loaves, and set to rise again; then bake.

EXCELLENT GRAHAM BREAD.

One quart of corn-meal, one pint of Graham flour, one cup of sour milk, one cup of molasses, one tea-spoonful of soda, one tea-spoonful of salt, and bake three hours.

GRAHAM ROLLS.

Boil two pounds of Irish potatoes, and mash through a colander; add to this one pint of water, one half cupful of yeast, and enough Graham flour to make a stiff dough. Set to rise all night, and in the morning mold into small cakes; let rise again, and then bake. Nice Graham rolls.

GRAHAM GEMS.

One cup of wheat flour, one cup of Graham flour, two eggs, two cups of fresh milk, half tea-spoonful of salt. Grease and heat the pans very hot. Bake about half an hour.

GRAHAM BREAD.—No. 1.

To one quart of lukewarm water add one tea spoonful of salt, two of brown sugar, and yeast as for flour bread; thicken to a batter with sifted Graham flour, and let it rise until morning. Then add one half pint of new milk, one fourth tea-cup of molasses, one third teaspoonful of soda, a small piece of lard, and sufficient Graham flour to mold soft. Put into deep tins, and let rise. As soon as little cracks come on the top, put into a hot oven and bake one third longer than flour bread. This bread is better not to mold very much.

GRAHAM BREAD.—No. 2.

To three pints of sifted Graham meal add one pint of sour milk or buttermilk, four table-spoonfuls of molasses, soda to sweeten the milk, a small piece of shortening, and a tea-spoonful of salt. Mold, and bake in a deep tin.

MILK-YEAST BREAD.—(Excellent.)

To one pint of boiling new milk add one pint of lukewarm water, one tea-spoonful of salt, two of sugar, and one tea-cup of fine cornmeal. Add the cornmeal first, then flour enough to make quite a stiff batter; place in a jar or pitcher, and put it where it will be kept more than milk-warm; stir occasionally until it begins to rise. It will then be ready to mold in less than half an hour. Mold soft, place in deep tins, and at once begin to heat the oven, as it rises very quickly. The sponge should be ready to mold in five hours.

RYE BREAD.

One pint of rye flour, one of cornmeal, one table-spoonful of lard, one tea-spoonful of salt, one tea-cup of good yeast; mix with water enough to make a stiff dough; knead well; set to rise. When well risen, knead again and form into loaves.

RUSK.—No. 1.

One quart of flour, one cup of yeast, one of milk, one of brown sugar, three eggs, one nutmeg, two table-spoonfuls of butter; rub the sugar, butter, and nutmeg in the flour, then add the eggs well beaten, next the yeast and milk. Make the dough at night, and if more flour is necessary, add it next morning. Make into rolls; let them rise a second time, and bake.

RUSK.—No. 2.

Beat an egg and a spoonful of sugar well; add a half pint of well-risen yeast; then add another well-beaten egg, a large cup of sugar, and one of butter; sift in sufficient flour to make a soft dough, and let rise till very light. Mold the rusk as you would rolls; fill the pan with them barely touching, and when well risen bake in a quick oven.

SALLY LUNN.

One quart of flour well beaten with three eggs, one cup of milk, half cup of butter, one tea-spoonful of salt, one of soda, and two of cream of tartar; dissolve the soda in a little warm water; rub the cream of tartar thoroughly into the dry flour; put in the salt, slice the butter into the milk, and dissolve over a gentle fire, adding to it the flour. Mix all well, to the consistency of pound-cake, then bake in a pan as you would cake.

HEALING SPRINGS, VIRGINIA, SALLY LUNN.

To three well-beaten eggs add one table-spoonful of butter, one of sugar, one pint of sweet milk, one half tea-cup of yeast; mix in one and a half pounds of flour; let it rise; then beat up again; and if too soft, beat in a little more flour. It should be the consistency of muffin batter. Make it up at night for morning.

CREAM-OF-TARTAR BISCUIT.

Stir into one quart of flour two tea-spoonfuls cream of tartar, a little salt, one table-spoonful of butter or lard, with enough milk or water to make a soft dough. A table-spoonful of cream will improve them. They do not need much working.

BISCUITS.

One quart of flour, one table-spoonful of butter or lard, soda the size of a pea, mixed with milk or water, well worked, will make fifteen good biscuits.

One heaping pint of flour, one tea-spoonful of salt, a piece of lard the size of a walnut, one half tea-cup of new milk, and the same quantity of cold water. This makes a stiff, dry dough. It must be beaten or worked until it is perfectly elastic, then made into biscuits or rolled thin for crackers.

BISCUIT WITH YEAST.

Boil two large potatoes, and mash them while warm; put in one tea-spoonful of sugar, one of salt, a dessert-spoonful of lard, one cup ot yeast or a yeast cake; thicken with flour to a thick dough. In the morning, work in a little more flour; puncture with a fork, and let rise.

YEAST-POWDER BISCUIT.

Three quarters of a pound of flour, four ounces of butter and lard mixed, one table-spoonful of yeast-powder. Rub the yeast-powder, salt, lard, and butter into the flour dry until well mixed; then add two gills of water; work very little, and bake in a quick oven.

CREAM BISCUIT.

To three coffee-cups of sifted flour add one cup of sweet cream, two tea-spoonfuls of yeast-powder, a little salt; mix, and mold as little as possible to get the dough in shape. Bake in a brisk oven. Should the cream be thin, melt a piece of butter and pour into it, as rubbing shortening into the flour makes the dough less spongy.

NICE BISCUIT-ROLLS FOR TEA

Make a nice biscuit dough, roll it out until it is about one eighth of an inch thick, butter it, then sprinkle well with sugar; begin at one end, as for jelly-cake, and roll; cut in pieces one and a half or two inches long; then bake.

SPLIT BISCUIT.

Two eggs, one pint of milk, two iron-spoonfuls of yeast, one table-spoonful of sugar, one of butter and lard mixed;

put in flour enough to make a soft dough; add a little salt; cover close to rise. Next morning, put on pastry-board and work it; roll it out half an inch thick, and cut them out with a biscuit-cutter. Put a piece of butter about the size of a pea in the center of each one, and put another biscuit on the top; grease your pan, and put your biscuits in an inch apart, and grease each one of them on the top; set in a warm place to rise. This recipe will amply repay any one for their trouble.

ST. JAMES BREAD.—(VERY NICE.)

One pint of flour, one pint of milk, two table-spoonfuls of lard (even full), two tablespoonfuls of sugar, two eggs, two tea-spoonfuls of yeast-powder, or a little soda and sour milk; mix the yeast-powder in the flour; beat the sugar and the yelks of the eggs together; add the whites well beaten; alternate flour and milk, putting in a little at a time; melt lard and pour in the batter. Bake in muffin-molds or baking-pans. Serve hot.

BELL FRITTERS.

Put into a stew-pan a piece of butter the size of an egg; pour over it a pint of boiling water, and set it on the stove until ready to come to a boil; then stir in a pint of flour, making a smooth paste; stir constantly until as thick as mush. When milk-warm, stir in one egg at a time until five are added; put in a little salt; make into small balls, and drop into boiling lard; fry until a light brown.

BREAKFAST PUFFS.

Take one pint of milk, one pint of flour, two eggs, a lump of butter the size of an egg, and a little salt; place the flour in a bowl; put the butter in the center of the flour; break in the eggs, and knead thoroughly; then gradually add the milk, so as to make a smooth batter. The puffs may be baked in a cast-iron pan with small divisions, or small patty-pans. These should be heated, buttered, and filled about two thirds full. Place in a quick oven. They take but a few minutes to bake.

COLONNADE PUFFS.

Put in one quart of milk two well-beaten eggs, with very thin batter and a little sait. Grease the cup thoroughly; put half full, and bake in a quick oven.

TURN-OVERS.

To two pints of flour add three well-beaten eggs, a table-spoonful of sugar, one yeast-cake, and a little salt; work it well, and put it to rise. In the morning, work in a small table-spoonful of butter; make into thin cakes, and turn half edges, not quite meeting.

PAPOOS.—(GOOD.)

One cup of flour, one cup of milk, one egg, and one tea-spoonful of salt. Bake in a quick oven in rings.

HOMINY BREAKFAST-DROPS.

Mix three table-spoonfuls of boiled hominy with two of flour, and half tea-spoonful of salt. Dissolve one table-spoonful of butter in a gill of milk, and pour it on the hominy; add flour enough to roll this into cakes, and cut out like biscuits. Bake quickly

DECEPTIONS.

Take the yelks of three eggs and the white of one worked up with as much flour as will make it as thick as biscuit-dough. Beat well; it must be very light. Divide in small pieces and roll very thin; have ready a skillet of boiling lard; put one in at a time, and turn as soon as done; then take out and put on a sifter or dish, and sprinkle sugar on them.

BANNOCKS.

Take four table-spoonfuls of meal, and dissolve in a little milk or water to a liquid; pour in a pint of boiling milk; add a little salt and a small piece of butter. When cold, beat up two eggs and stir them in; grease little muffin-pans, and bake in a quick oven. Very nice for breakfast.

CRUMPETS.—No. 1.

One quart of flour, two tea-spoonfuls cream of tartar sifted in the flour, two eggs beaten separately very light, one spoonful of salt, one quart of milk, and a tea-spoonful of soda dissolved in some of the milk, and put in last. Bake in round cakes to cover the bottom of a plate. Butter them, while hot, with melted butter.

CRUMPETS.—No. 2.

Beat the whites of two eggs with two table-spoonfuls of yeast; mix in one pound of flour; put a lump of sugar in a pint of warm milk; rub all together until free of lumps; let it stand near the fire until well risen. Bake in small cake-pans.

MUFFINS.—No. 1.

One quart of flour, two eggs beaten very light, one pint of milk, one table-spoonful of butter, one tea-spoonful of salt, one yeast-cake. Make up at night to rise; when risen, drop the batter from the spoon, first dipping the spoon in water to prevent sticking. Let rise in muffin-pans, and bake quickly.

MUFFINS.—No. 2.

Two eggs beaten lightly, a table-spoonful of butter, a pint of flour, half a cup of milk, one tea-spoonful of yeast-powder, a little salt. The same will do if you use yeast instead of yeast-powder, and let rise.

CREAM MUFFINS.

One tumbler of cream, one of flour, a little salt, two eggs, —the whites and yelks beaten separately. Bake quickly in patty-pans. These are excellent.

ST. CHARLES MUFFIN-BREAD.

One pint of meal, one pint of butter-milk, two eggs, one table-spoonful of butter (measure, and then melt), one half tea-spoonful of soda dissolved in the milk, a little salt. Bake in pans or rings.

MUFFINS WITHOUT EGGS.

One pint of sweet or sour milk, one half pint of flour, one tea-spoonful of soda, two tea-spoonfuls cream of tartar, one half tea-spoonful of salt. Beat well, and bake quickly.

WAFFLES.—No. 1.

To one pint of milk add two eggs, one pint of flour, a large table-spoonful of lard, a tea-spoonful of salt, and a tea-spoonful of carbonate of soda dissolved in the milk.

MRS. E.'s RECEIPT FOR WAFFLES.—No. 2.

One pint of milk, one pint of flour, two eggs, two large spoonfuls of melted lard, and half tea-spoonful of salt.

WAFFLES.—No. 3.

One pint of milk, half tea-spoonful of salt, flour enough to make it the consistency of cream, one tea-cup of boiled rice mashed into a smooth paste, with a table-spoonful of butter. Beat the whites of the eggs very light, and stir in just before baking.

WAFFLES.—No. 4.

Into one quart of flour sift one tea-spoonful of soda and one of salt. Then take one egg, one tea-spoonful of butter, and one table-spoonful of flour creamed together. Then add the sifted flour, and sufficient butter-milk to make a good waffle-batter.

SWEET-POTATO WAFFLES.

Two table-spoonfuls of mashed potatoes, one of butter, one of sugar, four of flour, a pint of milk, and a tea-spoonful of salt, well beaten together. Bake in waffle-irons.

WAFERS.

Put in a quart of sifted flour, two cups of butter; wet this with a tumbler of water, into which a tea-spoonful of salt has been dissolved; work very little; cut in small pieces; and if two large after closing the irons, trim the edges.

CRACKERS.

Rub eight ounces of butter into two pounds of flour, one tea-spoonful of salt, two of soda, and milk enough to make a stiff dough; beat it with a rolling-pin until it blisters; roll out thin, and cut with a tumbler; bake about fifteen minutes. They may be returned to the oven after they are all baked, and it will make them crisp.

CRACKNELS.

Take a quart of flour, half a nutmeg grated, the yelks of four eggs beaten with four spoonfuls of rose water; mix all to a stiff paste with cold water; rub in a pound of butter; make into cracknel shapes; put them into boiling water, and boil until they swim; take them out, and put them in cold water. When hardened, lay them out to dry, and then bake them in tin plates.

DUKE'S BUCKWHEATS.

Sift together one quart of buckwheat flour and one tea-cupful of cornmeal; add one table-spoonful of sugar, one tea-spoonful of salt; dissolve a table-spoonful of yeast-cake in tepid water, and mix with the flour into a stiff batter, using tepid water; let rise all night in a warm place. Before cooking, add a half tea-spoonful of soda, and then thin the batter to the proper consistency.

BUCKWHEAT CAKES

One pint of buckwheat mixed at night with a yeast-cake. In the morning, add one pint of buckwheat, a little milk, a tea-spoonful of soda, one egg, two table-spoonfuls of molasses.

FRENCH TOAST.

Beat four eggs very light, and stir them into a pint of cold rich milk. Slice some nice baker's bread; dip the slices into the eggs and milk, and then lay them into a skillet of hot lard and fry brown; sprinkle a little powdered sugar over them when taken out—and a little cinnamon also, if that spice is liked. Serve while hot. If nicely prepared, this is an excellent dish for breakfast or tea.

CREAM TOAST.

Boil one quart of milk; stir in a table-spoonful of butter and a little salt; take two table-spoonfuls of corn-starch or flour mixed with a little milk; pour it into the quart of milk, and let it boil a few minutes. Have ready the toasted bread on a dish, and pour the boiling mixture on it; send to the table hot.

FLANNEL CAKES.—No. 1.

One pint of fresh milk, a table-spoonful of butter melted, four eggs (the whites and yelks beaten separately), one spoonful of yeast, or a small piece of yeast-cake dissolved in a spoonful of tepid water. Put this in with the yelks, and thicken with a quart of flour. Lastly, after the whites are beaten, mix them with the butter and milk; then mix all together, and beat hard; set it a few hours to rise; season with salt to suit the taste.

FLANNEL CAKES.—No. 2.

Four eggs, one pint of sour cream, one pint of water, one pint and a half of flour, one tea-spoonful of baking-powder sifted with the flour, a tea-spoonful of salt.

FLANNEL CAKES.—No. 3.

One pint of nice clabber, one pint of flour, a piece of butter or lard the size of an egg, a tea-spoonful of soda stirred in the milk, two eggs, and a tea-spoonful of salt. Beat the eggs separately, and stir in the whites last. Very good.

BREAKFAST CAKES.

Take a saucerful of stale bread-crumbs, and mix with a tea-cupful of milk; add three eggs, and flour sufficient to make a good batter, a tea-spoonful of yeast-powders, a half tea-spoonful of salt. Bake immediately.

BATTER-CAKES.

Put a half tea-spoonful of lard in a pint of sifted meal; pour over this enough boiling water to thoroughly moisten it; add one quart of flour, a half tea-spoonful of salt, and enough sour milk to make a good batter, a half tea-spoonful of soda dissolved in sour milk, and one well-beaten egg.

CORN-CAKES.

One pint of sifted cornmeal, one tea-spoonful of salt, two spoonfuls of butter, four table-spoonfuls of cream, two eggs well beaten; add milk until it is a thin batter. Bake in pans.

OWENDON CORN-BREAD.

Two cups of boiled hominy; while hot, mix with it a large table-spoonful of butter or lard; next add a pint of milk stirred in gradually, a half pint of cornmeal, and four well-beaten eggs. The batter should be the consistency of rich boiled custard; if thicker, add more milk. Bake with a good deal of heat at the bottom of the oven, and not too much at the top, so as to allow it to rise. The pan ought to be a deep one, to allow for rising. It has the appearance, when cooked, of a batter-pudding.

RICE CORN-BREAD.

One pint of boiled rice, one pint of cornmeal, one ounce of butter, two eggs, one pint of sweet milk; beat the eggs very light; then add the milk and melted butter; beat the rice until perfectly smooth, and then add the eggs and milk. Lastly, add the cornmeal; beat all together very light, and bake in a quick oven.

CORN-BREAD.

Three eggs beaten separately, two cups of sour milk or butter-milk, one tea-spoonful of soda dissolved in boiling water, one table-spoonful of white sugar, one tea-spoonful of salt, and corn-meal enough to make a thin batter. Bake in a quick oven.

THE FAMOUS ST. CHARLES INDIAN-BREAD.

Beat two eggs very light; mix alternately with them one pint of sour milk or butter-milk, one pint of fine cornmeal; melt one table-spoonful of butter, and add to the mixture. Dissolve one tea-spoonful of soda or salaratus in a small quantity of the milk; then beat all hard, and bake in a quick oven.

SWEET-POTATO CORN-BREAD.

One quart of cornmeal, a half pint of milk, half a pound of sweet-potatoes, half a pound of butter, one pound of brown sugar, and eight eggs. Boil and mash the potatoes; rub the butter and sugar to a cream, and add them to the potatoes; next beat the eggs well, and stir them in the mixture; then add the milk, and then the meal. Beat all well together, and bake in a pan in a moderate oven.

PLAIN CORN-BREAD.

Mix the meal with cold water to a stiff dough; salt to suit the taste; shape with the hand in small cakes or loaves. Do not bake too long, or the crust will be too hard.

CAKES.

GENERAL DIRECTIONS FOR CAKE.

Cake, to be nice, should be made of the best materials. Butter and eggs should both be fresh. Some persons entertain the mistaken notion that butter which can not be eaten on bread will do very well for cake. On the contrary, the baking increases the bad flavor. It is a good plan to wash the butter in clear water before using it. The whites and yelks of the eggs should be beaten to a stiff froth, separately. Brown sugar will answer for some kinds of cake, if free from lumps and creamed well with the butter. When soda is used, dissolve before adding to the general mixture. Butter the baking-pan well, covering the bottom with buttered white paper. In cake-baking much of the success depends on the oven, which should be well and evenly heated before the cake is put in; and never allow the heat to diminish, or the cake will fall,—except fruit-cake, which should remain in the oven, while it cools down gradually. Avoid moving the cake while baking, as it tends to make it heavy. When the cake is done it will leave the sides of the pan. It is a good plan to put a pan filled with warm water on the top range of the stove after the cake rises, as it prevents burning or cooking too fast. To prevent browning too fast, lay a paper over the top of the cake. Avoid any contact of draft while baking.

FRUIT-CAKE.—No. 1.

One pound of sugar, one pound of butter, one pound of flour, twelve eggs, three pounds of raisins, three pounds of currants, two pounds of citron, three pounds of almonds, chopped, not *too* fine, one ounce of allspice, one ounce of cinnamon, one pint of brandy, half pint of rose-water, three table spoonfuls of cloves, and two nutmegs. The fruit should be dredged with sifted flour, before putting it in the batter, to prevent its sinking; stir in lightly. Put white paper in the bottom of pans—grease well with butter; then put in a layer of batter and a layer of citron, until the pans are full.

FRUIT-CAKE.—No. 2.

Toast pound-cake, roll very fine, and sift it; use one pound of this instead of flour, one pound of butter, one pound of white sugar, one dozen eggs, three pounds of raisins, two pounds of currants, one pound of citron, one pound of almonds blanched and chopped, not very fine, half a tumbler of good sherry or Madeira wine, half a tumbler of French brandy, one nutmeg, half a tea-spoonful of cloves, half a tea-spoonful of allspice, and half a tea-spoonful of cinnamon.

FRUIT-CAKE.—No. 3.

One pound of butter, one pound of sugar, ten eggs,—leaving out four whites,—one pound of flour, two pounds of raisins, stoned and chopped fine, two pounds of currants, three quarters of a pound of citron, half a cup of molasses, half a cup of sour cream, one gill of brandy, one ounce nutmeg, half ounce of cloves, half ounce of cinnamon, half ounce of allspice, half a tea-spoonful of soda. This makes one large loaf. Bake five hours.

WEDDING-CAKE.

Five pounds of flour, four pounds of sugar, three and one half pounds of butter, three dozen eggs, leaving out four whites, six pounds of washed and well-dried currants, two pounds of seeded raisins, two pounds of citron, two ounces of mace, one ounce of cinnamon, one ounce of cloves, one cup of molasses, one tea-spoonful of soda, two wine-glassfuls of good brandy. Cream the butter and sugar, then add the thoroughly beaten eggs; molasses, brandy, and spices should then be added. Stir the flour in gently. The fruit should be well rubbed in flour extra from the five pounds. Citron should be sliced thin and set in two or three thick layers, as the dough is put in the pans. Bake gently three or four hours.

WHITE FRUIT-CAKE.—No. 1.

One pound of sugar, one pound of citron, one pound of flour, half pound of butter, twelve eggs, yelks and whites beaten separately, two grated cocoa-nuts, one pound of blanched almonds, split, two tea-spoonfuls cream of tartar and one tea-spoonful of soda.

WHITE FRUIT-CAKE.—No. 2

Twelve eggs, one pound of butter, one pound of sugar, one pound of flour, two pounds of citron—some sliced, and some chopped fine; two pounds of blanched almonds, two grated cocoa-nuts, one wine-glassful of wine, one table-spoonful of mace, one table-spoonful of cinnamon, and two tea-spoonfuls of yeast-powder. Do not bake as long as black fruit-cake.

WHITE FRUIT-CAKE.—No. 3.

One pound of flour, one pound of butter, one pound of sugar, one pound of grated cocoa-nut, one pound of citron cut in small slices, one pound of almonds blanched and cut fine, one pound of English walnuts, and twelve eggs.

LOAF-CAKE.

Ten eggs, with three whites left out, one pound of sugar, one pound of butter, one pound of flour, one pound of citron, two pounds of currants, two table-spoonfuls cinnamon, one tea-spoonful of cloves, four grated nutmegs, one cup of molasses, and one wine-glass of brandy. Use the whites for frosting.

CUP FRUIT-CAKE.

Four cups of flour, one and a half cup of sugar, one half cup of molasses, four eggs, one large cup of butter, one pound of currants, one pound of raisins, one half pound of citron, one half tea-spoonful of soda, half tea-spoonful of cloves, half tea-spoonful cinnamon, half tea-spoonful spice, and one half tea-cup of wine, or water.

POUND-CAKE.—No. 1.

One pound of flour, one pound of eggs, one pound of sugar, and one pound of butter. Cream the butter and flour together till perfectly light. Beat the eggs separately, beating the sugar with the yelks; then add alternately the whites and creamed butter. Lastly, add one table-spoonful of lemon-juice, and one tea-spoonful of extract of lemon. Bake quickly.

POUND-CAKE.—No. 2.

Twelve eggs, one pound of butter, one pound of sugar, one pound of flour. Flavor with extract of lemon or vanilla, to taste.

POUND-CAKE.—No. 3.

Ten eggs, one pound of white sugar, one pound of flour, three quarters of a pound of butter, and the juice of one lemon. Rub the butter and sugar to a cream. Sift the flour, adding one tea-spoonful of yeast powder. Beat the yelks of the eggs and add them to the butter and sugar; then put in the juice of the lemon. Stir the whites to a stiff froth; then add the flour and whites alternately. Beat all together well. Bake one hour in a quick oven.

POUND-CAKE.—No. 4.

Ten eggs, one and quarter pound of flour, one pound of butter, one pound of sugar, one quarter ounce of ammonia dissolved in a gill of water.

POUND-CAKE.—No. 5.

Ten eggs, one pound of flour, one pound of sugar, three quarters pound of butter, one wine-glass of brandy, one nutmeg, one tea-spoonful of mace. Cream the butter, and rub in half the flour; add brandy, nutmeg, and mace. Beat the yelks of the eggs, and add the sugar; then the well-beaten whites and the remainder of the flour alternately. When thoroughly mixed, beat all half an hour.

POUND-CAKE.—No. 6.

Beat separately six eggs, one pound of sugar, half pound of butter, one pound of flour, one pint of sweet milk, one tea-spoonful of soda, and two of cream of tartar.

WHITE POUND-CAKE.

One pound of flour, one pound of white sugar, three fourths pound of butter washed and worked to a cream; ten eggs, leaving out three yelks; one half cup of cream—if sour stir in a little soda to sweeten. Flavor with vanilla or extract of almonds.

CORN-STARCH CAKE.

One quarter of a pound of corn-starch, one quarter of a pound of flour, half a pound of butter, one half pound of sugar, and the whites of eight eggs. Rub one tea-spoonful cream of tartar in the flour, dissolve one half tea-spoonful of soda in a *small* quantity of sweet milk, and put in last.

SPONGE-CAKE.—No. 1.

Beat the yelks of ten eggs, with one pound of sugar, then add the whites of the eggs, well beaten. Stir in a little over a half pound of flour, and bake with a moderate fire. Never beat after the flour is added.

SPONGE-CAKE.—No. 2.

Nine eggs, one pound of sugar, and half a pound of flour.

Flavor with the juice and grated rind of one lemon. Beat the eggs separately, and stir in the flour a little at a time. Add an extra table-spoonful of flour.

SPONGE-CAKE.—No. 3.

One pound of powdered sugar, twelve eggs, one pound two ounces of flour.

SPONGE-CAKE.—No. 4.

Take as many eggs as you please, the weight of the eggs in sugar, half their weight in flour.

WHITE SPONGE-CAKE.

Take the whites of twenty eggs, two and one half cups of sugar, one and one half cups of flour, one cup of corn-starch, and two tea-spoonfuls cream of tartar. Whip the eggs as light as possible; sift in the sugar, then the flour, corn-starch, and cream of tartar mixed together. Flavor to taste.

BOILED SPONGE-CAKE.

Seven eggs, three fourths of pound of sugar, half pound of flour; flavor to suit the taste. Pour two wine-glasses of water on the sugar, and boil till it feathers from the spoon. Have the whites and yelks well beaten; mix them and pour on them the boiling sugar, stirring briskly; beat until cold, and add the flour.

HOT-WATER SPONGE-CAKE.

Four eggs, three light cups of flour, two cups of sugar, half tea-spoonful of soda, and one tea-spoonful cream of tartar; add one half cup of boiling water just before baking.

CHEAP SPONGE-CAKE.

Three eggs beat with one cup and a half of sugar; add one cup of flour, beat three minutes, one half cup of milk, add one cup of flour with one tea-spoonful of yeast-powder. Flavor to taste.

SPONGE-CAKE.

Twelve eggs, the weight of ten in sugar and six in flour. Flavor with lemon. Bake the cake in a paste of ryemeal or Graham meal—the fine siftings of wheat-bran, mixed with a little flour, to make it roll, is just as good. Line the pan as for a meat pie; slightly butter the crust before putting in the batter. This will leave no crust upon the cake, and will prevent it from drying, if the cake is to be kept any length of time.

LADY-FINGERS.

One pound of sugar, one pound two ounces of flour; flavor to suit the taste; sixteen eggs—beat yelks and sugar together, and beat the whites to a stiff froth; stir in flour lightly, and never beat *any mixture* long after adding the flour, as it toughens it. Make a funnel-shaped bag of canvas, insert a tube (tin will answer) half inch in diameter, in the small end. Use this bag to shape your lady-fingers on the paper, then dust them lightly with powdered sugar. After they are done and cool, wet the paper, and they will come off easily; this will moisten the lady-fingers; stick two together, back to back, while moist.

GOLD-CAKE.—No. 1.

Beat the yelks of eight eggs, very light, and mix with them one cup of sugar and three fourths cup of butter, previously stirred to a cream. Add two cups of sifted flour, half a tea spoonful of soda dissolved in half a cup of sweet milk; when well mixed stir in one tea-spoonful cream of tartar. Flavor to taste.

GOLD-CAKE.—No. 2.

One pound of sugar, one pound of flour, three fourths pound butter, yelks of fourteen eggs. Work the butter and sugar well together, then add the eggs after being well beaten, one tea-spoonful of yeast-powder, then the flour.

When well mixed, add the grated rind and juice of two lemons.

SILVER-CAKE.—No. 1.

One pound of white sugar, three fourths pound flour, half pound of butter, whites of fourteen eggs. Beat the sugar and eggs till it looks like icing; cream the butter and flour well together; then mix with the icing. When well mixed add two tea-spoonfuls of yeast-powder, dissolved in wine. Flavor to taste.

SILVER-CAKE.—No. 2.

Two cups of white sugar, two and a half cups sifted flour, half cup of butter, three fourths cup sweet milk, half tea-spoonful soda, dissolved in the milk, one tea-spoonful cream of tartar, and the whites of eight eggs. Flavor with peach, vanilla, or rose-water. Stir the butter and sugar to a cream; add the eggs beaten stiff, then the flour, and the milk and soda. Stir the whole several minutes, then add the cream of tartar and essence.

SILVER-CAKE,—No. 3.

Whites of twelve eggs, three cups of white sugar, one and a half cup of butter, four and a half cups flour, and one fourth cup sour cream. Dissolve one tea-spoonful of soda in a table-spoonful of boiling water, two tea-spoonfuls cream of tartar, sifted in the flour; stir the butter and flour together; beat the eggs to a stiff froth; then add the sugar and beat it well; stir in the butter and flour and cream all together well. Flavor with peach; put the soda in last.

DELICATE-CAKE.—No. 1.

The whites of fourteen eggs, one pound of pulverized white sugar, one pound of flour, three quarters of a pound of butter. Beat the butter and sugar together, add the flour alternately with the eggs; a half cup of sweet milk. Bake quickly.

DELICATE-CAKE.—No. 2.

One cup of butter, two cups of sugar, three cups of flour, half cup of sweet milk, the whites of eight eggs, two tea-spoonfuls cream of tartar, and one tea-spoonful of soda. Flavor to taste.

LADY-CAKE.—No. 1.

The whites of eighteen eggs, one pound of sugar, one pound of butter, one and one fourth pounds of flour, one table-spoonful grated sweet almonds, and three tea-spoonfuls of extract of rose.

LADY-CAKE.—No. 2.

Whites of six eggs well beaten, four tea-cups of sifted flour, one cup of butter, one cup of sweet milk, two cups of white sugar, one tea-spoonful of soda, and two tea-spoonfuls cream of tartar. If sour milk is used, leave out the cream of tartar.

CUP-CAKE.—No. 1.

Six eggs, three cups of sugar, five light cups of sifted flour, one heaping cup of butter, one cup of milk and water,—two thirds milk and one third water,—and a tea-spoonful of yeast-powder. Flavor to taste.

CUP CAKE.—No. 2.

One cup of butter and three of sugar worked to a cream, a half wine-glassful of wine, five eggs beat separately, one tea-spoonful of soda sifted with five cups of sifted flour, a little nutmeg, and lastly a cup of sour cream. Bake in round tins, in a moderately quick oven. Fruit may be added if desired. Frost while the cake is warm, and it will keep some time without becoming stale.

CUP-CAKE.—No. 3.

One cup of butter, one cup of sweet milk, two of sugar, three of flour, four eggs, and one tea-spoonful of yeast-powder. Flavor with extract of vanilla.

CREAM CUP-CAKE.

Four cups of flour, two cups of sugar, three cups of cream, and four eggs. Beat well and bake in square tin-pans, and when cold cut in squares. Bake in a quick oven.

WHITE CUP-CAKE.

One large coffee-cup of cream or very rich milk—best when sour, one cup of fresh butter, four cups of sifted flour, and two cups of sugar. Stir the butter and sugar together until quite light, then by degrees add the cream alternately with half the flour. Beat five eggs separately, very light, and stir alternately with the remainder of the flour. Add essence of lemon, and lastly, a tea-spoonful of soda.

CUP CHOCOLATE-CAKE.

Six eggs, three cups of powdered sugar, four cups of flour, one cup of milk, one cup of butter, one and one half cups of grated chocolate, one tea-spoonful of yeast-powder.

COFFEE CUP-CAKE.

One cup of cold, strong coffee, one cup of sugar, one cup of molasses, one cup of stoned raisins, one cup of butter, five cups of flour, one tea-spoonful of soda, one tea-spoonful of allspice, and one tea-spoonful of cinnamon.

JELLY-CAKE.

Use cup-cake recipe, and bake in jelly-cake pans. When partially cold spread a layer of jelly or marmelade alternating with cake-layers, till it is the thickness desired. Let a layer of cake be on top.

ROLL JELLY-CAKE.

Four eggs, one cup of flour, one tea-spoonful cream of tartar, half tea-spoonful of soda, one cup of sugar, and a pinch of salt. This will make two cakes. Spread thin on long tins, and bake. When baked, turn from the tins; spread jelly quickly over the cake while warm, and roll immediately.

LEMON JELLY-CAKE.

Six eggs, two cups of sugar beaten well together, three cups of sifted flour, a small pinch of salt, eight table-spoonfuls of cold water and three tea-spoonfuls of yeast-powder. Bake in jelly-cake pans, in a quick oven. *Filling for above.*—Three eggs, one cup of sugar, two lemons, juice and grated rinds, one tea-cupful of water thickened to the consistency of rich cream, with flour. Let all boil together, and when cool spread between the cakes.

SPONGE LAYER-CAKE.

One coffee-cup of sugar, one coffee-cup of flour, one tea-spoonful of yeast-powder, or one tea-spoonful cream of tartar, half tea-spoonful of soda, one table-spoonful of milk, and two eggs. Bake in thin pans, as for jelly-cake. *Filling for cake.*—One pint of milk, one large table-spoonful of corn-starch, one cup of sugar, the yelks of three eggs; boil and flavor with vanilla. The whites of eggs save for merangue. When this is cold, lay alternate layers of cake and filling. The merangue is made by beating the whites of the three eggs with a small cup of pulverized white sugar; flavor with vanilla, and add a little citric acid to make it stiff and white; beat well. Lay this on the top cake, and put it in the oven to get hard, but not brown. Then put this on the others for the top layer.

MOUNTAIN-CAKE.

Six eggs, one pound and a half ounce of flour, half pound of butter, two tea-spoonfuls cream of tartar sifted in the flour, one tea-cupful of sweet milk, one tea-spoonful of soda dissolved in a little boiling water, to be added last. Bake in jelly-pans. When cold, put the following mixtures between the layers of cake. Beat the whites of two eggs, dampen one pound of white sugar with the milk of a cocoa-nut, and make this into hot icing, and thicken with grated cocoa-nut. Spread this on the cake, as for jelly-cake.

CHOCOLATE-CAKE.—No. 1.

Half cup of butter, one cup of milk, two cups of sugar, three cups of flour, four eggs, one tea-spoonful of soda, and two of cream of tartar. Bake in jelly-pans. Mix one cup of grated chocolate, one cup of sugar, one and a half cups of milk, and one egg. Boil until as thick as custard; when cool, flavor with vanilla; spread between layers of cake, as in jelly-cake.

CHOCOLATE-CAKE.—No. 2.

Two cups of sugar, one small cup of butter, four eggs—leaving out the whites of two, one cup of milk, three and a half cups of flour, one tea-spoonful cream of tartar, and half tea-spoonful of soda. Bake in jelly-cake pans. Prepare a filling to put between the layers of cake. Six table-spoonfuls of grated chocolate, whites of two eggs not beaten, one and a half cups of powdered sugar, and one tea-spoonful of vanilla. Mix the eggs and chocolate in a bowl; set the bowl in hot water on the stove, and stir the mixture until smooth and shining; then add sugar and vanilla.

COCOA-NUT-CAKE.—No. 1.

Twelve eggs,—whites only,—one pound of sugar, half pound of butter, half pound of cocoa-nut, three fourths pound of flour.

COCOA NUT-CAKE.—No. 2.

One coffee-cup of butter, two coffee-cups of powdered sugar, three coffee-cups of flour, ten eggs, one tea-spoonful cream of tartar, one half tea-spoonful of soda, and one cocoa-nut finely grated. Stir the butter and sugar together till it becomes creamy, then add the whites of the eggs, beaten to a stiff froth; next the yelks, beaten very light. Then stir in one cup of flour, then the soda, dry; then another cup of flour and the cream of tartar, dry; then the last cup of flour followed by the cocoa-nut stirred in very lightly. Put in the oven without delay. This cake requires very careful baking.

ANGEL'S FOOD.

Grate one cocoa-nut, one pound of grated chocolate; take the whites of four eggs and one pound of powdered sugar; let it cook as in boiled icing. When it begins to rope take half of it and mix with all the chocolate; the other half mix with the cocoa-nut, reserving enough of the nut to sprinkle on top of the cake. Have either pound or cup cake baked in jelly-cake pans. Put a layer of cake, chocolate, then cake, then cocoa-nut, cake, jelly, &c., till it is the size desired.

ORANGE-CAKE.

Two cups of sugar, three cups of flour, half cup of water or milk, the yelks of five eggs and the whites of three, one tea-spoonful of yeast-powder, and grated rind of an orange. Bake in jelly-cake tins. *Filling for above.*—The whites of two eggs well beaten with one pound of pulverized sugar, and the juice of the orange. Spread this icing between and on top of the cake. Lemon may be used instead of orange, if preferred.

CREAM-CAKES.

Half a pound of butter, one pound of flour, tea-spoonful of sugar, half tea spoonful of salt; rub them smoothly together, and stir into one quart of boiling milk; stir constantly over the fire, till it clears from the kettle; set aside to cool.

When cool break in ten eggs, stirring well; add a small tea-spoonful of soda in half a cup of cream. Drop on buttered pans; shape with the hands in turban form, and rub a beaten egg over them with a feather. Bake moderately twenty minutes; when done, open one side with a knife and fill with the following custard: One pint of water, one quarter pound of butter, and three quarters pound of flour. Put the butter in the water; while boiling, stir in the flour smoothly; then pour out to cool. Beat in ten eggs, one at a time.

CREAM-CAKES FOR DESSERT.

A pint of cold water or milk, three fourths pound of flour, and one fourth pound of butter. Boil the butter and milk together; while boiling, add the flour. When cool, add ten eggs and a small tea-spoonful of soda. Bake in jelly-pans. *Cream for cakes.*—One quart of milk, two cups of sugar, one cup of flour, and four eggs. Boil part of the milk and flour together; then add cold milk and eggs, and boil a few minutes. Flavor with lemon.

CREAM-CAKES.

One cup of butter, two cups of sugar, three cups of flour, one cup of milk, four eggs, a tea-spoonful of lemon,—or any extract desired,—and a table-spoonful of yeast-powder. Bake in jelly-pans. Make a custard of one pint of milk, two eggs, a half cup of sugar, a table-spoonful of corn starch, and a piece of butter the size of an egg. When cold, place between the cakes as you do jelly.

BOSTON CREAM-CAKES.

Half pound of butter, three fourths pound flour, eight eggs, and one pint of water. Stir the butter into the water, which should be warm; set it on the fire in a sauce-pan, and slowly bring to a boil, stirring it often. When it boils, put in the flour and boil one minute, stirring all the while; take from the fire, turn into a deep dish, and let it cool. Beat the eggs very light and whip into this cooled paste, first the yelks then the whites. Drop in a great spoonful upon buttered paper, taking care not to let them touch or run into each other, and bake ten minutes in a quick oven. *Cream for filling.*—One quart of milk, four table-spoonfuls of corn-starch, two eggs, two cups of sugar; wet the corn-starch with enough milk to work it into a smooth paste. Boil the rest of the milk; beat the eggs, add the sugar and corn-starch to them, and so soon as the milk boils pour in the mixture gradually, stirring all the time until smooth and thick. Drop in a tea-spoonful of butter, and when this is mixed in set the custard aside to cool. Then flavor with vanilla or lemon. Pass a sharp knife lightly around the puff; split them, and fill with the mixture.

MARBLE-CAKE.—No. 1.

DARK.—Yelks of seven eggs, two cups of brown sugar, one cup of butter, one cup of molasses, five cups of flour unsifted one cup of milk, one tea-spoonful of soda, cloves, nutmeg cinnamon, and allspice; dissolve the soda in molasses.

LIGHT.—Whites of seven eggs, two cups of white sugar, one cup of butter, three cups of flour, half cup of milk, one tea-spoonful cream of tartar, half tea-spoonful of soda. Put alternately about a handful of each, or any way the taste may dictate to be prettily marbled. A part of the light may be colored with cochineal, and put in with the light and dark with good effect.

MARBLE-CAKE.—No. 2.

THE WHITE.—Two cups of white sugar, one cup of butter, one of sweet milk, four of flour, whites of eight eggs well beaten, one tea-spoonful cream of tartar, and one half spoonful of soda, cream, butter, and sugar; add milk; then flour, with cream of tartar in it, alternating with white of egg; lastly, the soda well dissolved in a little of the milk.

The Brown Part.—One large cup of brown sugar, half a cup of butter, two thirds cup of milk, two and a half cups of flour with a tea spoonful cream of tartar rubbed into it, the yelks of eight eggs, half tea-spoonful of soda, two tea-spoonfuls of powdered cloves, four of cinnamon, four of allspice, and one grated nutmeg. If not dark enough, add more cinnamon and spice. Drop the white batter first into the bake-pan, and then the brown, having the white to finish off on the top.

SPICE-CAKE.

Three eggs, one cup of butter, three cups of sugar, four of flour, one of milk, one tea-spoonful of yeast-powder, one table-spoonful of allspice, ginger, cloves, cinnamon, and half a nutmeg

MOLASSES SPICE-CAKE

One dozen eggs, one pound of butter, one pound of sugar, a pint of molasses, two pounds of flour, a wine-glassful of spices, and a tea-spoonful of soda. Mix like pound-cake.

ALMOND-CAKE.

Ten eggs, one pound of sugar, three quarters of a pound of butter, and three quarters of a pound of flour. Add half a pound of almonds, blanched and beaten fine, with a wine-glassful of rose-water.

HICKORY-NUT CAKE.

One cup of sugar, two eggs, two thirds cup of sweet cream, two cups of flour, one tea-spoonful of soda, and two cream of tartar; season with lemon or cinnamon extract, or with grated nutmeg. Bake on jelly-tins, enough for four layers. *Filling between the layers.*—One cup of sweet, thin cream; put on a dish and bring to a boil; dissolve a table-spoonful of corn-starch in new milk, and stir into the heated cream; cook a few minutes, then add to the cooked cream a pint of hickory-nut meats sliced finely. Spread between the layers of cake while warm; frost the top layer of cake.

WASHINGTON-CAKE.

Two and a half pounds of flour, one and a half pounds of sugar, six eggs, three fourths of a pound of butter, half a gill of milk, half a gill of brandy, half a pound of citron, one nutmeg, one tea-spoonful of cloves, one of soda, one pound of raisins, and one pound of currants.

QUEEN-CAKE.

One pound of sugar, one pound of flour, half pound of butter, five eggs, one gill of cream, one nutmeg, half tea-spoonful of soda, and two pounds of chopped raisins.

IRENE-CAKE.

Five cups of flour, two of butter, four of sugar, one of milk, one of wine, six eggs, one tea-spoonful of soda, one of cloves, one orange-peel, one pound of citron, and two pounds of washed currants. Beat the whites and yelks separately

GRAHAM-CAKE.

One cup of sugar, one of sour cream, one egg, three cups of flour, soda, salt, and a little nutmeg.

CORN-STARCH CAKE.

Three fourths pound of butter, three fourths pound of sugar, six eggs, three fourths pound of corn-starch, and one fourth pound of flour. Beat into it one egg at a time. Flavor with lemon—a fresh lemon is best.

BEVERLY-CAKE.

Six cups of flour, three cups of sugar, one cup of butter, one cup of milk, half cup of molasses, four eggs, raisins, spice, a little salt, and a tea-spoonful of soda.

IMPERIAL-CAKE.

One pound of flour, one pound of sugar, one pound of butter, one pound of raisins stoned and chopped, half pound of blanched almonds, one fourth pound citron, eight eggs, two wine-glasses of wine, and half tea-spoonful of mace.

FRANCIS-CAKE.

Six eggs, one pound of sugar, half pound of butter, one pound of flour, half pint of sweet milk, two tea-spoonfuls of cream of tartar, and one of soda, dissolve in *extra* milk, just enough to dissolve it. The cream of tartar must be sifted dry into the flour; put the soda in just before cooking. Flavor with essence of lemon.

CROTON SPONGE-CAKE.

One pound of sugar, one pound of flour, half pound of butter, six eggs, one tea-spoonful of soda dissolved in a small tea-cupful of sweet milk, and two tea-spoonfuls cream of tartar sifted in flour. Bake quickly.

MEASURE-CAKE.

Three cups of sugar, six cups of flour, one and a half cups of butter, six eggs, three tea-spoonfuls cream of tartar, one and a half tea-spoonfuls of soda, and one and a half cups of milk.

SODA-CAKE.—No. 1.

Two and a half cups of sugar, one and a half cups of butter, one quart of flour, and seven eggs. After all are well mixed together, add a tea-spoonful of soda and two cream of tartar; dissolve each in half a cup of water. Bake in a quick oven; flavor with essence of lemon, to your taste.

SODA-CAKE.—No. 2.

One and a half cups of sugar, one cup of milk, two table-spoonfuls of butter, two tea-spoonfuls cream of tartar, one tea-spoonful of soda, three cups of flour, and two eggs; reserve the whites for merangue. Bake about an inch thick.

CURRANT-CAKE.

One and one quarter pound of sugar, one pound of butter twelve eggs, one quarter ounce of ammonia dissolved in a gill of water, two pounds two ounces of flour, and three quarters of a pound of washed and dried currants, put in just before baking.

PIPER-CAKE.

Two eggs, half cup of butter, one cup of sugar, one cup of molasses, one cup of milk, three cups of flour, one tea-spoonful of cloves, half a nutmeg, and one tea-spoonful of soda.

TURBAN-CAKE.

Two cups of milk, two eggs, a little salt, and flour enough to make a batter. Bake in cups fifteen minutes. Nice for lunch or tea, hot.

ONE-EGG CAKE.

One egg, one cup of sweet milk, one and a half cup of sugar, three cups of flour, one table-spoonful of butter, and one tea-spoonful of yeast-powder.

CAKE WITHOUT EGGS.

Three pounds of flour, one and a half pounds of sugar, one and a half pound of butter, one and a half pound of raisins, one nutmeg, one table-spoonful powdered cinnamon, two gills of wine, and one half pint of yeast. Put the milk, butter, flour, and yeast together, and let rise before adding the other ingredients.

TEA-CAKES.—No. 1.

Two eggs, one cup of sugar, one and a half table-spoonfuls of butter, two tea-spoonfuls cream of tartar, rubbed into the dry flour, one tea-spoonful of soda, dissolved in a little milk; flour sufficient to roll into a soft dough. Flavor with grated nutmeg, or to taste. Bake in a quick oven.

TEA-CAKES.—No. 2.

Three eggs, one cup of butter, one tea-spoonful of salt three cups of sugar, one tea-spoonful of soda, one cup of buttermilk, and flour sufficient for rolling. Flavor with cinnamon or other extract.

TEA-CAKES.—No. 3.

One pound of sugar, six ounces of butter and lard together (mix well), half ounce crystals of ammonia dissolved in half pint of water, two pounds of flour, and two eggs. Flavor with grated nutmeg.

SOFT TEA-CAKE.

Five eggs, half pound of butter, half pound of sugar, one pound of flour, one wine-glassful of brandy, one nutmeg, one tea-spoonful of soda. To be dropped in with a spoon.

FASCINATORS.

One cup of butter, two of sugar, four eggs, one tea-spoonful of soda, two cream of tartar, and flour enough to stiffen; roll very thin. Bake quickly

SUGAR-CAKES WITHOUT EGGS.

Three pounds of flour, one and a half pound of sugar, fourteen ounces of butter, a small tea-spoonful of soda or yeast-powder sifted with the flour, half pint of milk. Rub the the butter, sugar, and flour together; then wet with the milk and roll out thin. Flavor to suit the taste.

GINGER POUND-CAKE.

Five cups of flour, five eggs, two cups of butter, two cups of sugar, two cups of molasses, two table-spoonfuls of ginger, one of spice, one cup of sour milk, and one teaspoonful of soda.

SOFT GINGER-CAKE.—No. 1.

Three cups of flour, one of sugar, one of molasses, one of butter, six eggs, two table-spoonfuls of ginger, one tea-spoonful of soda dissolved in sour milk or vinegar. Bake in a moderate oven. With sauce it makes a nice dessert.

SOFT GINGER-CAKE.—No. 2.

Five eggs, four cups of flour, two of sugar, one of milk, one of butter, one of molasses, two table-spoonfuls of ginger, one tea-spoonful of soda.

HARD GINGER-CAKE.

One cup of butter, one of sugar, one of molasses, two of flour, five eggs, one table-spoonful of ginger, half a tea-spoonful of soda.

GINGER-SNAPS.—No. 1.

One pound of flour rubbed in one quarter pound of butter, three quarters pound of powdered sugar, one ounce ground ginger, and peel of a lemon. Work the ingredients well together, and roll thin and cut in small cakes. Bake as tea-cakes.

GINGER-SNAPS.—No. 2.

One pint of molasses, one cup of butter, one cup of lard, half cup of buttermilk, one table-spoonful of soda, three eggs, and four table-spoonfuls of ginger; add flour to make a moderately stiff dough. Roll the dough very thin, and cut with a ring the size of a half dollar.

GINGER-SNAPS.—No. 3.

Half pound of butter, half pound of sugar, two and a half pounds of flour, one pint of molasses, one tea-spoonful of soda, and ginger to taste. Boil the molasses.

SUGAR GINGER-CAKES.

Two cups of sugar, one cup of butter, one tea-spoonful of soda, one cup of cold water, flour sufficient to roll out very thin; ginger to the taste.

CRULLERS.—No. 1.

Six eggs, one cup of butter, one nutmeg, two cups of sugar, one cup of sour milk, one half tea-spoonful soda, and flour enough to roll. Fry in hot lard.

CRULLERS.—No. 2.

One pound of sugar, eight eggs, half ounce crystals of carbonate of ammonia dissolved in half pint of water, and two and a quarter pounds of flour. Flavor with lemon. Cut crullers in shapes to suit the fancy. Have the lard so hot that it will cease to bubble; then fry the crullers a light brown.

CRULLERS.—No. 3.

Four eggs, one and a half quarts of flour, one cup of milk, two cups of sugar, a table-spoonful of butter, one nutmeg and two tea-spoonfuls of yeast-powder. Have the lard boiling hot to fry them.

CRULLERS.—No. 4.

Two eggs, one cup of sugar, a small piece of butter, one and a half nutmeg, two cups of milk, two tea-spoonfuls cream of tartar and one of soda; flour to roll.

DOUGHNUTS.

One pint of yeast, one pint of water, two ounces of butter a tea-spoonful of soda, six ounces of sugar; flavor to taste; use sufficient flour to make a soft dough. Let this dough rise; roll out the doughnuts and permit to rise again; then fry.

SWEET WAFERS.—No. 1.

One egg, four table-spoonfuls of sugar, one table-spoonful of butter, four heaping table-spoonfuls of flour, made into batter and dropped into the irons. If the butter does not fur nish salt enough, add a little.

SWEET WAFERS.—No. 2.

Three cups of flour, one cup of sugar, one cup of butter, one cup of rich cream, and a little nutmeg.

SWEET WAFERS.—No. 3.

Four eggs, three tea-cupfuls of flour, two cups of sugar, and one cup of butter.

CHOCOLATE MACAROONS.

Scrape fine half a pound of Baker's chocolate. Beat stiff the whites of four eggs, and stir into the eggs one pound of powdered sugar and the scraped chocolate, adding a very little flour. Form the mixture into small, thick cakes, and lay them, not too close, on a buttered tin, and bake them a few minutes. Sift sugar over them while warm.

SUGAR-KISSES.

The whites of four eggs whisked to a stiff froth, and stir in half a pound of sifted white sugar. Flavor to taste. When stiff drop it on white paper, the shape and size desired, an inch apart. The paper should previously be laid on a clean board, half an inch thick; and put them into a hot oven, and bake until they are a light brown. Slip them off the paper with a table-knife, and stick the broad edges of every two of them together; and if pressed gently they will adhere. When finished they should be the size and shape of an egg.

BOILED ICING.

Dissolve one pound of loaf-sugar in a tea-cup of water. and

let it cook until it begins to rope. Try it frequently by dipping in a spoon. Have ready the whites of four eggs, beaten until they begin to froth; then pour the boiling sugar upon the eggs—pour slowly, beating constantly until perfectly white. Flavor with rose-water, or to taste. Add a little citric acid to whiten it. If the icing is too thin, put the bowl containing it in a large pan of boiling water, and place it upon the stove and let boil until perfectly thick.

ICING.

Beat the whites of four eggs to a stiff froth. Stir in one pound of pulverized white sugar; then put on the stove in a flat earthen dish, and cook until heated through, stirring all the time. Spread on your cake while the icing is hot, keeping the knife hot by dipping in hot water, which will make it perfectly smooth, having no ridges.

COLD ICING.—No 1.

Whites of three eggs; when partially beaten stir in one pound of powdered sugar, and juice of one lemon; then beat till white and thick. Before icing tops of cakes rub them slightly with flour. Spread on the icing with a knife, dipping constantly in cold water to make the icing smooth.

COLD ICING.—No. 2.

Four eggs, one pound of powdered sugar, and a very little acetic acid.

CHOCOLATE ICING.

Beat whites of four eggs, and when partly beaten add gradually one pound of powdered sugar and one full cup of grated chocolate. This is nice to spread between layer-cakes instead of jelly, using cup-cake recipe for the cake.

CHOCOLATE CREAM.

Mix one cup of grated chocolate, one cup of sugar, one and

a half of milk, and one egg together. Boil till thick as custard, and flavor with vanilla. Spread between the cakes, as in cream-cakes.

PIES.

GENERAL RULES FOR PASTRY.

Pastry should be made on a cold, smooth substance, such as marble, mixing with a knife. It should be made quickly; much handling makes it heavy. Great nicety is required in wetting the paste, too little moisture rendering it dry and crumbly, while too much makes it tough and heavy. Reserve half of the butter and a fourth of the flour to be used in rolling out the paste. Roll it out lightly, dredge with flour, and spread with butter; fold, and roll again, repeating the same three or four times, always rolling fast and pressing on lightly. When you see the surface of the paste covered with blisters, you may be sure that it is a success; that is, if it is baked properly, for the quality of the paste depends much on the baking. The oven should be well and evenly heated before baking, and not allowed to cool.

PUFF-PASTE.—No. 1.

One pound of flour, one pound of butter, one egg; mix the flour with two table-spoonfuls of butter, and make a dough with cold water and the egg; divide the remainder of the butter into six equal parts; roll the paste, and spread on one part of the butter, dredging it with flour; repeat until all the butter is rolled in. Great care is necessary to prevent the butter from bursting through. Handle as little as possible. It is improved by standing awhile on ice before baking.

PUFF-PASTE.—No. 2.

One pound of flour, three quarters of a pound butter; rub into the flour two ounces of butter; then make a dough with cold water; then proceed to roll in butter and flour according to the general directions given above.

PASTRY.

One quart of flour, quarter of a pound of butter, quarter of a pound of lard; make a dough of the flour and lard, using as little water as possible; roll it out lightly; dredge with flour; spread with butter in bits; fold and roll again; repeat until the butter is all used.

PLAIN PASTRY.

Three cups or flour, one cup of butter, one cup of lard, one cup of cold water. Mix with a knife; roll from you. This is enough for two pies, with crusts top and bottom.

PLAIN PIE-CRUST.

Nine ounces of lard, one pound of flour, a pinch of salt. Rub the lard and flour well together; add water sufficient to make a dough, and roll out into thin sheets. Bake in a quick oven.

PASTRY FOR MEAT-PIES.

One quart of flour, half pound of lard. Dissolve a teaspoonful of soda in a cup of sour milk, and mix with a knife, stirring as little as possible.

POTATO-PASTE.

Take equal quantities of mashed potatoes and sifted flour; wet with sour milk, into which enough soda has been stirred to sweeten it. A little salt and butter may be added. Roll out thin. This is nice for apple-dumplings or pot-pies.

BOILED APPLE-DUMPLINGS.

Pare and core ten or twelve apples; cover each apple separately with potato-paste; tie up in thin cloths. Boil until tender.

EXCELLENT APPLE-DUMPLINGS.

Mix well together one egg, one pint of buttermilk, one teaspoonful of soda, salt, and flour enough to make a stiff batter. Into well-greased cups drop a small piece of butter, and into each cup an apple, quartered and cored and put together again; pour the batter over each apple, and set the cups in a steamer over boiling warm, and steam them till done. Eat them with sauce.

BAKED APPLE-DUMPLINGS.

Pare, quarter, and core eight or ten apples; roll out pieces of paste the size of a common saucer; place an apple upon each piece, and close the edges of the paste around the fruit; put the dumplings in a large dish; pour over them a sauce made of one cup of butter and three cups of sugar well creamed together; flavor with nutmeg; bake one hour. Peach-dumplings may be made in the same way.

POTATO FRITTERS

Boil two large potatoes; mash them fine; beat four yolks and three whites of eggs, and add to the above; one large spoonful of cream, another of sweet wine, the juice of one lemon, and a little nutmeg. Beat this batter for half an hour at least. Put a good quantity of fresh lard in a stew-pan, and drop a spoonful of the batter at a time into it, and fry a light brown. Serve with sauce.

ALTONA FRITTERS.

Make a batter of eight eggs, half pint of milk, six large spoonfuls of sifted flour, one tea-spoonful of salt. Into this batter put half a dozen apples pared, cored, and cut in quarters; let each piece of apple be well covered with the batter. Then put each piece into boiling lard, and fry a light brown. Serve with sauce.

SLICED SWEET-POTATO PIE.

Parboil and slice two medium-sized potatoes; put them into a deep pie-plate that has been previously lined with puff-paste; pour over the potatoes a sauce made of one cup of sugar, half cup of butter, and one cup of boiling water; flavor with a tea-spoonful of cinnamon, tea-spoonful of cloves and allspice mixed, and the juice and grated rinds of two lemons; cover with paste. Bake in a slow oven.

SWEET-POTATO PIE.

One pound of potatoes boiled and rubbed smooth, half pound of sugar, a small cup of cream, one fourth pound of butter, four eggs; nutmeg and lemon to suit the taste; bake in a crust. This quantity will make two large pies.

IRISH-POTATO PIE.

Two cupfuls of boiled potatoes nicely strained through a colander, one cup of butter, one of milk, two of sugar, six eggs; flavor with wine and nutmeg. Bake on pastry, or in a dish like a pudding.

A DELICIOUS APPLE-PIE.

Six apples of medium size, a tumblerful of crushed sugar, three table-spoonfuls of butter or two tumblerfuls of rich cream, six eggs, the juice and grated rind of one lemon; peel the apples, and grate them; cream the butter and sugar together; beat the whites and yelks of the eggs separately; mix as for cake. Bake in paste.

APPLE-PIE.

Peel, core, and stew the apples until transparent; pass through a sieve; sweeten to taste; add one cup of cream; fla vor with lemon; bake in puff-paste; have ready the whites of four eggs beaten to a stiff froth, with six table-spoonfuls of sugar; flavor with lemon; spread over the pies, return to the oven, and brown lightly.

FRUIT-PIES IN VARIETY.

Prepare and stew your fruit; sweeten to taste. They need no flavoring. Bake between thin crusts. Plums require more sugar than any other fruit. Serve with cream.

RHUBARB-PIE.

Put the rhubarb in deep plates lined with pie-crust, with a thick layer of sugar to each layer of rhubarb. A little grated lemon-peel may be added. Place over the top a thin crust; press tight around the edge of the plate. Bake about an hour in a slow oven. Rhubarb-pie must not be baked quick.

DRIED-FRUIT PIE.

Beat six eggs and six table-spoonfuls of sugar together; add one cup of milk and one table-spoonful of butter; have a cup of dried fruit, peaches or apples, stewed until very soft, and rubbed through a sifter; sweeten to taste, and add to the other ingredients; flavor with lemon. Bake in paste.

DRIED-APPLE PIE.

Soak the apples over night in warm water; stew in cider or water until tender. When cool, sweeten and flavor with the juice and grated peel of one lemon to every two pieces; add a table-spoonful of butter.

COCOA-NUT PIE.—No. I.

The well-beaten whites of six eggs; cream one fourth of a pound of butter with six table-spoonfuls of sugar; add one half pound of grated cocoa-nut; stir in the whites of the eggs; flavor with a wine-glass of wine and a little rose-water. Bake in paste.

COCOA-NUT PIE.—No. 2.

One cocoa-nut, six eggs, one pound of sugar, two ounces of flour, one ounce of butter; beat the eggs well; add the sugar, flour, and butter; beat all very light, and then add the grated cocoa-nut; flavor with lemon; fill the pastry; dust powdered sugar on the top of the custard, and bake.

COCOA-NUT CUSTARD.

Eight eggs, one half pound of butter, one pound of sugar, one large cocoa-nut and the milk of it; cream the butter and sugar together; stir in the other ingredients; flavor with lemon. Bake in paste.

ALMOND-PIE.

One half pound of butter, one half pound of sugar beaten to a cream, six eggs beaten very light, a little rose-water, one half pound of blanched almonds pounded fine, with rose-water or brandy to prevent oiling. Mix all well, and bake in puff-paste.

LEMON-PIE.—(EXCELLENT.)

The yelks of five eggs and the white of one; stir together with one half pound of sugar, one quarter of a pound of butter, the grated rind of three lemons and the juice of two, one table-spoonful of sifted flour mixed with a little water. Bake on paste in tin plates before putting in the mixture; bake the paste until it turns white; pour in the custard and bake slowly. Use the four remaining whites for a marangue; flavor with the juice of one lemon; put on top of pie when done, return to the oven, and brown lightly. Orange-pie may be made in the same way, using oranges instead of lemons.

LEMON-CREAM PIE.

The juice and grated peel of two lemons, four eggs, one quarter of a pound of butter, one pound of sugar; beat all well together; place on the fire, and cook until it becomes the consistency of custard. Bake with under crust.

LEMON-PIE.

The yelks of six eggs, four tea-cupfuls of sugar, one table-spoonful of butter, two tea-cupfuls of milk, the juice and grated rinds of four lemons, four table-spoonfuls of corn-starch or arrow-root; stir well together; bake on paste. When done, have ready the six whites, beaten to a stiff froth, with eight table-spoonfuls of pounded sugar; flavor with lemon; spread over the pies, return to the oven, and brown lightly.

LEMON AND POTATO PIE.

Three sweet-potatoes of medium size; boil well and rub through a sifter; one pint of rich milk, one quarter pound of butter, one pound of sugar, the juice of three lemons and the grated rind of one, the yelks of six eggs beaten well; mix all well together, and bake in puff-paste. Use the whites for a marangue, and spread over the pies after they are cooked; return them to the oven and brown.

ORANGE-PIE.

One half pound of butter and half a pound of sugar beaten to cream, four eggs, whites and yelks beaten separately; grate the rind of a sweet orange, and scrape the pulp from the inner skin, and stir with the butter, sugar, and eggs. Bake in puff-paste.

SOUR-ORANGE PIE.

Three eggs, the whites and yelks beaten separately, half a pint of boiling water, one table-spoonful of corn-starch wet and cooked liked starch, three cups of brown sugar, one table-spoonful of butter, the juice of two or three oranges. Bake in an open shell.

PUMPKIN-PIE.

One cup of sugar, one cup of stewed pumpkin, two cup of sweet milk, three eggs; flavor with ginger, nutmeg, and lemon-peel. Bake in an open shell.

MOLASSES-PIE.

One cup of molasses, one cup of sugar, half cup of milk, three eggs, a table-spoonful of butter; flavor with ginger, orange, or lemon. Bake on paste.

TRANSPARENT PIE.—No. 1.

One dozen eggs, whites and yelks beaten separately, one pound of sugar, one pound of butter. Mix the ingredients nicely, and place on the fire; stir gently until done; bake in puff-paste. Before putting in the mixture, bake the paste until it turns white.

TRANSPARENT PIE.—No. 2.

Beat eight eggs; put them into a sauce-pan with a pound of powdered sugar, one half pound of butter, and a little nutmeg. Mix well; set on the fire; stir constantly until it thickens; set aside to cool. Make a rich puff-paste, line a pie-dish with it, and spread on a layer of sliced citron or preserved ginger; pour over the custard, and bake an hour in a moderate oven.

MINCE-MEAT.

Two pounds of well-boiled beef or tongue chopped fine, to which add three pounds of raisins, three pounds of currants, one pound of citron chopped, the juice of six oranges with the peel chopped fine, one quart of preserved cranberries, four dozen pippin apples chopped, four table-spoonfuls of powdered cinnamon, three table-spoonfuls of allspice, six nutmegs;

mix together and chop well. Put in a sauce-pan two pounds of butter, two pounds of sugar, three pints of cooking brandy, three pints of sweet cider; simmer this ten or fifteen minutes, and pour over the mince-meat boiling hot; stir thoroughly, and put away in stone jars until wanted. It is better to put in the apples fresh as you use the mince-meat. Three large ones to the pint.

MOCK MINCE-MEAT.

Three soda-crackers rolled fine, one cup of cold water, one half cup of molasses, half cup brown sugar, three quarters of a cup of melted butter, half cup of raisins seeded and chopped, half cup of currants, one egg beaten light, half table-spoonful of powdered cinnamon, one table spoonful of allspice and cloves mixed, one tea-spoonful of black pepper and salt mixed, half a glass of wine or brandy.

PUDDINGS.

GENERAL RULES.

In boiling puddings, mind that the cloth be perfectly clean. Dip it in hot water and dredge well with flour, by sifting the flour over it. When bagged, tie the string tight, leaving sufficient room in the bag for expansion by swelling. Flour and Indian puddings require much room. Put the pudding in a pot of boiling water, placing an old plate on the bottom. Keep sufficient water in the pot to cover the pudding, being careful not to let the boiling cease one second. A tea-kettle of boiling water should be at hand to add as the water boils away. Dip the pudding into cold water immediately upon taking out, which prevents its adhering to the cloth. Make your pudding-bag of thick cloth; if it is thin, it will admit the water and deteriorate the pudding. If you use a pudding-mold, grease well with butter from which the salt has been carefully washed.

CONFEDERATE PUDDING.

Rub thoroughly into four tea-cupfuls of sifted flour one ea-cupful of suet shredded and chopped fine, one tea-cupful of raisins seeded and chopped, the same quantity of currants washed and dried the day previous, and one tea-spoonful of cinnamon; stir into this one tea-cupful of molasses, and the same quantity of milk. Pour into a pudding-mold, and boil two hours. Eat hot, with sauce.

BOILED CAKE-PUDDING.

One pound of sugar, one pound of flour, half pound of butter, six eggs, one tea-cupful of milk, one tea-spoonful cream of tartar, half tea-spoonful of soda; sift the cream of tartar with the flour; mix the soda in the milk, and add it to the other ingredients when they are all mixed together. It is good with sliced citron, or raisins and currants. If plain, boil two hours; if with fruit, three hours. Serve with wine-sauce.

MINISTER'S PUDDING

Three eggs, an equal weight of sugar and butter, and the weight of two eggs in flour; cream the butter and sugar well together; beat the eggs, and mix with the butter and sugar, beating the whole to a stiff froth; then add the flour by degrees, and the grated rind of a lemon. Pour in a mold, and boil gently for an hour. To be eaten with sauce.

BOILED BATTER-PUDDING.—No. 1.

Nine eggs beaten until very light; then sift in a pint of flour; add a tea-spoonful of salt; lastly, add a quart of milk. Pour in a pudding-mold, and boil two hours. Eat with rich wine-sauce.

BOILED BATTER-PUDDING.—No. 2.

Eight eggs, eight table-spoonfuls of flour, one quart of milk. Boil one hour, and serve with sauce.

ENGLISH PLUM-PUDDING.

Eight eggs, one pound and a half of raisins, one pound of currants, one pound of brown sugar, one pound of bread-crumbs, one pound of suet chopped fine, half pound of citron, or any candied fruit, quarter pound blanched almonds, one nutmeg grated, table-spoonful of powdered cinnamon, tea-spoonful of powdered cloves, tea-spoonful of powdered mace, the grated rind of a lemon, half pint of brandy, wine-glass of wine, wine-glass of rose-water. Put in a pudding-mold, and boil four hours. Pour brandy over the pudding, and bring to the table burning. Serve with sauce.

AN EXCELLENT PLUM-PUDDING.

One pint of bread-crumbs, one pint of flour, one pound of fresh suet chopped very fine, one pound of sugar, nine eggs, one pint of milk, half pint of wine and brandy mixed, one pound of raisins, one pound of currants, half pound of citron chopped fine, one nutmeg, one table-spoonful of cinnamon, one table spoonful of mixed spice and cloves, one tea-cupful of molasses. Dredge the fruit well with a portion of this flour to prevent its sinking to the bottom of the pan. Boil five hours according to the general directions. Serve with plum-pudding sauce.

PLUM-PUDDING.

One loaf of baker's bread sliced, buttered, and cut into pieces one inch square; put a layer of bread in the pudding-mold, and then a layer composed of raisins, citron, cloves, cinnamon, and nutmeg; then another layer of bread, then the fruit and spices, and so on until the mold is full. Then make a custard of five eggs, one quart of milk, and a cup and a half of sugar; pour the custard over the pudding, and boil six hours. Serve with sauce.

STEAM-PUDDING.

One tea-cupful of raisins stoned and cut fine, one of beef suet, one cup of molasses, one tea-spoonful of soda, one cup of milk, four cups of flour, a pinch of salt; cover close; keep over steamer for three hours. Serve with wine-sauce.

REBEL PUDDING.

One cup of molasses, half cup of butter, one cup of sweet milk, one tea-spoonful of ground cloves, the same of cinnamon, two tea-spoonfuls of allspice, small tea-spoonful of soda dissolved in vinegar, enough flour to make a stiff batter. Boil four hours.

SPONGE-CAKE PUDDING.

Butter a mold well, and ornament it with dried cherries or raisins; then fill three fourths full with sponge-cake. Pour over this a custard made of halt a pint of milk, two eggs, half a cup of sugar. Boil or steam for half an hour. Serve with wine-sauce.

BOILED ALMOND-PUDDING.

Blanch one pound of almonds; beat them to a smooth paste, with two tea-spoonfuls of rose-water; add one gill of wine, one pint of cream, one one gill of milk, one egg, one table-spoonful of flour. Boil half an hour. Serve with sauce.

FIG-PUDDING.

One pound of figs peeled and chopped fine, quarter of a pound of suet chopped fine; dredge with flour; one pound of bread-crumbs, quarter of a pound of sugar, two eggs, one tea-cupful of milk; mix all well together; boil four hours. Ornament the pudding with blanched almonds, and serve with wine or brandy sauce.

BAKED ALMOND-PUDDING.

Blanch one pound of almonds; beat them in a mortar to a smooth paste, with two tea-spoonfuls of rose-water; add one gill of wine, one gill of cream thickened with one large table-spoonful of bread-crumbs, half pound of sugar, seven eggs, and one nutmeg. Bake a light brown.

QUEEN'S PUDDING.

One quart of milk, one pint of bread-crumbs, one cup of sugar, yelks of four eggs, butter the size of an egg, and the grated rind of a lemon; pour in a pudding-dish, and bake. When done, spread over the top jelly or preserves; then beat the whites of four eggs to a stiff froth, with one cup of sugar and the juice of one lemon; pour over the pudding, and bake a light brown.

PRINCE ALBERT PUDDING.

Half pound of bread-crumbs, half pound of sugar, half pound of butter, six eggs beaten separately, the juice of one lemon and grated rind of two, one wine-glass of brandy, four table-spoonfuls of any kind of preserves; bake in a moderate oven. Serve with wine-sauce.

APPLE-PUDDING.—(EXCELLENT.)

Peel and core eight or nine apples of medium size; put them into a stew-pan, with half a tumbler of water, a wine-glass of wine, a heaped table-spoonful of sugar, a little cinnamon, mace, and lemon-peel. Cover the pan, and stew slowly until the apples are tender; take them up, and let them get cold. Fill the bottom of an earthen dish with the apples, and pour over them a rich custard made by beating together the whites and yelks of six eggs, with one quart of milk; sweeten to taste; bake in a moderate oven. Serve with solid or liquid sauce.

APPLE-PUDDING.

Pare and chop half a dozen good sour apples. Butter a pudding-dish, and put in a layer of grated bread half an inch thick; add small bits of butter; put in a layer of chopped apples, with sugar and nutmeg, and repeat until the dish is full. Pour over the whole a tea-cup of cold water, and bake thirty minutes. No sauce

BIRD'S-NEST PUDDING.

Put into three pints of boiling milk six crackers pounded fine—stir in carefully, to prevent lumping; add a pint of raisins; boil a few minutes; set aside to cool, after which add five well-beaten eggs, and sugar to taste; peel and core eight or ten apples, place them in regular order in a pudding-dish, and pour over them the custard; bake a light brown. Serve with sauce.

A NICE APPLE-PUDDING.

Butter a deep baking-dish, and fill it with alternate layers of thin slices of bread and butter and stewed apples. Pour over this a custard made of one pint of milk sweetened to taste, and the beaten yelks of four eggs. Bake in a moderate oven. Beat the whites of four eggs to a stiff froth, with eight table-spoonfuls of sugar; flavor with lemon or nutmeg; spread over the top of the pudding, return to the oven, and brown.

TAPIOCA-PUDDING WITH APPLES.

Five table-spoonfuls of tapioca, two quarts of water, one and one half cups of sugar, table-spoonful of butter, twelve large apples; soak the tapioca in the water several hours; then pare and core the apples, and place them in a pudding-dish, with two lemons sliced; pour over the other ingredients, and bake until the apples are done. Serve with sweetened cream. A nice dish, cold for tea, served in a glass bowl.

PEACH-PUDDING.

Five eggs well beaten, five table-spoonfuls of flour, five of sugar, five of milk, two and a half spoonfuls of butter, wine-glass of brandy or wine, one soup-plate of peaches chopped fine. Bake, and serve with wine-sauce or sweetened cream.

SWEET-POTATO PUDDING.

Two tea-cupfuls of grated sweet-potatoes, one cup of butter, one cup of brown sugar, one cup of cream, one wine-glass of wine and brandy mixed, one wine-glass of rose-water; nutmeg and cinnamon to taste. Bake slowly.

LEMON-PUDDING.—No. 1.

One and a half pounds of sugar, the juice and grated rind of three lemons, eight eggs, one cup of butter, table-spoonful of flour. Beat all well together. Bake as soon as prepared.

LEMON-PUDDING.—No. 2.

The juice and grated rinds of two lemons, five table-spoonfuls of sugar, one table.spoonful of butter, one large Irish potato boiled and mashed, five eggs; add sufficient milk to make a thin batter. Bake in a moderate oven.

TAPIOCA-PUDDING WITH COCOA-NUT.

Soak over night three table-spoonfuls of tapioca in cold water; pour off the water, and pour over the tapioca one quart of boiling milk, and boil ten minutes. Beat the yelks of four eggs with one cup of sugar and three table-spoonfuls of grated cocoa-nut; add to the boiling milk, and boil five minutes longer; pour in a pudding-dish; beat the whites of three eggs to a stiff froth, with half a cup of white sugar; spread this over the top of the pudding; sprinkle thick with cocoa-nut. Bake a light brown.

TAPIOCA-PUDDING.

Soak over night one tea-cupful of tapioca in a pint of milk. The next morning pour over the tapioca one pint of boiling milk, and add one cup of sugar, four well beaten eggs, a wine-glass of rose-water, one table-spoonful of butter, and a little nutmeg; pour in a pudding-dish, and bake half an hour. Sago may be prepared in the same way.

RICE-PUDDING.—No. 1.

Boil four ounces of rice in a quart of milk until soft; stir in four ounces of butter; take it from the fire; add a pint of cold milk, two tea-spoonfuls of salt, and a grated nutmeg. When it is lukewarm, beat four eggs with eight ounces of sugar, and stir it in, adding eight ounces of raisins. Pour the whole into a buttered pudding-dish, and bake forty-five minutes.

RICE-PUDDING.—No. 2.

Boil a cup of rice in a quart of milk until soft. When it is cooled a little, add the well beaten yelks of three eggs, two table-spoonfuls of butter, one cup of sugar, and a pinch of salt; pour in a pudding dish, and bake; beat the whites of the eggs to a stiff froth with eight table-spoonfuls of sugar; flavor with the juice of a lemon; spread this over the top of the pudding; return to the oven and brown.

SPONGE-PUDDING.

One fourth pound of flour, one fourth pound of sugar, one quart of sweet milk; boil these ingredients; then add one fourth pound of butter, and twelve eggs well-beaten. Stir all well together; pour in a pudding-dish; place in a pan of hot water, and bake one hour.

SOUFFLI PUDDING.

Boil together one pint of milk and two table-spoonfuls of of flour, stirring to prevent burning; turn out to cool when done. Stir into the boiled milk ten table-spoonfuls of powdered sugar; then add the yelks of six eggs well beaten; half a wine-glass of sherry; last, the whites of the eggs beaten very light. Bake in a deep dish thirty minutes

CHAMBLISS PUDDING.

Three eggs, one small cup of butter one cup of sugar, two

cups of sifted flour; beat the yelks of the eggs with the sugar; cream the flour and butter together; add the whites of the eggs and a desert-spoonful of yeast-powder. Bake in a quick oven. Serve with liquid sauce.

DIXIE PUDDING.

One cup of preserves, one cup of butter, one cup of sugar, half cup of flour, five eggs; cream the butter and sugar together; add the flour and eggs well beaten; lastly, the preserves. Bake in a quick oven. Serve with sauce.

A PLAIN PUDDING.

Six eggs, six table-spoonfuls of sugar, six table-spoonfuls of butter, one cup of flour, one cup of milk; beat well, and flavor with nutmeg or lemon. Bake in a moderate oven. Serve with wine-sauce.

DELICIOUS PUDDING.

Slice a sponge-cake; butter the slices, and put in a pudding-dish; pour over this a rich custard made of a pint of milk, four eggs, and a cup of sugar. Bake half an hour.

CAKE-PUDDING.

Put a layer of sponge-cake in a pudding-dish, and then a a layer of raisins, currants, and citron mixed (any kind of fruit—stewed apples are very good); another layer of cake, and so on until the dish is nearly full. Pour over this a custard made of a quart of milk and six eggs; sugar to taste. Bake a light brown. Serve with wine-sauce.

INDIAN-MEAL PUDDING.

One pint of molasses, three well-beaten eggs, one teaspoonful of soda, one large spoonful of butter; stir in a sufficient quantity of boiled meal to make a thick batter; flavor with ginger. Bake a nice brown. Serve with liquid sauce.

MOLASSES-PUDDING.

Four eggs, three cups of flour, two cups of molasses, one cup of butter, one cup of milk, one tea-spoonful of soda dissolved in milk; mix molasses, eggs, and butter; then add the milk and soda; lastly, the flour. Bake in a moderate oven, and serve with sauce.

POOR AUTHOR'S PUDDING.

Flavor a quart of new milk by boiling in it for a few minutes half a stick of well-bruised cinnamon, or the rind of a small lemon; add a few grains of salt, and sweeten to taste; turn the whole into a deep basin. When it is quite cold, add six well-beaten eggs, and strain into a pudding-dish; cover the top entirely with slices of bread free from crust, and half an inch thick; cut so as to join neatly, and butter on both sides Bake in a moderate oven for half an hour. Simple, and very good.

BIDDLE PUDDING.

One pint of milk, four table-spoonfuls of flour, four eggs; pour into a well-buttered pudding-dish, and bake twenty-five minutes. Bring it directly from the oven to the table, or it falls. Serve with sauce.

TWO-EGG PUDDING.

Two eggs, one cup of sugar, one table-spoonful of butter, one cup of milk, flour enough to make a stiff batter. Bake in a quick oven, and serve with wine-sauce.

BUTTERMILK PUDDING.

Three cups of buttermilk, one and one half cups of sugar, two cups of flour, half cup of butter, three eggs, tea-spoonful of soda; flavor with nutmeg. Bake a nice brown, and serve with sauce.

CHOCOLATE PUDDING.

One quart of milk, three ounces of chocolate boiled in the milk; flavor with two tea-spoonfuls of vanilla, and sweeten to taste. When cool, add the beaten whites of three and the yelks of six eggs. Bake in a moderate oven. Sweeten the three remaining whites, beat to a stiff froth, pile on the pud ding, and bake a light brown.

POTATO-PONE

One quart of grated sweet-potato, one cup of sugar or molasses, two table-spoonfuls of butter. One table-spoonful of ginger, one tea-spoonful of cloves and cinnamon mixed, half tea-cup of sweet milk, and a pinch of salt. Bake two hours and a half.

CRACKER FRUIT-PUDDING.

Mix six crackers pounded fine with one quart of boiling milk; add one table-spoonful butter, one tea-cup brown sugar, six eggs well beaten, half pound of raisins and currants each. Bake in a moderate oven. Serve with wine-sauce.

MACAROON-PUDDING.

Butter a deep pudding-dish, and it with alternate layers of macaroons and preserves; pour over this white wine until the whole is perfectly saturated; then add a rich custard made of a pint of milk sweetened to taste, and the well-beaten yelks of four eggs. Bake a rich brown. Beat the whites of the eggs to a stiff froth, with a cup of white sugar; spread this over the top of the pudding, and brown.

SNOW PUDDING.—No. I

Take a box of gelatine; pour on it a pint of cold water. When soft, add a quart of boiling water, the juice of four lemons, and half a pound of sugar; strain and put aside to cool; when it begins to congeal, beat in the whites of six eggs whipped to a stiff froth. It must be beaten until very light, and well mixed. Pour into a mold, and set aside to congeal. Serve with syllabub.

SNOW PUDDING.—No. 2.

One box of gelatine dissolved in one pint of cold water; then add one pint of boiling water. When entirely dissolved, add a pint of good wine, half a pound of sugar, one nutmeg, and the juice of one lemon; let come to a boil; then strain. Beat to a stiff froth the whites of six eggs, and mix with the jelly after it is partly congealed. Serve with a rich boiled custard.

JELLIED APPLES.

One pound of apples peeled and cored, one pound of sugar, and a pint of water; make a sirup of the sugar and water, and simmer the apples in it until they can be pierced with a straw. Then take out the fruit in a glass bowl, and add half an ounce of gelatine to the sirup, and boil ten or fifteen minutes. When the sirup is nearly cold, pour it over the apples, and let it congeal. Serve with syllabub.

SWEET OR PUDDING SAUCES.

WINE-SAUCE.

Two ounces of butter, two tea-spoonfuls of flour, half pint of boiling water, one gill of wine, quarter of a pound of sugar, and half a nutmeg. Mix the flour and butter, pour in the boiling water, let it boil for a few minutes, then add sugar and wine.

BOILED SAUCE.

Dissolve three cups of loaf-sugar in two cups of water, and boil to a thick sirup. Flavor with ground cinnamon and grated nutmeg.

HARD SAUCE.

Stir to a cream one cup of butter and two of sugar; add a wine-glass of wine or brandy, one tea-spoonful of essence of lemon.

CREAM-SAUCE.

Rub together, till very light, half a pound of butter and the same quantity of sugar; add a well-beaten yelk of an egg and half of a goblet of wine. Warm through, stirring constantly. Flavor with nutmeg.

MILK-SAUCE.

In one cup of boiling milk dissolve two cups of loaf-sugar; add one quarter of a pound of butter, one wine-glassful of brandy, one wine-glassful of wine, and half a grated nutmeg.

PUDDING-SAUCE.—No. 1.

Beat to a cream one cup of butter, and two of sugar; place over the fire and stir constantly until dissolved; flavor with extract of lemon or wine. Pour in the sauce on a half tea-cup of any tart jelly; stirring thoroughly.

PUDDING-SAUCE.—No. 2.

Beat together four eggs and two cups of sugar; add one pint of wine, lemon and cinnamon to taste. Heat thoroughly, but do not let boil.

PLUM-PUDDING SAUCE.

One cup of butter, two cups of sugar, yelks of two eggs, and two table-spoonfuls of flour. Beat all well together, and add one wine-glassful of wine and one of brandy. Pour on all two tea-cupfuls of boiling water. Simmer well, but do not boil.

APPLE-SAUCE.

Pare, core, and quarter the apples, let them stew in just enough water to cook them without burning them; cook until perfectly soft; mash well, and when done stir in the sugar or any seasoning you may like. Lemon-peel or sliced lemon is a great advantage where the apples are not well flavored. Nutmeg is always agreeable.

SAUCE FOR FRUITS.

Whisk one half pint of cream and a tea-cup of white sugar; flavor with nutmeg.

LEMON-SAUCE.

Beat to a cream one cup of butter and two of white sugar; stir in the juice and grated rind of one lemon. Grate nutmeg on sauce.

SAUCE.

Three cups of sugar, one of cream, three table-spoonfuls of water. Boil, and when nearly done flavor to taste.

ICES.

ICE-CREAM.—No. 1.

Three pints of cream, three pints of milk, nine eggs, one and a half pounds of white sugar; flavor to the taste. Put the sugar in the milk, and let it come to a boil; have the eggs whipped up lightly, whites and yelks together, and pour the boiling milk over it, stirring constantly to prevent curdling; then pour it into the pan and put on the fire and let it thicken. Stir all the time from the bottom, to keep from sticking to the pan. When cold, put in two table-spoonfuls of vanilla and the cream. Freeze. For flavoring with lemon squeeze the juice and grate the rinds of four large lemons, and pour it over one and a quarter pounds of powdered loaf-sugar; let it stand until the sugar is dissolved, then strain and add to the cream, after it is in the freezer.

ICE-CREAM.—No. 2.

Two quarts and a half of milk, twelve eggs beaten together, two table-spoonfuls of sugar to each egg, and one table-spoonful of corn-starch. Beat sugar and eggs well together pour on the boiling milk, and put back on the fire; simmer gently until of the desired consistency. Flavor when cold, and add a quart of sweetened cream. Freeze.

QUEEN'S ICE-CREAM.

Fifteen eggs, three pints of milk, sugar to the tase. Use only four yelks and all the whites; beat very light and make like any other custard. Do not use arrow-root or any thickening. Have the same quantity of rich cream whipped very light; flavor to taste, and freeze.

ICE-CREAM WITHOUT EGGS.

Two quarts of milk, two quarts of whipped cream, one pound of powdered sugar, one box of condensed milk, and vanilla to the taste. Freeze

CHOCOLATE ICE-CREAM.

Make ice-cream as in No. 2, and before freezing add eight table-spoonfuls of grated chocolate, dissolved in sufficient milk or water to make a smooth paste.

STRAWBERRY ICE CREAM.

Sweeten and boil one gallon of sweet milk. Set it aside to cool; when ready to freeze stir in a quart of cream, whipped to a froth. After the cream begins to freeze, stir in the juice of two quarts of strawberries that have been strained and sweetened.

FROZEN PEACHES.

Make a rich custard, as for ice-cream; when cold, put in a quart of ripe fruit that has been sweetened and mashed very fine. Freeze. Other fruits may be frozen in the same way.

TUTTI FRUTTI ICE-CREAM.

One pint of milk, one quart of cream, yelks of five eggs, beaten light with the sugar, three cups of sugar, one lemon-juice and grated peel, one glass of sherry, and one half pound of crystallized fruits chopped. Heat the milk to boiling, pour slowly over the eggs and sugar, beating all together well. Return to the fire and boil until sufficiently thick. When cold, beat in the cream, and partly freeze before you stir in the fruit and wine. Then freeze hard.

APPLE, QUINCE, AND PEAR CREAM.

Take juicy fruit and boil till very tender; mash and rub

through a sieve. Stir into a rich custard, with the addition of cream well sweetened, and freeze.

MACAROON ICE-CREAM.

Make a custard of one quart of milk, four eggs, and sweeten to your taste. When cool, add a quart of cream, sweetened and whipped light. Stir in two dozen macaroons, powdered very fine, and freeze.

COFFEE FROZEN.

Prepare the coffee as for the table; add cream and sugar, making it sweeter than for the table. Freeze and serve in after dinner coffee-cups.

COCOA-NUT ICE-CREAM.

Make boiled custard, putting six eggs to a quart of milk. Just before freezing grate one cocoa-nut into half a gallon of custard. The milk of the cocoa-nut must not be used, nor cream, as it will be too rich.

FROZEN PLUM-PUDDING.

Two quarts of well-frozen ice-cream in a freezer, two ounces of raisins chopped, two ounces of currants, two ounces of citron cut very thin, one and a half ounce of chocolate grated fine, and one pint of Madeira wine. Put these ingredients into a stew-pan, and set it on the fire; let it stew slowly half an hour; when cold, mix with the ice-cream, to which you may add one cup of strawberry preserves, one of peach, and one of cherries; then let it freeze. Serve with whipped cream, flavored with vanilla or with maraschino.

WHITE ICE-CREAM.

Two quarts of fresh milk, twelve ounces of sugar, whites of eight eggs whipped, and two table-spoonfuls of arrow-root. Boil all together until thick as custard, and when cold add one quart of whipped cream.

FROZEN BUTTERMILK.

Strain the buttermilk through a thin cloth, so as to remove all lumps and particles of butter, add sugar until *very*, very sweet, and flavor with vanilla. Freeze as you would ice-cream.

PINE-APPLE SHERBET, OR ICE.

Take four pine-apples, pare them, and cut in thin slices; put in a bowl with two pounds of loaf-sugar; let it stand one hour, then separate the slices from the juice and pour over them three quarts of boiling water. When cold, strain through a coarse cloth, squeeze hard, then add the juice and freeze.

PINE-APPLE SHERBET.

Two cans of pine-apple; cut off the dark spots from the slices; chop very fine, and pour over it two quarts of boiling water; strain into this the juice; also, the juice of four lemons, five tea-cupfuls of white sugar, and just before freezing beat in the whites of six eggs, which have been whipped to a stiff froth.

FROZEN CLARET.

Make a sweet sangaree; flavor with lemon-juice and peel. Freeze.

LEMON SHERBET.

Make a rich lemonade of twelve lemons; strain through a thick cloth and add the whites of six eggs beaten to a froth Freeze.

ITALIAN SNOW.

Make a lemonade, putting in as much sugar as the lemonade will dissolve; add the whites of twelve eggs to each quart. Freeze.

ORANGE ICE.

One dozen oranges, juice of two lemons, two quarts of

water, and sugar to the taste. Rind of four oranges grated on sugar. Freeze.

BISQUE GLACE'.—No. 1.

Beat well together the yelks of eight eggs, and eight ounces of powdered sugar. Flavor one pint of good milk with vanilla, and boil it. Dissolve in a vessel set in hot water one and a half ounce of gelatine, and as soon as it is dissolved mix with the boiling milk; pour the boiling milk slowly on to the eggs and sugar, stirring all the time; when well mixed pass through a sieve and put in a very cold place to cool. This is called "apperiel," or preparation. Beat one pint of cream to a stiff froth, and when well beaten add it slowly to the mixture already prepared, which should be quite cold. To freeze, you must have a tin mold, either square or rectangular; fill this with little paper molds, which must fit the tin mold exactly in every part. Fill the little paper cases with the mixture, and cover the tin mold with a hermetically fitting top. In the bottom of a box made for the purpose, put about eight inches of pounded ice and coarse salt in alternate layers; in this place your tin mold of Bisque Glace' and another eight inches of ice and salt; cover the whole with a thick, heavy cloth, and let it stand six or eight hours. The box containing the ice and salt should have a small hole, to allow the escape of the water from the melted ice. When the mold is taken from the ice, wipe well before opening, to prevent any salt-water getting in. It is then ready to serve.

BISQUE GLACE'.—No. 2.

Take some pieces of broken sugar, and rub off the rind of four lemons; then pulverize the sugar and mix with half a pound of pulverized loaf-sugar, moistened with the juice of the lemons. Beat six eggs very light; stir them gradually into a quart of cream, in turn with the sugar and lemons.

Have ready some stale sponge-cake, grated very fine; stir into the mixture until it is a thick batter, which must be beaten until perfectly free from lumps. Put into a porcelain kettle, and let it boil up once, stirring it nearly all the time; then freeze as ice-cream.

CARAMEL ICE-CREAM.—No. 1.

One gallon of sweet cream, four tea-cups of powdered sugar, and five table-spoonfuls of caramels. *Caramels.*—Put in a stew-pan one tea-cup of nice brown sugar, and half a cup of water. Stew over a hot fire till it burns a little.

CARAMEL ICE-CREAM.—No. 2.

Make a rich custard of one pint of milk and five or six eggs. Put two pints of brown sugar in a skillet, and stir constantly over a brisk fire until it is dissolved; do not let it burn. Stir into the custard while both are hot. When cold, pour it into three quarts of cream well beaten. Freeze

---

CREAMS, JELLIES, &c.

CHARLOTTE RUSSE.—No. 1.

Soak in a pint of fresh milk one box of Cox's refined gelatine. Make a boiled custard of one pint of milk, two eggs, and one fourth pound of powdered sugar. Put the gelatine that is soaked in the milk on the fire, stirring constantly until it is dissolved. After it gets boiling hot strain into a large bowl. The custard may be strained into this as soon as it is made. Stand in a cool place, and have two pints of pure cream, with sugar enough to sweeten, whipped to a stiff froth; add this just before it congeals; flavor according to taste with vanilla or other extract. The whites of four or five eggs whipped to a stiff froth, and stirred very hard and rapidly into the Charlotte, after the cream has been put in, makes it very light and delicate. Have the mold lined with lady-fingers, and pour the Charlotte Russe in just as it begins to congeal. Do not let the cake project above the Charlotte, as it would prevent its standing nicely when turned out. If the cakes should be too long cut them off evenly, and push the little ends into the surface. Unless the weather is cold, the mold should be placed on ice. In a few hours it will be ready to turn out on the stand, and ready to be served.

CHARLOTTE RUSSE.—No. 2.

One quart of thick cream, one half pint of milk, one ounce of gelatine, whites of seven eggs, yelks of five eggs, twelve ounces of sugar. Dissolve the gelatine in the boiling milk; take off the fire, stir in the yelks, and then the sugar and the flavoring. When the custard is cold, but not congealed, stir in the cream, which has been beaten to a stiff froth, and lastly the whites of the eggs.

CHARLOTTE RUSSE.—No. 3.

Dissolve three fourths box of Nelson's gelatine in a pint of warm milk. Make a thick custard of one pint of milk, one fourth pound of powdered sugar, the whites of four eggs, and yelks of two. When done, add the gelatine, stirring all till cool; flavor with one tea-spoonful of vanilla. Whip three pints of cream, sweetened with powdered sugar, to a stiff froth, and add to the custard and gelatine. Do not whip after they are well mixed, but pour into a mold lined with lady-fingers, or sliced sponge-cake.

CHARLOTTE RUSSE WITHOUT EGGS.

Two thirds of a box of Cox's gelatine, dissolved in a tea-cup of sweet milk. Beat to a stiff froth one quart of sweet cream sweetened, and flavored with vanilla. After the gelatine is dissolved and cool, stir it into the cream and beat all well together. Put into a mold lined with lady-fingers.

CHARLOTTE RUSSE.

Beat separately the yelks and whites of five eggs. Add to the yelks three fourths pound of loaf-sugar, beat well. Soak in not quite a half a pint of water a half box of gelatine, and put it on to boil. Whip very light one quart of cream. Flavor the custard. Pour the boiling water and gelatine over the yelks and sugar, beating all the time. When cold enough, add the cream.

CHARLOTTE RUSSE WITHOUT CREAM.

Half a box of gelatine in a large cup of water, one pint of milk, one cup of sugar, and four eggs. Beat the yelks and sugar, stir into the boiling milk; let this cook until nearly as thick as boiled custard, then add the gelatine. When nearly cold add the whites of the eggs, whipped to a froth. Flavor with vanilla.

BLANC-MANCE.

Boil a quart of milk and sweeten to the taste. Dissolve an ounce of isinglass or gelatine, and pour it into the milk; at the same time remove the milk from the fire. When nearly cold flavor with vanilla and pour into a mold. Set it on ice to harden.

CHOCOLATE BLANC-MANGE.

In one pint of water dissolve one ounce of gelatine. Boil one quart of milk, four ounces of grated chocolate, and three fourths pound of sugar together for five minutes; then add the gelatine, and stirring constantly boil five minutes longer. Flavor with one tea-spoonful of vanilla, and pour into a mold. To be eaten with sweet cream.

NEAPOLITAN BLANC-MANGE.

One quart of milk, one ounce of gelatine, three ounces of

almonds blanched and pounded in a mortar with one table-spoonful of rose-water, to prevent oiling, and three fourths cup of sugar. Heat the milk to boiling, having previously soaked the gelatine in a cup of it for an hour. Put this in when the milk is boiling hot; add the pounded almonds, and stir all together ten minutes before putting in the sugar. When the gelatine has dissolved, strain through a thin muslin bag, pressing it well to get out the flavor of the almonds. There should be three or four bitter ones among them. Separate the *blanc-mange* into four different portions. Into one part beat one large table-spoonful of chocolate wet with a very little boiling water, and rubbed to a smooth paste, for the brown; beat into the other part a large table-spoonful of currant jelly for the pink (or currant or cranberry juice), yelk of an egg, beaten light for the yellow. Leave the fourth part uncolored. Return each part, except the fourth, to the fire, stirring until very hot, but not boiling. When cold and a little stiff, pour carefully into a wet mold, the white first, then the pink, next the yellow, and the chocolate last. Set in a cool place. Loosen, when firm, by dipping the mold in warm water for a moment, and turn out on your stand, when the order of colors will be reversed. Put a little vanilla with the chocolate.

SYLLABUB.—No. 1.

Have a quart of very rich cream; wash and wipe four lemons, and with a very sharp knife pare off the entire rind. Mix one half pint of Madeira wine with half pint of white sugar, powdered, and the lemon-peels; let it stand to extract the flavor of the lemons; then add it slowly to the cream, and whip up the whole.

SYLLABUB.—No. 2.

One quart of cream, the whites of four eggs, one glass of white wine, and two tea-cups of powdered sugar. Whip half the sugar into the cream; the remainder into the eggs. Mix these, add the wine, and flavor to the taste.

TO WHIP CREAM.

Sweeten the cream with powdered white sugar; flavor with any extract, or with lemon or orange, by rubbing sugar on the peel. Set a bowl near with a sieve over it, then whip the cream, and as it rises to a froth take it off with a skimmer, and put it into the sieve to drain; whip also the cream which drains off. If the cream is a little sour, it may be sweetened by adding a small quantity of soda.

ALMOND-CREAM.

Beat four ounces of sweet almonds, and a few bitter ones, in a mortar, with a tea-spoonful of water, to prevent oiling,—both having been blanched. Put the paste to a quart of cream, and add the juice of three lemons, and sweeten to the taste; beat it to a froth, which take off on the shallow part of a sieve. Fill glasses with some of the liquor and froth.

IMPERIAL CREAM.

Boil a quart of cream, with the thin rind of a lemon, and stir it until nearly cold. Have ready in a bowl or dish that you are going to serve it in, the juice of three lemons strained, with as much sugar as will sweeten the cream, which pour into the dish from a large tea-pot, holding it high, and moving it about to mix with the juice. It should be made at least six hours before it is used; and a day is better.

ITALIAN CREAM.—No. 1.

One quart of cream, two boxes of gelatine, one pound of sugar, yelks of ten eggs, and flavor the cream to the taste—strawberry flavoring is the nicest. Whip the cream to a stiff froth. Beat the eggs very light, and mix in the sugar well; then pour in the cream. Dissolve the gelatine in sufficient warm water to cover it, and when it begins to congeal add it to the mixture. Pour all into the mold, and when stiff cover with grated cocoa-nut or syllabub, ornamented with bright jellies or preserves.

ITALIAN CREAM.—Nc. 2.

Three three pints of cream or milk, and sweeten with sugar to the taste; flavor with vanilla, and add one paper of gelatine. Stir constantly until it boils; beat in the yelks of eight eggs, and stir them well into the boiling milk; strain it into a mold, and let it stand on ice five or six hours. Serve with sweetened cream.

BAVARIAN CREAM.—No. 1.

Take half a box of gelatine; pour on it one pint of cold milk; when soft pour on a pint of hot milk, and sweeten to your taste. While this is congealing churn up a quart of rich cream; sweeten and flavor to your taste. When the gelatine begins to thicken, beat in the syllabub, which must be churned very thick. You may add a little milk if the cream is too thick. Do not put in any of the thin part of the syllabub, as it will make it heavy.

BAVARIAN CREAM.—No. 2.

One quart of thick cream, one pint of milk, two eggs well beaten, half box of Cox's sparkling gelatine. First, pour a small cup of milk on the gelatine; let this stand while the cream is being whipped. Flavor the cream with wine and sugar, as you would syllabub. Put the pint of milk on the fire; as soon as it is hot pour the soft gelatine into it and immediately put in the beaten eggs. Stir them rapidly in until the custard is done. Pour out, sweeten and flavor with vanilla; when cold, whip up the cream, and before the custard congeals stir it rapidly in.

SPANISH CREAM.

Three pints of milk, one ounce of gelatine, six eggs, twelve table-spoonfuls of sugar. Beat the yelks and sugar together. Soak the gelatine in about half a pint of cold water, pour the boiling milk on the eggs and sugar, then stir in the gelatine; put it on the fire and let come to a boil, take off and place to cool; flavor with vanilla. When it commences to congeal, stir in the whites, which have been beaten to a froth.

RASPBERRY CREAM.

Put two large table-spoonfuls of raspberry jam in a fine sieve, pour over, and work through one pint of cream, then whisk it until it thickens. Meanwhile dissolve half an ounce of gelatine, two ounces of white sugar in a tea-cup of milk, and add gradually to the cream. When quite thick turn into a mold.

CHARLOTTE POLONAISE.

Boil over a slow fire one and a half pints of cream. While it is boiling have ready six yelks; stir them gradually into the boiling cream—take care to have it smooth and free from lumps. Let this mixture boil ten minutes, then divide it by putting into two sauce-pans. Mix into one pan six ounces of chocolate grated fine, two ounces of loaf-sugar, one fourth pound of macaroons broken fine. Put into the other pan one dozen bitter almonds, four ounces of shelled sweet almonds blanched and pounded, one ounce of citron cut fine, and four ounces of pounded sugar. Stir this in well; let it come to a boil and set aside to cool. Cut a large sponge-cake into slices half an inch thick; spread one slice thickly with chocolate cream, and one with almond cream. Do this alternately until all the cream is used up. Serve cold.

AMBROSIA.—No. 1.

Eight or a dozen oranges peeled and sliced, one cocoa-nut

grated, one pine-apple sliced. Alternate layers of each with sugar and wine.

AMBROSIA.—No. 2.

Alternate layers of sliced oranges and grated cocoa-nut, sugar sprinkled upon each layer of orange; have the top of cocoa-nut.

APPLE-FLOAT.

A quart of stewed apples mashed fine and passed through a fine sieve, sweetened with white sugar to the taste, flavored with vanilla or lemon—grating the rind in the apples if flavored with lemon. Stir in the well-beaten whites of four eggs. Beat until very light. Serve with rich cream; or pile on glass bowl half filled with cream or rich custard. Very nice mixed with cream and frozen.

APPLE ME′RINGUE.

To three or four cups of nice mashed apples, add beaten yelks of two eggs, half cup of sugar, a little milk, one and a half table-spoonfuls of butter. Mix well and bake a few minutes; when cold, spread evenly on top a me′ringue made of whites of eggs, beaten to a stiff froth and sweetened.

PORCUPINE.

Eight eggs to a pint and a half of milk. Take out four whites. Boil the milk and pour it on the beaten eggs. When just ready to boil take off and stir till cool, or it will curdle. Sweeten to taste, and flavor as you choose. Put a loaf of sponge-cake into a deep dish, soak thoroughly with wine, and then stick over it blanched almonds cut in pieces. Pour over the custard just before sending to the table.

APPLE-SOUFFLE′.

Twelve large apples, half pound of sugar, six eggs, one pint of milk, and one lemon. Pare and core the apples, stew them with the lemon-peel and sugar until quite soft; press through a sieve. Make a custard with the yelks of the eggs and milk. Half fill a pie-dish with the apples, and cover with the custard. Beat the whites of the eggs to a stiff froth, and spread on the custard. Sift a table-spoonful of white sugar over all, and bake in a moderate oven for ten minutes.

CATEAN POMMES.

Boil in a pint of water one pound and a half of loaf-sugar, till it becomes a rich sirup. Weigh two pounds of apples after they have been peeled, cored, and cut small; boil them in the sirup with the grated peel and juice of a large lemon, till they are reduced to a pulp; then put it into a mold. The following day serve it turned out in a glass dish, with a rich custard.

BOILED CUSTARD.

To each quart of milk allow five eggs and five table-spoonfuls of sugar. Put the milk on the fire with half the sugar; whip the whites to a stiff froth, and when the milk is scalding hot put it in the whites with a skimmer, and when partially set take them out. Have the yelks well beaten with the balance of the sugar, and put in the milk, stirring constantly till thick, to prevent scorching. When sufficiently thick take up and flavor to the taste. Serve in cups or glasses, laying the whites on the top, and grating nutmeg over it.

BAKED APPLES.

Pare, core, and cut in thin slices, sprinkle sugar between each layer and bake. They will be candied and excellent. Peaches and pears prepared in the same way are very nice.

BAKED PEARS.

Peel and core the pears, place them in a baking-dish, and fill the middle of each with brown sugar; also, strew sugar over the pan about an inch thick. The juice of lemon or orange-peel, or stick of cinnamon inserted in the center of each piece, will improve the flavor. Add enough water to dissolve the sugar. Bake until quite soft. Serve with cream or milk.

TIPSY-CAKE.—No. 1.

Cut a sponge-cake through twice, to make three pieces; put layer upon layer in a dish, with wine and jelly between each piece; make a rich custard to pour over the whole. The above is a good way to utilize not only stale sponge-cake, but cup or pound cake.

TIPSY-CAKE.—No. 2.

Pour over a jelly-cake as much white wine as it will absorb, and stick it all over with blanched sweet almonds. Serve with whipped cream.

LEMON-JELLY

One box of Cox's gelatine dissolved in one pint of cold water, the juice and rind of three lemons if large, four if small, one and three fourth pounds of loaf-sugar, three pints of boiling water, five wine-glasses of wine (sherry, cooking-wine, or Champagne). When nearly cold, strain and set aside to congeal.

WINE-JELLY.—No. 1.

One package of gelatine, one quart of water, three fourths of a pound of white sugar, four lemons, half pint of sherry or good Madeira wine, one ounce of mixed spice—cloves, allspice, mace, and cinnamon. Put the gelatine, sugar, water, spices, juice and peel of the lemons into a brass or porcelain-lined kettle; set on the fire, stirring occasionally, until the gelatine is perfectly dissolved. Have ready the stiffly-beaten whites of two eggs, with which you have mixed a dozen or fifteen pieces of charcoal, each piece about the size of the end of your finger; empty the eggs and charcoal into the mixture on the fire; stir well, and just before it begins to boil add the wine. Remove from the fire just as soon as it boils up once; let it stand in the kettle about five minutes, and then strain through a flannel jelly-bag until clear. If you wish to have it a beautiful amber color, drop in just before taking from the fire a few drops of liquid burned sugar. By using more or less of the burned sugar you can obtain any shade of amber you wish

WINE-JELLY.—No. 2.

To one pint of cold water add one ounce of gelatine, the juice and slices of two lemons; let it stand until the gelatine softens, and pour over one pint of boiling water, one full pint of loaf-sugar; stir till thoroughly dissolved, and pour in a pint of wine; strain through a flannel-bag, and set aside to congeal. In this way jelly can be made with little time and trouble.

JELLY AND FRUIT.

Line a charlotte or jelly-mold with various kinds of fruit, such as stoned cherries, strawberries, pieces of peaches, etc., by dipping the fruit in jelly and sticking it to the sides. Arrange in any design wished; then fill the mold with wine-jelly, and place on ice. This makes a beautiful dish, if the fruit is arranged with taste.

JELLY OF IRISH MOSS.

Half an ounce of Irish moss, a pint and a half of fresh milk; boil down to a pint, and remove any sediment by straining. Add one tea-cupful of sugar; lemon-juice or peach-water to give an agreeable flavor.

CALF OR HOG FOOT JELLY.

Have four feet scalded and scraped; split them, and boil them in a gallon of water until they have gone to pieces, and the liquor reduced to one half. Skim off all grease; strain the liquor through a jelly-bag; set aside to cool, when it will be a firm cake of jelly. To each quart allow a pound of sugar, a pint of Madeira wine and a wine-glass of brandy, three sticks of cinnamon, juice and grated peel of four lemons, the whites of four eggs; boil twenty minutes; do not stir; then add a tea-cup of cold water, and boil five minutes longer. Strain through a flannel bag; but do not squeeze or press the bag, as it will render the jelly cloudy.

MARASCHINO JELLY.

Add to some nice, clear gelatine jelly *maraschino* enough to flavor it. Put the mold into a vessel, with ice and salt around it; then put the mold one fourth full of jelly; place in it as it cools a layer of Malaga grapes. When this is congealed, pour on some more jelly which is cold, but not congealed; then another layer of grapes; fill up the mold in this way. Serve when stiff. If in preparing it the jelly stiffens too rapidly, set it in warm water. Other kinds of fruit can be substituted for the grapes.

PRESERVES AND JELLIES.

In making preserves, procure firm, ripe fruit, as it is desirable to have the natural flavor of the fruit, which can not be obtained from hard, unripe fruit. Use the best loaf-sugar; but if not convenient, good brown sugar will do by clarifying, which may be done by stirring in the sirup the whites of one or two eggs, carefully taking off the scum as it rises, until the sirup is clear.

It is not well to expose the fruit long to the action of the sun, as it has a tendency to toughen it. Have your jars well cleaned by washing in weak lye, or soda-water. Put your preserves in the jars hot, which may be done without risk by placing the jars on a towel folded in several thickness saturated with cold water. Cover the top with a paper cut to fit inside the mouth of the jars; wet in brandy or whisky; cork tightly.

FIG PRESERVES.

Drop them in a weak salaratus-water, and let remain for fifteen minutes; wipe them dry, and to a pound of figs allow three quarters of a pound of sugar. When the sirup has well boiled, put in the figs, and boil them until they look clear; take out the fruit, and sun it for two hours; then return to the sirup, and boil a little while before taking off.

They may be flavored with either ginger, mace, cinnamon, or lemon. If lemons are used, do not put them in the boiling sirup, as that will make them hard. Slice them, take out the seeds, and put in a vessel with a very little water, and boil until tender; then pour the lemon and the water in which it was boiled into the sirup. If lemons can not be obtained, use the oil of lemon, which should be put in when taken from the fire.

TO PRESERVE BLUE FIGS.

Peel, and throw into a solution of lime-water (one tablespoonful of air-slacked lime to half a bucket of water). Let them remain for nearly an hour; drain well. To every pound of figs add three quarters of a pound of white sugar. Slice lemons very thin; take out the seeds, and strain in the preserving-kettle until tender; use as little water as will dissolve the sugar; then put in the figs, and let them boil until cooked through. Seal up in jars while boiling hot.

FIG MARMALADE.

Use ripe figs; place them in cooking soda-water for a few minutes; wipe dry with a coarse cloth; then put them on to boil, with just water enough to cover them; boil until soft, mashing often. When soft, put three quarters of a pound of sugar to a pound of figs; cook slowly; stir frequently to prevent burning. Flavor with oil of lemon, or anything preferred.

TOMATO PRESERVES.

The impression generally prevails that these preserves are *very* indifferent, but, if *properly* prepared, they will rival any fruit. Take half a bushel of ripe tomatoes; scald and peel, and as they are peeled plunge into cold water; cut them in halves (across the tomato), so as to extract any seed; throw again in cold water, and when cleansed and thoroughly washed, weigh, allowing one pound of loaf-sugar to the same of fruit. Make a sirup of sugar and sufficient water; when thick enough, add the tomatoes; cook slowly until done. Be careful when they are nearly done, or they will burn. Flavor with sliced lemon cut in the preserves when about half done.

STRAWBERRY PRESERVES.

Stem and wash the fruit carefully, and to every pound of fruit allow a pound of loaf-sugar. Put in a kettle a layer of fruit and a layer of sugar; let stand about an hour, and they will make sufficient juice without adding water. (Do not let them stand too long, or they will have a shrunken appearance.) Boil until done, but not too fast. Blackberries may be preserved in the same way.

BLACKBERRY JAM.

Weigh the fruit, and press it through a colander. To every pound of berries add a little more than half a pound of sugar. Boil slowly until as thick as desired, stirring constantly.

APPLE PRESERVES.

Pare and slice your apples; weigh them and your sugar, allowing a pound of crushed sugar to a pound of fruit. In a stone jar place a layer of apples, then a layer of sugar, sprinkling every layer with enough water to moisten the sugar; let this stand all night. In the morning, remove the apples; put the sirup in a kettle, adding a little more water —enough to cook the apples. Clarify the sugar with the whites of two eggs; strain it, and return to the kettle; place on the fire; when nearly boing hot, put in the apples; give them a good scald, but do not allow them to remain long enough to break; remove from the sirup, place them in dishes, and *sun* them until a little tough; return to the sirup, boil a short time, and sun *again*; then return to the sirup, and boil until quite clear and the sirup is thick. Flavor with lemons sliced, or with ginger. Seal tight.

CRAB-APPLE PRESERVES.

Boil in clear water until the core can be easily removed.

A small tin tube is the best arrangement for taking out the cores. Make a sirup, allowing two pounds of sugar to one pound of fruit; put in the fruit and boil until clear; sun a short time, and boil again.

PEAR PRESERVES.

To one pound of pears put three quarters of a pound of sugar. Peel and quarter your fruit; then drop into the boiling sirup. After boiling awhile, take out and put in the sun; then put in the sirup some race ginger, or cloves if liked; return the fruit to the boiling sirup, and boil until done.

PLUM PRESERVES.

Have the plums nearly ripe; allow a pound of sugar to a pound of fruit. Put the plums in a kettle of cold water, and let it heat gradually until it boils; pour off this water, and do not use it, as it will impair the flavor of the preserves. Make a sirup of the sugar and enough water to cook them in. When the sirup has boiled a few minutes put in the fruit, and let it boil until done.

QUINCE PRESERVES.

Pare and core the quinces, taking out the defective parts; cut in halves or quarters; place them in a preserving-kettle, with enough water to cover them; lay a plate over the top to keep in the steam, and boil until tender. Take out the fruit; strain the liquor, and retain it to make your sirup of, allowing a pound of sugar to the same of fruit. The weight should be taken before boiling the fruit. When the sirup has boiled twenty minutes, and been well skimmed, put in the quinces, and boil half an hour.. Take them up, lay on a dish, and expose to the sun for an hour; then return the fruit to the sirup, and boil until done.

QUINCE MARMALADE.

Wash and quarter the quinces, taking out the cores, but do not pare; put them in a kettle with sufficient water to stew them in; boil until soft; run through a sieve, and to each pound of this pulp put a pound of sugar. Return to the kettle, cook slowly, and stir constantly until done.

WATER-MELON PRESERVES.

To a bucket of cold water add two handfuls of lime. Cut your rinds, either water-melon or cantaloup; let it remain in the lime-water twenty-four hours, turning it often from the bottom. Take out of the lime-water, and soak in clear water to remove the lime, changing the water frequently. Scald in strong alum-water, with grape or butter bean-leaves, keeping the vessel well covered that the rind may have a good green color. Let them boil in this about ten minutes; then drop the rind in cold water; boil in a strong ginger-tea, making enough to cover the rind well, and long enough to impart a flavor of ginger to the rind. Make a sirup, using two pounds of white sugar to one pound of rind, and water sufficient to boil the rind until perfectly transparent. Do not put in the fruit until the sirup boils; then cook slowly. The rind should be weighed as soon as cut. Sliced lemon is a great improvement; when not at hand, the oil of lemon may be used, but not until the preserves have been taken from the fire—while hot.

PEACHES PRESERVED IN THEIR JUICE.

Wash, wipe, and pare with a silver or fine steel knife; halve, and remove the pits; to each pound of the fruit use one half pound of the best loaf-sugar. Sprinkle a little sugar in a deep earthen bowl; then put in a layer of peaches; alternate with sugar until all are closely packed, covering the top with sugar, cover tightly, and set aside for ten or twelve hours. Pour all into a preserving-kettle; let them come to a boil, and as fast as the pieces swell sufficiently take out with a silver spoon and place in a glass, air-tight, preserving-jar. As soon as the jars are filled, pour the boiling sirup over the peaches, filling the jars to the top; seal at once.

I have kept peaches and other fruit prepared in this way perfectly good three and four years.

PEACHES PRESERVED WHOLE.

Take the large, white clingstones; pare evenly; to every pound of fruit allow a pound of powdered loaf-sugar; place them in large earthen tureens,—a layer of fruit, and one of sugar; let them remain over night; then boil over a gradual fire until transparent; then pour the fruit and sirup into large dishes; place them in the sun until the sirup is almost a jelly and the fruit well cooked; put them in jars. See that no bubbles of air are left in the jars. Place a brandy paper on the top. Seal carefully.

BRANDY PEACHES.

Select ripe peaches, but not soft; drop in lye or soda-water to remove the furze, and wipe with a coarse towel. Make a thick sirup, allowing a half pound of sugar to one of fruit, and one half pint of water. Put the peaches in the sirup, and boil five minutes. After taking the fruit out, if the sirup is too thin add more sugar, and boil until a thick sirup is made. Put the peaches in a jar, and to a measure of sirup put a measure of brandy, ond pour over the fruit.

PEACH-CHIPS.

Take ripe peaches; peel, and cut from the seed. Make a thin sirup; boil the peaches in this until they look clear; then lay them on a sieve to drain; roll in dry brown sugar, and expose to the sun in dishes; change to dry dishes, and dip in sugar again until entirely dried and crystallized. The sirup may be kept and used for more peaches.

PEACH-LEATHER.

Prepare the peaches as you would to eat with milk; then strain through a sieve; butter panes of glass and spread it out thin on them, and put in the sun. The second day turn it.

PUMPKIN-CHIPS.

Weigh equal quantities of sugar and pumpkin cut thin or shaved with a plane; sprinkle the sugar over the pumpkin, and let it remain over night. It will not need any water. To every pound add one orange or lemon cut into thin slices. Some prefer ginger as a flavoring. Boil until the pumpkin is perfectly clear, and the orange-peel is soft; take all out, and lay on a dish in the sun for half an hour; boil the sirup quite thick; then put the preserves back.

WATER-MELON OR CITRON PRESERVES.

Pare the rinds, and soak in salt-water one night, then in clear water until all the salt is extracted; then scald in alum-water, with grape or butter-bean leaves, and a lump of alum the size of a hickory-nut; then throw in cold water; boil in clear water; then boil in ginger-tea. Make a sirup, allowing one pound of sugar to a pint of water. When the sirup boils, put in the fruit, and cook until tender and transparent; then take out the fruit, and boil the sirup until thick. The above is for ten pounds of fruit.

CANTALOUP PRESERVES.

Select sound fruit; pare, and divide into quarters, and cut each quarter into several pieces; take the seeds out carefully; weigh the fruit, and to every pound allow half a pound of the best loaf-sugar. Put the fruit in a preserving-kettle, and boil in water for half an hour, or until quite clear; drain, and place them on a large dish; put the sugar into the kettle, and add water enough to dampen the sugar; boil until quite clear; then add the fruit, and boil slowly until it becomes almost transparent, and soft enough to allow a straw to pierce through without breaking. A few lemons sliced and boiled with the fruit in the sirup, and a few ginger-roots added to the sirup while boiling, will improve the flavor. Put the fruit in jars, and pour the boiling sirup over it.

SOUR-ORANGE MARMALADE.

Rasp the orange on a vegetable grater to remove the deep yellow. Then peel the oranges; quarter the peel, and boil until tender enough to pierce with a straw. While boiling, change the water three or four times, using each time boiling water. Get all the pulp and juice free from the skin; pour over the seeds a pint of boiling water, and let it stand until jelly-like; pour this off, and save; pour more water on the seeds until all the jelly is extracted. Cut the peel into straw-like strips; weigh the peel, pulp, and jelly-water, and to each pound of this allow a pound of sugar. Boil all until jelly-like.

ORANGE-PEEL PRESERVES.

Put the peel in salt-water for twenty-four hours; then soak in clear water; boil in weak alum-water, then in clear water. Make a sirup of a pound of sugar to the same of peel, and boil until clear.

SCOTCH-ORANGE MARMALADE.

Take large, ripe oranges, and weigh them, and to each pound of fruit allow one pound of crushed sugar. Pare off the yellow rind of half the oranges, and put it over the fire; cover tightly, and let it simmer slowly until tender. Grate off the yellow rind of the remaining oranges; quarter the fruit, squeeze out all the juice and pulp, and remove the seeds and skin. To each pound of sugar add half a pint of cold water, and the white of one egg to every two pounds of sugar; let the sugar stand until nearly dissolved; then boil slowly, and skim off what rises. Pound the boiled parings in a mortar, or chop them very fine, and turn into the sirup after it has become very thick; then boil ten minutes, stirring often; put in the juice, pulp, and grated rind, and boil for half an hour, or until transparent. Lemons can be mixed with the oranges—one to every fifteen—and a little more sugar added with good effect.

This recipe makes the famous Scotch marmalade used so much for a breakfast dish. It is sold in all large groceries in cities, but can be made at home at much more reasonable rates. Try a little of it with good bread and butter for a dessert dish, and you will not sigh for pie.

PINE-APPLE PRESERVES.

Pare and slice the fruit. Make a sirup of half a pound of sugar to a pound of fruit; when the sirup boils, put in the fruit, and let it remain until a little tender. Fill the jars with the hot fruit, and pour on the sirup. To be kept in air-tight jars. Prepared in this way, much of the flavor of the fruit is preserved.

APPLE-JELLY.

Wash and cut up the apples, leaving the cores; put them in a kettle with enough water to cover; boil until tender; then strain through a flannel bag. If the apples are very tart, allow one pound of the best white sugar to a pint of sirup; then boil until it jellies, which may be ascertained by trying in a cup of cold water. In case the apples are not tart, allow half a pound of sugar to a pint of sirup. Two lemons cut up and added to the fruit while boiling will impart a pleasant flavor. In general, twenty minutes will be long enough to boil after the sugar is added. It will be more economical, and the jelly will be lighter, if only a small quantity is boiled after the sirup is mixed with the sugar—say a quart at a time.

PLUM-JELLY.

Have your plums thoroughly ripe; put them in a kettle, with two pints of water to half a bushel, three pints to a bushel; let them boil until done, stirring all the time. When they have all burst they are done, and should be poured slowly through a sieve. After all the juice has dripped out, strain it through a piece of flannel. To every pint of juice put one pound of loaf-sugar; put it on, and let it boil until it jellies.

Take the fruit that is left, and place on the fire, allowing a pound of sugar to the same of fruit, or a *little more* weight of *sugar*; cook until done. This will make very nice marmalade.

GRAPE-JELLY.

Pick and wash your grapes; put them in a kettle, and to six pounds of fruit put half a pint of cold water. Place the kettle on the fire, and steam until the grapes have yielded their juices; then strain, and to each pint of juice add one pound of loaf-sugar. Cook fifteen or twenty minutes.

QUINCE-JELLY

Wash and cut up the quinces, taking out the cores; boil in clear water until tender; strain through a flannel bag, and to each pint of the liquid allow a pound of loaf-sugar. Boil until done.

CANDY.

SUGAR-CANDY.—No. 1.

Six cups of sugar, two cups of water, one cup of vinegar, one table-spoonful of butter. Boil without stirring. Begin to pull it as soon as it can be handled, using only the fingers, and not the hands; pull rapidly. Do not grease the hands if you can pull it without.

SUGAR-CANDY.—No. 2.

Dissolve two pounds of loaf-sugar in two cups of water; stir in one tea-spoonful cream of tartar, table-spoonful of extract of vanilla, two table-spoonfuls of vinegar, and one full table-spoonful of butter. Do not stir the mixture after it boils, or it will sugar. When done, pull until white, handling as little as possible.

HOARHOUND CANDY.

In one quart of water boil one package of dried hoarhound, as obtained from the druggist, till reduced to one pint. Strain this tea on four pounds of brown sugar; boil as sugar-candy, —without stirring,—and when nearly done, add a table-spoonful of butter. Pull very little. This is excellent for a cough.

PEA-NUT CANDY.—No. 1.

To two pounds of sugar add one tumbler of water, one talbe-spoonful of butter; boil, stirring constantly. Just before taking off, stir in a pint of parched and pounded pea-nuts (measure after prepared). Drop with a spoon upon buttered plate.

PEA-NUT CANDY.—No. 2.

Make sugar candy as No. 1, leaving out the vinegar. Do not stir it. When done, pour thinly upon buttered plates covered with parched pea-nuts from which the thin skins have been taken.

COCOA-NUT CANDY.

Dissolve two pounds of loaf-sugar in the milk of one large cocoa-nut; let it boil, and when nearly done stir in the grated cocoa-nut. This must be stirred constantly until done. Drop from a spoon on buttered dishes.

COCOA-NUT DROPS.

To a grated cocoa-nut add half the weight in sugar, and the white of five eggs beaten to a stiff froth. Drop the mixture in small cakes on buttered paper, and sift sugar over them. Bake them fifteen minutes in a slow oven.

TAFFY.

One pound of sugar, one quart of good molasses, half pound butter; let this boil until nearly or quite done; then stir in one grated cocoa-nut. Grease your biscuit-board, and pour the taffy on; then pour essence of lemon over it. When cold, take a large knife and cut in squares.

ALMOND-TAFFY.

One pound of sugar, quarter of a pound of butter, the grated rind of a lemon; boil until done; pour this in a dish sprinkled thickly with blanched almonds cut fine, but not pounded. When nearly cold, mark off with a buttered knife, but do not raise it until perfectly cold.

CARAMELS.—No. 1.

Two and half pounds of brown sugar in sufficient water

to dissolve it, quarter of a pound of butter; boil these together or fifteen minutes, and add one and a quarter pounds of grated chocolate dissolved in have a pint of creamor milk; cook slowly one hour. Pour on buttered plates, and when nearly cold mark off in small squares.

CARAMELS.—No. 2.

One fourth pound of grated chocolate, one and a fourth pounds of brown sugar, one fourth pound of butter, one tea-cup of cream or milk; boil the whole briskly half an hour, stirring. Have ready buttered plates; pour out on them, and when nearly cold mark off in small squares.

HONEY CREAM-CANDY.

Ten pounds of white sugar, with just enough water to dissolve it. When nearly done, add a tea-cup of molasses; cook till well done; then add half a tea-cup of butter. Flavor with oil of lemon to suit the taste. To prevent graining, put in a tea-spoonful cream of tartar. Pull rapidly, and handle lightly.

MOLASSES-CANDY.

Dissolve one cup of sugar in half a cup of vinegar; mix with one quart of molasses, and boil until it hardens when dropped from the spoon into cold water; then stir in a table-spoonful of butter, and one tea-spoonful of soda dissolved in hot water. Give one hard final stir, and pour into buttered dishes. Pull hard until white, using only the tips of the fingers.

WHITE NOUGAT.

Ten pounds of white sugar, half a gallon of strained honey, three pounds of blanched almonds, one table-spoonful of oil of lemon. After the sugar is melted and strained, cook until nearly done; have the honey boiling, and pour on the sugar in the kettle; set it on the fire again, and when it boils up well pour out on a greased marble; add the oil of lemon. When cool enough to handle, turn it up and bleach on a candy-hook; when white, take off and spread it out on the marble, and sprinkle the blanched almonds all over it; fold it up, and spread out again with more almonds. Continue working it over the same way until all the almonds are worked in; then form into a long bar, and cut up in square pieces.

CATCHUP, SAUCES, AND PICKLES.

VINEGAR.

To eight gallons of water add one gallon of molasses and a half gallon of spirits. Put into a cask, shake well a few times, then add a pint of good yeast, or two yeast-cakes Keep in a warm place; in ten days slip a sheet of brown paper—which has been rolled up and dipped in molasses—into the bung-hole of the barrel. Cover the bung-hole with a piece of muslin until the vinegar is good; then close it with a cork.

EXCELLENT VINEGAR.

Take four gallons of rain-water, one gallon of Louisiana or Florida sirup, and two yeast-cakes three inches square. Put these together in a jar. Do not exclude the air while fermentation is going on. A little sunshine on it will hasten the making of the vinegar.

SPICED VINEGAR.

To four gallons of strong vinegar add one pound of ginger, one dozen cloves, one ounce each of mace, nutmeg, black pepper, allspice, and red pepper; also, a little turmeric, and one pound of grated horse-radish. The spices should be ground and inclosed in a muslin bag. It is better to make your spiced vinegar and keep it on hand ready for pickles, as it improves from standing. Prepare pickles in the usual way, and pour this vinegar over them. Pickles keep better when the vinegar is not boiled.

TOMATO CATCHUP. (Good.)

Cut any quantity of ripe tomatoes across the middle, put them in a large kettle, and let them simmer till soft; strain them first through a colander, then through a sieve. Boil the liquid again until the watery substance ceases to rise on the surface. To every half gallon of tomato-juice add one quart of vinegar, four table-spoonfuls of salt, two table-spoonfuls each of black pepper and dry mustard, one tea-spoonful of cayenne pepper, one tea-spoonful of whole cloves, and one clove of garlic. Boil again until it is thick. Cook and seal while hot. Use a porcelain kettle.

TOMATO CATCHUP.—No. 1.

Take one bushel of ripe tomatoes, remove the stems, cut them into two pieces, and cook them in a porcelain kettle until they are tender; then strain them through a sieve; add half a gallon of white wine vinegar, four cloves of garlic well chopped, one pound of sugar, one table-spoonful each of allspice, cloves, mace,—these must be ground,—and one small cup of salt. Bring this mixture to a boil; when cool, bottle and seal well.

TOMATO CATCHUP.—No. 2.

Wash the tomatoes, cut them up, put them in a porcelain kettle, boil half an hour, and then strain them through a sieve. To four quarts of liquid add one quart of vinegar, eight pods of green pepper, and two onions chopped fine, two table-spoonfuls each of ground black pepper and salt, two table-spoonfuls of whole cloves and allspice. Boil until it becomes brown. Stir it well.

CUCUMBER CATCHUP.

Peel, grate, and squeeze through a cloth, until all the water is exhausted, one peck of full-grown cucumbers. Then add cider-vinegar, salt, pepper, and onion to taste.

Put in glass jars, pour a table-spoonful of olive-oil in each, and seal them well.

PEPPER CATCHUP.—No. 1.

Take four dozen large red pepper-pods, three quarts of vinegar, three table-spoonfuls of grated horse-radish, five onions andone clove of garlic. Boil until soft, and strain through a sieve. Then add two table-spoonfuls of black pepper, all-spice, mace, cloves, and salt. Boil again ten minutes; then bottle. Some add one quart of tomatoes and one cup of sugar.

PEPPER CATCHUP.—No. 2.

Take fifty large red peppers, one gallon of vinegar, and one table-spoonful of salt. Boil until the peppers are well done. Strain them through a sieve, getting as much pulp as possible.

GRAPE CATCHUP.

Take five pounds of grapes, boil and strain them through a colander; add to the grape-juice one pint of vinegar, two and a half pounds of sugar, one table-spoonful each of cinnamon, cloves, allspice, pepper, and half a table-spoonful of salt. Boil again until the catchup is a little thick.

FRENCH MUSTARD.

One pound of Coleman's mustard, one half gallon of vinegar, one half-pint bottle of Worcestershire sauce, and one tea-spoonful of salt. Mix these, then boil to the consistency of French mustard; add to this, while boiling, one jar of French mustard.

ITALIAN MUSTARD

One large onion, one half-tumbler of water, one tea-spoonful each of brown sugar and black pepper, one half tea-spoonful of salt, and two table spoonfuls of mustard. Boil the onion, put the other ingredients in a cup, and add enough of the water in which the onion has been boiled, to mix them; then add a little vinegar and a small glass of claret.

CITRON SWEET PICKLE.

Put the cut rind of water-melon in strong brine; let it remain nine days; then in strong alum-water twenty-four hours; then in clear water twenty-four hours, changing the water several times. To one quart of vinegar add two and a half pounds of brown sugar, one table-spoonful of allspice, whole, and one tea-spoonful of cloves. Let these ingredients boil; then add the fruit, and let it boil until you can easily stick a fork in it.

BLACKBERRY SWEET PICKLE.

To one pound and a half of half-ripe berries put one pound of sugar, one pint of vinegar, and spices to suit the taste. Boil twenty minutes.

DAMSON PICKLE.

Four pounds of fruit, one pound of sugar, and spices to the taste. Pour boiling vinegar over them nine mornings in succession.

GERMAN PICKLE.

To seven pounds of fruit take three pounds of sugar, one quart of cider-vinegar, one ounce each of cloves and mace. Let the vinegar and sugar come to a boil; pour this over the fruit; repeat the process three mornings. Let it boil fifteen minutes, when the pickle will be ready for use.

SWEET PICKLED FIGS.—No. 1.

Pluck ripe, but not full-ripe figs, stems on. Put in a jar; sprinkle on salt—one half pound to a peck of fruit. Pour boiling water sufficient to cover figs, then let it stand twelve hours; then drain in a colander. If too salt, rinse with fresh water. Fill jars with the fruit, and pour over it hot boiling vinegar that has had added to it, a pound of sugar to the gallon, and boiled. Put sticks of cinnamon and some cloves in the jar.

SWEET PICKLED FIGS.—No. 2.

Gather five quarts of figs, with stems. Let them be only half ripe. Put them in salt-water, and let them stand twelve hours. Dry them, then parboil in alum-water, using a piece of alum half the size of a nutmeg. Be careful not to let them break; when soft, take them out and wash in three buckets of clear water, to take the alum out. Dry them well. Make a sirup with a pint of strong vinegar, a very little water, and a pound of sugar. Flavor with mace and cloves. When the sirup has boiled well put the figs into it. Use glass jars. These pickles will keep for years.

SWEET PICKLED PEACHES.

Remove the skin from the peaches by making a mixture of boiling water and concentrated lye. Put in the peaches and let them remain until the rough skin begins to dissolve. Have ready a pan of cold water to drop them in; wash them thoroughly, then put them on dishes to dry. To each pound of peaches use one quarter of a pound of sugar, half a pint of white wine vinegar, two ounces of allspice, and one ounce each of cloves and mace. Put the vinegar, sugar, and spices in a kettle to boil; then put the peaches in; cook them until you can pass a straw through them. Be careful not to let them break in cooking.

SWEET-PICKLE PEACHES.

Take seven pounds of fruit, three pounds of sugar, and one pint of vinegar. When boiling, put in the fruit; add a few cloves, spice, and some cinnamon; put these in a muslin bag. Boil twenty minutes.

SWEET PLUM PICKLE.

To ten quarts of ripe plums use seven pounds of sugar, one pint of strong vinegar, half ounce each of allspice and mace, and two grated nutmegs. Make a sirup of the vinegar and sugar and spices. Pour this over the plums for three days, taking care to have the jars well closed. The fourth day boil the fruit with the sirup, until it is almost a jelly.

RIPE CANTALOUP PICKLE.

To three pounds of fruit add two pounds of sugar, one and a quarter pints of vinegar, a dozen cloves, a piece of cinnamon, four pieces of white ginger, a tea-spoonful each of celery-seed and salt. Boil all together.

MELON PICKLE.

Take ripe cantaloups, peel and slice, drop into vinegar, and let it stand twelve hours. Take out, and to one gallon of vinegar add three pounds of sugar and one tea-cupful of cloves, spice, and cinnamon mixed. Boil this, and while boiling drop in the melon and let it remain ten minutes. Pour it off into a jar, and the next day boil the vinegar again and pour over the melon while hot.

OIL MANGOES.

Gather the melons a size larger than a goose-egg; cut a slit from the stem to the blossom, and take the seed carefully out; fill them with salt and let them remain two weeks, turning them over frequently. Then wash them in cold water two or three times, to remove all salt, and spread on dishes to dry. *Stuffing.*—Wash one pound of white ginger in boiling water; when soft, slice thin one pound of grated horse-radish, one pound of onions chopped fine, one pound of white mustard-seed, one ounce of mace, one ounce of nutmegs, two ounces of turmeric, and one handful of whole black pepper. Make these ingredients into a paste with a quarter of a pound of dry mustard and a large cupful of olive-oil. Put a clove of garlic in each melon; sew the melons up after stuffing, and pack in jars with the caps up. Strew some of the stuffing over each layer of mangoes, and cover with cold vinegar, adding another cup of olive-oil. Notice at intervals, and if needed add more vinegar. They should be kept in a dry place, and closely covered.

PEPPER MANGOES.

Gather your pepper when green. Cut a slit in each pepper; take the seed out carefully and wash them. Pour weak, boiling brine over them, and let them stand four days; renew the brine daily, and always have it boiling hot. Freshen the peppers, and stuff them with cabbage that has been chopped very fine, and seasoned with cinnamon, mace, and cloves that have been pounded fine, and with whole, white mustard-seed. After stuffing the peppers tie a cord around each one; pack them in a jar and pour strong, boiling vinegar over them three weeks in succession. The last time add a small piece of alum to the vinegar.

PEPPER MANGOES WITH OIL.

Cut a slit in each pepper; take the seed out, and put the peppers in salt-water; let them remain two days. Freshen the peppers and stuff them with the following mixture: Chop onions and pickled cucumbers very fine. Add a tea-cupful each of mustard and cabbage-seed, a tea-spoonful of dry mustard, and the same of black pepper; also, one tea-cupful of sweet-oil. Sew the peppers up. Put them in a jar and pour boiling vinegar over them.

CUCUMBER MANGOES.

Prepare two gallons of cucumbers as you would other melons for mangoes. Make stuffing of two pounds of sugar, a small piece of horse-radish grated, one and a half ounce each of white and black mustard-seed, and the same quantity of celery-seed. Mix well and stuff the cucumbers; place them in a jar and pour on them five quarts of apple-vinegar, sweetened to taste.

PEACH MANGOES.

Gather one peck of clear-stone peaches before they are fully ripe. To remove the rough skin drop them in boiling lye, then in cold water; wash them in several waters, then wipe them dry. Cut the peaches on one side and remove the stone. Make the dressing of white-head cabbage chopped fine, half a pound of white mustard-seed, two tablespoonfuls each of allspice and grated horse-radish, one tablespoonful each of cloves, mace, and a little salt. Fill the peaches, put them in a jar, then cover well with boiling vinegar.

CUCUMBER PICKLE.

Take small cucumbers; put them in a strong brine for forty-eight hours. Pour off the brine and wash the cucumbers in cold water. Lay butter-bean leaves in the bottom of a kettle; put in the cucumbers, and cover them with water in which a piece of alum the size of a hickory-nut has been dissolved; cover them closely with more leaves; simmer slowly until the cucumbers are green. Drain the cucumbers. To every fifty allow four quarts of vinegar, one ounce each of ginger, allspice, cloves, cinnamon, black pepper, celery-seed, and a few small onions. Boil the vinegar and spices together, pour over the cucumbers boiling hot, and simmer a few minutes.

SPANISH PICKLE.

One peck of cucumbers, one half peck of green tomatoes. four cabbages, three handfuls of onions, eight pods of green pepper—all these chopped fine; three quarters of a pound of white mustard-seed, a handful of black pepper, one ounce of celery-seed, a small tea-cup of each; mace and allspice. One pound of brown sugar, one pint of molasses, one table-spoonful of salt, and one gallon of vinegar. Mix these ingredients in a kettle, and let them simmer. Pour over the pickles.

CABBAGE PICKLE.—No. 1.

Take on quart of finely-chopped onions, three table-spoonfuls each of cloves, white mustard-seed, black pepper, celery seed, and ground mustard, half a pound of brown sugar, and three quarts of strong vinegar. Simmer this compound until it begins to thicken. Pour it over one gallon of finely-chopped cabbage, and boil a few minutes.

CABBAGE PICKLE.—No. 2.

Take red or white cabbage; remove the leaves from the stalk, wash them thoroughly, put them in a wooden tray, and chop it fine; sprinkle well with salt, and let it stand twelve hours; then wash all the salt out of it, put it on trays or dishes to drain off the water. Put in a kettle a sufficient quantity of white wine vinegar, to cover the cabbage. Flavor with whole allspice; when the vinegar comes to a boil put in the cabbage and let it boil three quarters of an hour. When cool, put it in air-tight jars.

JERUSALEM ARTICHOKE PICKLE.

Scrape the artichokes well and soak them several hours in brine. Boil together vinegar, allspice, cloves, celery-seed mustard-seed, mace, and black pepper, in quantities to suit your taste. When boiling hot pour over the artichokes. Cover closely.

WALNUT PICKLE.

Select walnuts before the shells begin to harden. Make a strong brine of salt and cold water, using a quarter of a pound of salt to a quart of water; soak the walnuts in this a week, then put them in the sun until they turn black. Take half a pound of mustard-seed, half ounce each of allspice, cloves, and mace, two ounces of black pepper, and four large spoonfuls of grated horse-radish. Boil all these ingredients in one gallon of vinegar; pour over the walnuts, covering them entirely. Pickled walnuts improve with age.

RAILROAD PICKLE.

Take one peck of cucumbers, cut them in pieces one inch thick, and four onions sliced. Lay these in a kettle, adding the following ingredients: Three ounces of turmeric, two pounds of sugar, half a cup of black pepper, two table-spoonfuls of dry mustard, one half ounce of mace, one cup of allspice, and two table-spoonfuls of ginger. The spices must be ground. Cover well with vinegar. Cook two hours.

CHOWCHOW.

Take a peck of white cabbage and cut fine, three dozen onions sliced thin, sprinkle both with salt and let them stand twelve hours; then press out the salt-water and spread them on dishes to dry. For seasoning take a half box of mustard, two ounces of turmeric, a very little red pepper, half a pound of white mustard-seed, and a small piece of horse-radish. Beat the following spices fine, and add two table-spoonfuls of each: Cloves, mace, ginger, nutmeg, and celery-seed. Put cabbage and all the ingredients in a kettle, cover well with strong vinegar, and let it come to a boil. After taking from the fire add one pint of salad-oil.

ONION PICKLE.

Take small onions, peel and drop them into cold water to prevent changing color; then drain them and boil them in equal parts of milk and water; drain and cover with best vinegar. Season with red pepper and white ginger-root.

MUSTARD PICKLE.

After your fruit has been in brine, soak it in clear water

until the salt is out. Take a kettle that holds a little more than a gallon; put in the bottom a layer of grape-leaves. Sprinkle in pulverized alum,—a piece the size of a nutmeg,—a teaspoonful each of cinnamon, allspice, black and red pepper; also, two table-spoonfuls of sugar, then a layer of fruit. Continue these layers until you fill the kettle; cover with vinegar and let it simmer over a slow fire until green. Mix smoothly with vinegar five boxes of mustard, seven and a half cups of sugar; to this add one table-spoonful each of cloves, mace, allspice, celery-seed, cinnamon, turmeric, and four table-spoonfuls of salad-oil; mix well. Drain off the first vinegar from your fruit, and pour this mixture over it. Allow the whole to boil a few minutes. In three weeks it will be ready for use.

GREEN-TOMATO SAUCE.

One peck of green tomatoes, twelve large onions; slice them and lay on dishes, sprinkling each layer with salt. Set them aside for twenty-four hours. Drain them through a sieve until they are perfectly dry. Put them in a kettle and cover with strong vinegar. Let them simmer, but not boil, until quite tender. To flavor them, add one quarter of a pound of white mustard-seed, three pods of red pepper sliced thin, one ounce each of allspice, mace, cloves, black pepper, and celery-seed; also, three table-spoonfuls of sugar. After removing it from the fire add a half pint of brandy, and a half tea-cup of sweet-oil.

PICKLE-SAUCE.

Take six quarts of green tomatoes, two quarts of green pepper, and one quart of onions; slice them up separately, sprinkle them with salt, and let them stand two days. Then strain them from the brine; add one gallon of vinegar, one tea-cup of sugar, one box of dry mustard, a half pound of white mustard-seed, two spoonfuls of each black pepper, cinnamon, cloves, allspice, and mace. The spices must be ground. Boil fifteen minutes.

REGENT PICKLE.

Take two gallons each of cucumbers and cabbage, one pint of onions. Chop all these very fine; then add a quarter of a pint of salt, one pound of sugar, two table-spoonfuls each of allspice and cloves, five table-spoonfuls of dry mustard, one paper of celery-seed, and two gills of white mustard-seed. Mix all well, and put it over the fire a few minutes. Stir it constantly.

BEVERAGES.

TO PREPARE. COFFEE.—No. 1.

Pick over the grains to remove all imperfect ones; wash, drain, and dry. Parch always on top of the stove, stirring constantly. In this way it is done rapidly and evenly. When a good brown, and just after taking off the stove, before emptying from the pan, stir in a table-spoonful of butter; this quantity to two or three pounds of coffee.

TO PREPARE COFFEE.—No. 2.

Scald the green coffee, and dry in the oven; leave in till parched a good brown. When done, have the whites of one or two eggs beaten to a stiff froth; stir in the coffee, and set back in the oven a minute to dry. Parched coffee should always be kept in a close can or jar.

HOW TO MAKE COFFEE.

To every half pint of water allow one table-spoonful of ground coffee. Do not grind too fine, either for boiled or dripped coffee.

TO MAKE TEA.

First scald the tea-pot with boiling water. Allow a tea-spoonful of tea for each person, or each half pint of water. After putting the tea in the tea-pot, only pour on a little of the boiling water at first; allow to steep a few minutes, and then pour on the balance of the water.

Hot or iced tea is best made of mixed tea—equal quantities of black and green.

CHOCOLATE.—No. 1.

Mix two heaping table-spoonfuls of chocolate to a smooth paste with water. Stir in half a pint of water, and allow to boil five minutes; then add half a pint of milk. Serve hot.

CHOCOLATE.—No. 2.

Dissolve two squares of Baker's chocolate in a cupful of hot water; beat well the yelks of four eggs with six table-spoonfuls of sugar, and mix in the chocolate. Have boiling a quart of new milk; stir the mixture in the milk, and let boil a few minutes till it thickens. Serve very hot, and on the top of each cup lay a spoonful of the whites of the eggs beaten to a stiff froth.

MILK-PUNCH.—No. 1.

Stir in a glass of new milk one table-spoonful of white sugar, the same of brandy; grate nutmeg on the top. Milk-punch is generally prepared in this way for invalids.

MILK-PUNCH.—No. 2.

One glass of fresh milk (must be very fresh, or it will curdle), one egg beaten very light, with one table-spoonful of sugar. Mix with the egg and sugar one table-spoonful of brandy; pour on the milk, and grate nutmeg on the top.

HOT MILK-PUNCH.

Beat together, very light, the yelks of two eggs and two table-spoonfuls of sugar; add two table-spoonfuls of sherry wine or brandy, and pour over all one pint of boiling fresh milk, and grate nutmeg on it. Drink as hot as possible.

CREAM NECTAR.

Put into a porcelain kettle three pounds of loaf-sugar, two ounces of tartaric acid, one quart of water; set it on the fire; when warm, add the whites of two eggs beaten to a froth; stir it well for a few minutes, but do not let it boil. When cool, strain it, and add a tea-spoonful of essence of lemon, and bottle. Put two table-spoonfuls in a glass, fill it half full of cold water, and stir in one fourth tea-spoonful of soda. Drink while effervescing.

CHAMPAGNE CUPS.

Two bottles of champagne, two dessert-spoonfuls of white sugar, two bottles soda-water, a half lemon squeezed, a half lemon sliced, one wine-glass curacoa, a few sprigs of borage, and plentifully iced. Cut lemon very thin, and throw in the peel.

CLARET CUP.

Two bottles of claret, two table-spoonfuls of white sugar, two bottles of soda-water, half a lemon squeezed, half a lemon sliced, two wine-glasses of sherry, one wine-glass of *maraschino* wine, or cordial; use ice plentifully. Slice lemons thin, and throw in the peel.

EGGNOG.—No. 1.

To each egg allow one table-spoonful of sugar and one table-spoonful of brandy or whisky; beat the eggs, whites and yelks together; when partially beaten, add the sugar; then beat till very light; add the brandy last. When the eggs are beaten in this way it requires more time; but they are not so likely to separate. For an invalid, sherry wine is a delicate substitute for brandy.

EGGNOG.—No. 2.

Allow the same proportions as above. Beat the whites and yelks of the eggs separately, the whites to a stiff froth. For about twelve eggs beat very light a pint of sweet cream, and stir in just before eating.

EGGNOG.—No. 3.

To each egg allow one small wine glass of brandy, one table-spoonful of sugar; beat the whites and yelks separately. After beating the yelks well, gradually add the sugar, then the brandy; also allow about three wine-glasses of rum to about one dozen eggs; pour in the milk, as much as you like, —say a quart to a dozen eggs,—and last stir in the whites, when they are as light as they can be beaten.

SHERRY-COBBLER.

In a tumbler of lemonade stir in a wine-glass of sherry wine, and pounded ice. Sliced pine-apple may be put in if desired.

A GOOD COCK-TAIL.

Dissolve four square lumps of white sugar in one table-spoonful of water; add one small wine-glassful of whisky and one tea-spoonful of Boker's Bitters. Add ice.

WHISKY PUNCH.

Six quarts of water, one quart of strong green tea, two pounds of sugar, two dozen sliced lemons, two sliced pine-apples, one bottle extract of vanilla, one grated nutmeg, and one gallon of whisky.

PRINCE REGENT PUNCH.

Six quarts of water, one quart of strong green tea, two dozen lemons sliced, one gallon of whisky, one quart of curacoa cordial, two pine-apples sliced, and two pounds of loaf-sugar. Float strawberries over the top, if in season.

ROMAN PUNCH.

One gallon of water, one pint of wine, one pint of old rum, half pint of brandy, four lemons, and sweeten it well. Add more brandy if needed. Ice abundantly, or freeze.

A PLEASANT DRINK, OR BEER.

Three pounds of brown sugar, one and a half pints of molasses, four ounces of tartaric acid; mix in two quarts of boiling water; strain it, and when cold it is fit for use. Take two table-spoonfuls for a tumbler two-thirds full of water; add half a tea-spoonful of soda; flavor with any extract you like, as you use it.

CORN BEER.

Two gallons of water, one quart of boiled corn well cooked, two quarts of molasses, a small quantity of ginger. Let it stand until ready for use.

BLACKBERRY CORDIAL.—No. 1.

Boil the blackberries in a little water about fifteen minutes; then strain them. To one quart of juice put three fourths of a pound of sugar; season with cloves, cinnamon, and allspice, and boil three quarters of an hour. To three quarts of the juice put in one quart of brandy.

BLACKBERRY CORDIAL.—No. 2.

To each quart of blackberry-juice add one pound of white sugar, half an ounce of cinnamon, one fourth an ounce of mace, two table-spoonfuls of cloves. Boil this mixture twenty minutes; strain, and when cold put to each quart a pint of French brandy.

BLACKBERRY CORDIAL.—No. 3.

Fill a demijohn with blackberries perfectly ripe, and pour on as much whisky or brandy as it will hold; spices to the taste—about a handful of cinnamon, two of allspice, and a dessert-spoonful of cloves to a five-gallon jar. Allow it to stand about three weeks, after which pour off the liquor, and sweeten to the taste.

BLACKBERRY OR PEACH CORDIAL.

Nearly fill your glass jars with fresh-gathered berries, or peaches cut up; fill up with whisky, and let it stand six months or more. Pour off the whisky, mash the berries well, strain, and put in their juice. Put sugar into a brass kettle, and cover with enough water to make a thick sirup; tie in a piece of muslin some mace, cloves, and any other spices you wish; drop in and boil fifteen or twenty minutes. Pour into the whisky, and bottle.

MINT CORDIAL.

After the mint is washed, bruise it slightly, and put in a stone jar or other vessel and cover it with whisky. Let it stand twenty-four hours; then strain, and to a quart of it put a pint of loaf-sugar. Bottle.

CHERRY CORDIAL.

Put cherries in your jar, and cover with whisky. Let it stand two weeks; mash and strain through a cloth; then add sugar to make a thick sirup.

SCUPPERNONG WINE.—No. 1.

To one gallon of the juice of the grape add two pounds of white sugar. When the sugar is dissolved, pour into demijohns or kegs, reserving a small quantity to fill up the demijohn, which must be kept well filled and uncorked until the wine ceases to ferment. The best plan is to fill them every morning. When fermentation ceases, strain it carefully and bottle it, being careful not to cork it too tightly. In drawing it for use, be particular not to shake the bottle, or the wine will mix with the lees and become muddy.

SCUPPERNONG WINE.—No. 2.

Press the juice from the grape, and to every gallon put three pounds of good sugar; put into an open-mouthed vessel, with a thin cloth over it, and let stand three or four days;

skim, and put in jugs, taking care not to cork tightly until the fermentation ceases. Set away for six or eight weeks; then bottle for use.

BLACKBERRY WINE.—No. 1.

Measure your berries, and bruise them. To every gallon add one quart of boiling water; let the mixture stand twenty-four hours, stirring occasionally. To every gallon put two pounds of sugar. Cork tightly, and let stand till the following October, when it will be ready for use.

BLACKBERRY WINE.—No. 2.

Measure and bruise your berries, and to every gallon add one quart of boiling water; let stand twenty-four hours, stirring occasionally. Strain off the liquor into an open vessel, to every gallon adding three pounds of good brown sugar. Let it remain open about ten days, skimming it frequently; then put it into jugs. Do not cork tightly. Let it remain so for three or four weeks, when fermentation will be over. Cork tightly. In the fall it will be ready for use.

SOUR-ORANGE WINE.—No. 1.

Peel the oranges; cut across in halves, and squeeze; strain, and to every gallon of juice add five gallons of water and twenty-five pounds of sugar. Ferment and bottle as you would other wines. Use for this the sour, not bitter-sweet orange.

SOUR-ORANGE WINE.—No. 2.

Three quarts of water, one quart of orange-juice, three pounds of sugar, and the beaten white of an egg.

COMFORTS FOR THE SICK.

"I own that nothing like good cheer succeeds."

Always endeavor to have the food for the sick as attractive in appearance as in taste. Prepare and serve in small quantities, as fresh as possible. Avoid consulting the patient as to what he would like to eat. Study all the peculiarities of the patient, and humor him whenever by so doing you do not interfere with the instructions of the physician.

BEEF-TEA.

About three pounds of lean, juicy beef cut in small pieces. Put in a strong bottle or wide-mouthed jar; place the jar in a vessel of cold water, and put on the fire, with a weight on top to keep it down in the water, having previously corked it closely. Boil for three or four hours; pour off the tea, and season with salt. If desired, add one dozen allspice and half a dozen cloves before boiling. Any grease rising on the top must be carefully skimmed off. A small tin bucket closely covered, with a flat-iron placed on top as a weight, is an excellent substitute for the orthodox bottle or jar, as in the old way the bottle is often broken by the heat just as it is ready to take up, and all the tea is lost. The bucket should be new, and very clean.

HASTY BEEF-TEA.

Cut up in very small pieces lean, juicy beef, and pour on

just enough cold water to prevent burning. Watch closely to prevent scorching. When done, season with salt. If beef-tea is allowed to cool, any grease in it can be readily detected and taken off. Heat only the quantity desired to give the patient at one time

CHICKEN-ESSENCE.

Take a whole small chicken or half of a large one; mangle it, so as to crush the bones; pour on it a pint and a half of cold water, and drop in three allspice. Place it over a fire, and notice what time it begins to boil; allow it to continue boiling twenty five minutes, when the water will have extracted all the strength of the chicken, and will be palatable to anybody after the addition of a very little salt. This is most nutritious, and has never been known to be distasteful to a sick person when well made and offered hot. A spoonful every hour will suffice for a very weak person, without other nourishment; yet it may be safely taken in larger quantities, if the patient wishes it.

CHICKEN-BROTH.

Cut up half of a chicken, and pour on one quart of cold water. Place over the fire, and allow to boil slowly two hours. After boiling one hour, add a table-spoonful of rice; salt and pepper to taste. Skim carefully while boiling.

MUTTON-BROTH.

One pound of mutton or lamb cut in small pieces. Pour on this one quart of cold water, and allow it to boil till the meat falls to pieces; cover close while boiling; strain, and add a table-spoonful of rice and a little parsley or thyme, boil half an hour, stirring frequently; then add pepper and salt to taste, and four table-spoonfuls of milk.

EGG-TEA.

Beat one egg very light, with sufficient sugar to sweeten.

Pour on this a tumbler of boiling water and a wine-glass of sherry or other liquor, according to taste. After adding the water, etc., have another vessel ready, and pour the tea rapidly and repeatedly from one vessel to the other to prevent curdling, Drink warm.

SOUP MAIGRE.

Take of butter half a pound; put it in a deep stew-pan, place it on a gentle fire till it melts, shake it about, and let it stand till it has done making a noise. Have ready six medium-sized onions peeled and cut up small; throw them in and shake them about. Take a bunch of celery cut in pieces about an inch long, a large handful of spinach cut small, and a little bundle of parsley chopped fine; sprinkle these into the pan, and shake them about for a quarter of an hour; then sprinkle in a little flour, and stir it up. Pour into the pan two quarts of boiling water, and add a handful of dry bread-crust broken in pieces, a tea-spoonful of pepper, and three blades of mace beaten fine; boil gently another half hour; then beat up the yelks of two eggs, with a tea-spoonful of vinegar; stir them in, and the soup is ready. The order in which the ingredients are added is very important.

EEG-SOUP.

One pint of water, the yelks of two eggs, a lump of butter as large as a big walnut, sugar according to taste; beat them up together over a slow fire, gradually adding the water. When it begins to boil, pour it backward and forward between the sauce-pan and bowl till quite smooth and frothy

BEEF AND CHICKEN TEA.

Take one pound of lean beef, one half of a hen, boned; pound together in a mortar; add one fourth of an ounce of salt; put in a stew-pan with two and a half pints of water; stir over the fire till boiling. Then add carrots, onions, leeks, and celery, cut fine. Boil half an hour; strain, and serve.

Beef-tea and broth should not be kept hot, but heated up as required It may be warmed, but never prepared in the sick-room, for nothing sets an invalid against food as much as cooking.

NUTRIENT ENEMA.

Take of beef-tea half a pint, and thicken it with a teaspoonful of tapioca. Reduce one and three fourths ounces of raw beef to a fine pulp, pass it through a fine colander, and mix the whole up with twenty grains of acid pepsin and a dessert-spoonful of malt flour. It should have a bright rose tint, and exhale a rich meaty odor. Not more than a quarter of a pint should be used at a time, and that slowly. Thus frequent repetition is facilitated. If the pepsin and malt are not at hand, the other portion of the liquor may be administered alone.

ANOTHER EGG-TEA.

Beat the yelk of one egg with a dessert-spoonful of sugar; add a spoonful of brandy, stirring all the time. Grate in a little nutmeg, and pour on half a pint of boiling milk.

EGGNOG.

One egg well beaten with a dessert-spoonful of sugar; add one table-spoonful of brandy or wine and half a cup of cream.

ICED EGG.

Beat very light the yelk of one egg, with a table-spoonful of sugar; stir in this a tumblerful of very finely-crushed ice; add a table-spoonful of brandy and a little grated nutmeg. Beat well together, and drink immediately.

BLANC-MANGE.

Two table-spoonfuls of corn-starch thoroughly beaten with one egg. Stir this into a pint of milk when nearly boiling;

add a little salt, sugar, and flavoring to taste. Boil a few minutes, and pour into a mold to congeal. To be eaten with cream.

BREAD-PUDDING.—No. 1.

Take of crumbs of bread two ounces, one third of a pint of new milk boiling hot; pour the hot milk on the bread, and let it stand about an hour covered up; then add the yelk of an egg well beaten; then a tea-spoonful of rose or orange-flower water, a little nutmeg, and half an ounce of sugar. Beat all up together. Tie up and boil, or steam, or bake three quarters of an hour.

BREAD-PUDDING.—No. 2.

Pour half a pint of boiling milk over a French roll, and let it stand covered up till it has soaked up the milk. Tie lightly in a cloth, and boil twenty minutes.

HARTSHORN JELLY.

Boil half a pound of hartshorn shavings (not "raspings," which are adulterated with bone-dust), or an equal weight of ivory turnings, in three pints of water down to a pint; strain, and add three ounces of white sugar-candy and an ounce of lemon-juice. Heat up again to the boiling-point. As a variety in flavoring, white capri, moselle, or champagne may be used in quantity not exceeding two table-spoonfuls.

ARROW-ROOT.

Stir into a pint of boiling milk a large table-spoonful of arrow-root well mixed with a little cold milk; boil it three or four minutes. Sweeten to taste, and flavor with nutmeg.

ARROW-ROOT JELLY.

Put into one pint of boiling water two table-spoonfuls of arrow-root previously dissolved in a little water; boil a few minutes. After taking from the fire, pour in a wine-glass of sherry or Madeira wine. Sweeten and flavor to taste.

SAGO JELLY.

Put to soak over night one cupful of sago in a tumbler of cold water. In the morning, add one pint of boiling water and the juice and rind of one lemon; boil gently twenty-five or thirty minutes. Sweeten to taste; add a wine-glass of sherry, and set aside to congeal.

CUSTARD AND TOAST.

Beat together till very light one egg and a dessert-spoonful of powdered sugar; pour on this a cup of boiling milk, and stir till thick. When done, pour into a dish over a slice of toasted bread. Grate on a little nutmeg.

TOAST-WATER.

Cut about a quarter of a pound of bread in thin slices, and toast an even brown, being careful not to burn. Put into a pitcher, and pour on three pints of boiling water. Cover till cool, and strain into another pitcher. Do not allow the toast to remain in the water after it is cold.

GRUEL.

Allow two table-spoonfuls of meal to one pint of water. Pour the water, cold, on the meal, a little at a time, stirring constantly to avoid lumps. When well mixed, boil twenty minutes; add salt to taste, and, if desired, sugar. Straining after it is boiled is a decided improvement. Gruel made with milk instead of water is more nourishing and palatable.

BARLEY WATER.

Wash a table-spoonful of pearl-barley through several waters till perfectly clean, and put it in a jug or pitcher. Rub several lumps of sugar on a lemon to absorb all the oil, and throw into the jug with the barley. Peel the lemon, leaving as little of the white pulp on the rind as possible; put this also into the jug, and pour on boiling water till the vessel is full. In half an hour it is ready for use. This is a palatable beverage.

FLAXSEED TEA.

Put a tablespoonful of flaxseed in a pitcher, and pour on one pint of boiling water; let stand till it thickens, and strain. Squeeze in the juice of a lemon, and sweeten to taste. This should be drank warm for colds or fevers, but cold and without the lemon-juice for bowel complaints.

SLIPPERY-ELM WATER

Is prepared by putting the bark in cold water, and allowing it to stand till it thickens; sweeten to taste. Benne-water is prepared in the same way from the leaves of the plant. Both are excellent for inflammation of the bowels.

ORANGE-LEAF TEA.

Thoroughly wash a large handful of orange-leaves, and put in a pitcher. Pour on a quart of boiling water, and cover closely. When well steeped, pour off and sweeten to taste. Drink while warm. An excellent fever-drink, and much used in yellow fever.

WINE-WHEY.

Stir into a pint of boiling milk one half pint of wine; let it boil one minute. Take from the fire, and let stand until the curd has settled; then pour off the whey, and sweeten it with loaf-sugar. Lemon, vinegar, and alum whey are made in like manner.

GUM-ARABIC WATER.

Take one ounce of gum arabic, and pour on it a pint of boiling water; stir while dissolving; sweeten to taste. The juice of a lemon squeezed in is an improvement. This is given to persons suffering from inflammation of the stomach.

APPLE-WATER.

Pare and core one half dozen juicy apples, and bake them until quite soft; put them in a pitcher, and pour over enough hot water to make a pleasant drink; sweeten to taste. When cold, it is ready for use.

BOILED FLOUR.

Tie tightly in a close linen cloth one pound of flour. After tying, moisten with water, and dredge well with flour till a coating is formed to prevent the water entering the flour. Boil four or five hours, and let the flour remain tied in the cloth until it is cold. It will be a hard, solid lump, and is a substitute for arrow-root. Prepare by grating. Excellent in diarrhea or other bowel affections.

DIET FOR INFANTS.

(As Prepared by Dr. J. F. Meigs.)

Dissolve a piece of gelatine an inch square in half a gill of warm water; when dissolved, add a gill of milk; put on the fire, and when boiling add half a tea-spoonful of arrow-root or boiled flour-ball. When sufficiently boiled, take off the fire, and stir in two table-spoonfuls of sweet cream. This may be given to very young infants; and as they grow older the food may be made stronger by using more milk and cream.

PANADA.

Toast nicely a slice of bread, and pour over it a hot brandy toddy; grate over it nutmeg.

ANOTHER PANADA

One ounce of bread-crumbs, once blade of mace, one pint of water; boil without stirring till they mix and turn smooth; then add a grate of nutmeg, a small piece of butter, a table-spoonful of sherry, and sugar according to taste.

RICE FLUMMERY.

Take rice in proportion to the quantity required; put it in

a broad pan; cover with water; stir up together, and let stand twelve hours. Then pour off the water as long as it runs clear. Add fresh water, mix, and let stand twelve hours more. Repeat the same process a third time. When the rice has thus been macerated thirty-six hours, strain it through a hair-sieve and boil it, stirring it vigorously till it is quite thick. Pour it in a dish to cool, and eat it cold, with milk or a little wine and sugar.

CRACKER AND CREAM

A nicely-toasted cracker, with sweet cream poured over it, is delicate and nourishing for an invalid.

TAPIOCA.

Soak over night two table-spoonfuls of tapioca in two cups of water. In the morning, add one pint of milk, sugar to taste, and a pinch of salt; simmer till soft, stirring frequently. When dished, add a table-spoonful of wine, and grate over a little nutmeg.

LEMON-JELLY.

One half box of gelatine dissolved in three gills of warm water, with a good half pint of loaf-sugar. Squeeze and slice two lemons, extracting the seeds, in three gills of water, and boil till the lemons are soft or their strength is extracted. Mix this with the gelatine and sugar, and strain; set aside to congeal. To be eaten with cream.

"SOFKY."

To a quart of well-washed, well-beaten hominy put a gallon of cold water; keep it boiling steadily but slowly until the hominy begins to get soft. Then add good strong lye, sufficient to discolor a silver spoon when the mixture is stirred with it. Mash the hominy with a spoon or roller, and let boil half an hour; then the liquor will be as thick as gruel. Take it off. and when you serve the liquor to the patient, add salt, sugar, milk, or wine. Do not mix or flavor more than the patient can eat at once, or about a tea-cupful. The lye should be made fresh from good wood-ashes. "Big hominy" should be used for making sofky, not grits.

ALKALINE DRINK.

Cut the rind of a lemon very thin, and put it in a jug with a table-spoonful of powdered sugar-candy. Pour on it a little boiling water, and, when it is dissolved, half a pint of Vichy water and half a pint of common water.

MALT-TEA.

Boil three ounces of malt in a quart of water.

CLARET-CUP FOR INVALIDS.

Half a bottle of claret to a bottle of soda-water. Half a dozen drops of sweet spirits of niter put into the jug first gives a fruity flavor.

SAGE-TEA.

Take half an ounce of leaves of green sage plucked from the stalks and washed clean, one ounce of sugar, quarter of an ounce of the outer rind of lemon-peel finely pared from the white; put them in two pints of boiling water; let them stand near the fire half an hour; then strain. When the sage is dried, it must be used in rather less quantity than above mentioned.

In the same manner, teas may be made of rosemary, balm, southern-wood, etc., and are convenient to prevent a thirsty patient taking too much tea and coffee when not good for him. The use of acid is also avoided.

MASHED POTATOES.

Boil one pound of potatoes with their jackets on till they are tender or brittle; peel them, and rub them through a fine sieve. When cool, add a small tea-cupful of fresh cream and a little salt, beating the *puree* up lightly as you go on till it is quite smooth, and warming it up gently for use.

POTATO SURPRISE.

Scoop out the inside of a sound potato, leaving the skin; attached on one side to the hole as a lid. Mince up fine the lean of a juicy mutton-chop, with a little salt and pepper put it in the potato, pin down the lid, and bake or roast. Before serving (in the skin), add a little hot gravy, if the mince seems too dry.

MEDICINAL.

COUGH MIXTURES.

Fifteen drops of oil of tar, half an ounce of balsam of fir, and alcohol sufficient to dissolve it. Boil one tea-cup of molasses for several minutes, and pour it in the above mixture, together with a pint of the best whisky, and shake it until well mixed. Dose: A table-spoonful two or three times a day.

ANOTHER.

Take one ounce of hops, one pint of water, and one table-spoonful of flax-seed. Put all in a vessel and boil till reduced one half. Strain it off; add one half pint of molasses and one quarter of a pound of brown sugar. Boil till it becomes a thick sirup. Dose: One table-spoonful at a time.

ANOTHER.

Take one dime-package of hoarhound, put it in one quart of water, and boil down to a pint. Strain and add one pint of honey or sirup, one stick of licorice, and boil down to a pint. When cool, thin to the proper consistency with whisky. Dose: A dessert-spoonful when the cough is troublesome; when very bad, add a little paregoric to the dose.

ANOTHER.

One pint of cider vinegar; drop in over night an unbroken egg, shell and all. In the morning beat it well till all is dissolved; then sweeten with loaf-sugar to the taste. Strain and bottle. Shake well before taking. Dose: A table-spoonful when the cough is troublesome.

ANOTHER

One ounce of elecampane and one ounce of comfrey-root soaked in one quart of water; boil to a pint. Strain and add one pint of molasses or honey, and thin with one pint of good whisky. Boil one stick of licorice with it. When done, add half an ounce of sirup of squills, and half an ounce of paregoric. Give a table-spoonful every hour or two, or when the cough is troublesome. For a child, two tea-spoonfuls is a dose. This is perfectly harmless, and has never been known to fail in curing a cough.

ANOTHER.

One pound of wet brown sugar, one table-spoonful of cook ing-soda and one of fine tar. Stir well together, and pour one pint of boiling water on it. Prepare at night, let it stand until morning, then pour off and bottle. Dose for an adult: One table-spoonful early in the morning.

WHOOPING-COUGH SIRUP.

One ounce each of boneset, slippery elm, stick licorice, and flax-seed. Simmer all together in one quart of water, until the strength is entirely extracted; then strain and add one pint of molasses and half a pound of white sugar. Simmer all well together. When cold, bottle and cork tightly. This sirup is excellent for any bad cough.

REMEDY FOR CROUP.

A tea-spoonful of powdered alum, mixed with twice the quantity of sugar. Give as quickly as possible. This affords almost instantaneous relief.

FOR HOARSENESS.

To a pint of whisky put as much rock-candy as it will dissolve. Dose: A tea-spoonful at a time.

GARGLE FOR SORE THROAT.

Make a tea of red-oak bark, with a little alum dissolved in it.

ANOTHER.

One tea-spoonful of chlorate of potash, dissolved in a tumbler of warm water, is an excellent gargle. Swallowing a little of the mixture occasionally will be beneficial.

ANOTHER.

Make a strong sage-tea, and add one tea-spoonful of borax and one of alum. Make very sweet with honey.

ANOTHER REMEDY.

Take old bacon, roll it full of salt, and bind it on the throat. It will take all the inflammation out. Use alum-water to gargle the throat. If you have no bacon, mix lard and salt together, spread it on a flannel cloth, and apply to the throat.

BINKERD'S SALVE FOR BURNS.

Take of yellow wax, melted and strained, three ounces linseed-oil, raw, one and a half pints; tannic acid, half an ounce; bicarbonate bismuth, one dram; powdered opium, one scruple; carbolic acid, thirty drops. Take a common fruit-can, not oxidized, cleanse it thoroughly, melt the wax in it, then add the oil, keeping it very liquid by heat, stirring it vigorously all the while. After all the oil has been poured in, stir it for five or ten minutes; then set it off to cool, agitating it as before. When it begins to chill, add the tannic acid; later, put in the bismuth, opium, and carbolic acid. The quantity of oil must depend on the season; less in summer and more in winter.

FOR BURNS.

Great relief is sometimes afforded in case of a burn by sprinkling thickly with carbonate of soda, and laying over this a soft linen cloth, saturated with water.

Linseed-oil and lime-water, mixed in equal quantities, are also excellent for a burn.

DR. W. H. PANCOAST'S LINIMENT.

Camphor, one and a half dram; olive-oil, one ounce; aqua ammonia, one ounce; tincture aconite root, one ounce; oil origanum, one half ounce; laudanum, one half ounce.

A GOOD LINIMENT.

Gum camphor, one ounce; chloroform, one fluid ounce; tincture of aconite root, half a fluid ounce; tincture of arnica, two fluid ounces; soap liniment enough to make six fluid ounces.

ANOTHER.

One pint of alcohol, two ounces of spirits ammonia, one ounce gum camphor, one half ounce tincture arnica, and one ounce of sweet-oil.

CURE FOR FEVER AND AGUE

Twenty grains of quinine, ten grains of blue vitriol, and five grains of opium. To be made into twenty pills. Dose—Two pills three times a day.

ANOTHER.

Twenty grains of quinine, twenty grains of peruvian bark, half a dram elixir of vitriol, in one pint of good whisky. Dose for an adult: Half a wine-glassful three times each day.

FOR DYSENTERY.

One tea-spoonful of common salt, one of epsom salts, twenty drops of laudanum, fifteen drops of camphor, in a goblet of water. Dose: A dessert-spoonful every hour.

ANOTHER.

One table-spoonful of epsom salts, and one tea-spoonful of laudanum, in a tumbler of water. Take a table-spoonful of the mixture every two hours, and one after *each discharge* from the bowels until the disease is checked.

FOR SUMMER-COMPLAINT IN INFANTS.

One ounce sirup of rhubarb, one dessert-spoonful of paregoric, one tea-spoonful of sup. carbonate of soda, well mixed. Dose: From ten to fifteen drops.

HEADACHE.

To cure a simple headache, immerse the feet in hot water and keep them there for twenty minutes. If the pain is severe, add two table-spoonfuls of dry mustard, keeping the water as hot as can be borne.

SICK-HEADACHE.—Two tea-spoonfuls of finely-powdered charcoal, drank in a half tumbler of water, will often give relief, when caused by superabundance of acid in the stomach.

TO STOP VOMITING.

A mustard plaster; or a warm plaster made of toasted bread dipped in brandy, with nutmeg grated over it; or a plaster made of all the spices pounded, and moistened with brandy; either of these applied to the chest, will generally give relief. A julep made very strong with bruised mint is also good.

ANOTHER.

A tea-spoonful of carbonate of soda, a table-spoonful of spirits of lavender, in half a goblet of water. Take a spoonful frequently.

TO STOP BLEEDING.

AT THE NOSE.—Fold a piece of paper about as thick as your little finger, and about two inches long, and place between your lips and gums, just under the nose. Keep it pressed tightly there by holding your finger on your lip, and it will generally relieve in a short time.

AT A WOUND.—Mix equal parts of wheat flour and common salt, and bind on with a cloth.

ANOTHER.

Take the fine dust of tea, or the scrapings of the inside of tanned leather, and bind it close upon the wound. After the blood has ceased to flow, laudanum may be applied advantageously.

FOR SPRAINED ANKLE.

Make a poultice of flour and vinegar, of the consistency of pudding-batter, and bind on the ankle; keep wet with vinegar, renewing when dry. Sit with the foot elevated.

CURE FOR EARACHE.

Take a bit of cotton batting, put upon it a pinch of black pepper; gather it up and tie it; dip it in sweet-oil, and insert it in the ear. Put a flannel bandage over the head to keep it warm. It will give immediate relief.

ANOTHER.

Take an onion and roast it well; pour on it a little laudanum and sweet-oil. Put a few drops of the juice in the ear, and stop it with wool; bind the warm onion to it.

FOR TOOTHACHE.

A few drops of sodique, or oil of cloves, or creosote, or chloroform, on a piece of cotton, placed in the cavity of the tooth, will generally give relief.

FOR NIGHT-SWEAT.

Make a strong tea of sage; strain and sweeten to the taste. A tumblerful taken before going to sleep will prevent the sweat common to very feeble persons.

AN EXCELLENT ENEMA.

One quart of warm water, one cup of molasses, one cup of table-salt, and a table-spoonful of lard.

FOR FAINTING.

If a person faints, place him on the flat of the back and give plenty of fresh air. Do not crowd around him.

PLASTER FOR A RISEN BREAST.

One table-spoonful of melted bees-wax, one table-spoonful of linseed-oil, one table-spoonful of sassafras-oil.

ANOTHER.

Take equal parts of bees-wax, mutton-suet, and camphor.

FLAXSEED POULTICE.

To make a poultice sufficiently large for the chest or stomach, stir into about one pint of boiling water sufficient flaxseed meal to thicken. Boil till thick and smooth, stirring constantly. Pour into a swiss-muslin bag, securing the opening so that the poultice will not escape. Apply as warm as can be borne. Lay over the poultices one or two thicknesses of flannel, or a piece of oil-silk, to prevent the dampness reaching the clothing, and to retain the heat.

TO MAKE A MUSTARD-PLASTER.

For an ordinary plaster use one part flour and two parts mustard—say one table-spoonful of flour and two of mustard; mix with a little warm water. If wanted to draw rapidly use no flour, and mix with vinegar or whisky. A plaster made of mustard alone, and mixed with the white of an egg, will draw perfectly, and not produce a blister.

NOTE.—This may be the contributor's experience, but it is not every one's. We know and have felt whereof we speak. After the plaster is spread lay a piece of this muslin over it, so that the plaster will not come in contact with the skin.

CURE FOR BONE FELON.

One table-spoonful of saltpeter, one of copperas, one of salt pulverized, mixed with a table-spoonful soft soap, one red onion roasted; mash all well together, making a poultice; apply to the felon, and let it remain a day. If it does not relieve entirely apply another the next day.

ANOTHER.

Take of blue flag-root and white hellebore, cut up very fine, equal parts; boil them in milk and water. Hold the finger in this as hot as it can be borne, about fifteen minutes; then lay the hot roots on the felon, and let them remain about one hour. Renew the application several times, or until the pain is removed. The above recipe has been proved by the contributor.

ANOTHER.

A small Spanish-fly blister applied in the first stages of the felon is said to be a certain cure.

ANOTHER.

Bathing the felon with tincture of lobelia sometimes gives great relief.

TO CURE A STY ON THE EYE.

Apply the rotten part of an apple as a poultice to the eye. It is both cooling and healing, and removes the inflammation.

ANOTHER.

Put a tea-spoonful of black tea in a small muslin bag. Pour on it just enough boiling water to moisten it; then put it on the eye pretty warm, and keep it on all night. If the sty is not removed in the morning, a second application will effect a cure.

TO DESTROY WARTS.

Dissolve as much common washing-soda as the water will take up. Wash the warts with this for a minute or two, and let them dry without wiping. Keep the water in a bottle, and frequently repeat the washing.

ANOTHER.

Lunar caustic carefully applied so as not to touch the skin, will destroy warts.

CURE FOR CORNS.

Mix smoothly together a tea-spoonful of pulverized indigo, the same of brown soap and mutton-suet. Spread on a piece of kid and apply to the corn.

ANOTHER.

Apply a good coat of gum-arabic mucilage to the corn, every evening on going to bed.

LIP-SALVE.

Spermaceti, virgin wax, and lard, one ounce each; balsam of Peru, half an ounce; six sweet almonds, six fresh raisins, loaf-sugar the size of a hickory-nut. Melt over the fire and stir constantly. Strain when melted.

FOR CHAPPED HANDS AND LIPS.

Melt together equal quantities of sweet-oil, white wax, spermaceti, and mutton-suet.

ANOTHER.

Take of honey any quantity, oil of sweet almonds sufficient to make a thin paste; rub the oil in gradually until well mixed. After washing the hands, and while still wet, take a small quantity and rub thoroughly on the parts affected; then wipe the hands dry.

CURE FOR TETTER.

One poke-root boiled to a strong decoction; take one pound of the best loaf-sugar; boil with the poke-root to a thick sirup. Dissolve twenty grains of iodide of potash in a little water, and mix with the poke-root sirup. Dose: One table-spoonful three times a day.

ANOTHER.

Corrosive sublimate, one grain; oil of lavender, one dram castor-oil, one dram; alcohol, two ounces. Mix and apply externally. Do not let it get into the eyes or mouth.

HAIR-TONIC.

One half ounce tincture cantharides, tnree ounces of castor-oil, and one pint of alcohol.

ANOTHER.

One ounce of borax, one half ounce of gum camphor, beaten up fine; pour on one pint of boiling water. When cool, it will be ready for use.

ANOTHER.

Sixty grains of quinine put into a quart of bay rum.

GLYCERINE HAIR-TONIC.

Glycerine, bay rum, each one ounce; tincture cantharides half an ounce; rose-water, four ounces; aqua ammonia, one fourth ounce. Mix.

This tonic will stop the hair from falling out, will effectually remove dandruff, and as a dressing will far surpass any of the pomatums or greasy preparations now in use.

FOR BITE OF INSECTS.

A lump of wet saleratus applied to the sting of a wasp, spider, or bee, will stop the pain almost immediately, and prevent all swelling of the part.

ANOTHER.

Tobacco, slightly moistened with water, and applied to the sting, will afford instant relief.

ANTIDOTES FOR POISONS.

Make the patient vomit by giving a tumbler of warm water with a tea-spoonful of mustard in it, and then send for the doctor. If it be necessary to act without the doctor, and the poison is *arsenic*, give large quantities of milk and raw eggs, or flour and water. If the poison is an *acid*, give magnesia and water, or chalk and water, and plenty of warm water besides. If it is an *alkali*, like potash, give vinegar and water, lemon-juice, or some other safe acid. Always remember the emetic first. If it be *laudanum*, strong coffee is a good thing to give until the doctor comes. Keep the patient awake.

CURE FOR COLDS IN THE HEAD.

A snuff composed of the following ingredients: Hydrochlorate of morphia, two grains; scacia powder, two drams; trisnitrate of bismuth, six drams. A pinch of the powder inhaled through the nose five or six times a day will greatly alleviate a cold in the head.

FOR A BRUISE.

Mix sweet-oil and laudanum in equal quantities and apply to the bruise. It will relieve the soreness and prevent discoloration.

MISCELLANEOUS.

HOUSEKEEPER'S ALPHABET.

Apples: Keep in a dry place, as cool as possible without freezing.

Brooms: Hang up by the handle.

Cranberries: Keep under water in cellar; change water monthly.

Dish of hot water set in oven prevents cakes, etc., from scorching.

Economize time, health, and means.

Flour: Keep cool, dry, and securely covered.

Glass: Clean with a quart of water mixed with a tablespoonful of ammonia.

Herbs: Gather when beginning to blossom; keep in paper sacks.

Ink-stains: Wet with spirits of turpentine; after three hours, rub well.

Jam: Currant and red raspberry jam are excellent.

Keep an account of all supplies, with cost and date of purchase.

Love lightens labor.

Money: Count carefully when you receive change.

Nutmegs: Prick with a pin, and, if good, oil will come out.

Orange and lemon peel: Dry, pound, and keep in corked bottles.

Parsnips: Keep in the ground until spring.

Quicksilver and white of an egg destroy bed-bugs.

Rice: Select large, with a clear, fresh look; old rice may have insects.

Sugar: For general family use the granulated is the best.

Tea: Equal parts of Japan and green are as good as English breakfast.

Use a cement made of ashes, salt, and water for cracks in the stove.

Variety is the best culinary spice.

Watch your back yard for dirt and bones.

Xantippe was a scold; do not imitate her.

Youth is best preserved by a cheerful temper.

Zinc-lined sinks are better than wooden ones.

GOOD YEAST-POWDER.

Two pounds cream of tartar, one pound carbonate of soda, one pound of seconds of wheat; all well mixed and sifted. Put up in jars or tin boxes.

PICKLE FOR BEEF.

Six gallons of water, three pounds of brown sugar, one quart of molasses, nine pounds of coarse salt, four pounds of fine salt, one ounce of pearlash, and a small quantity of saltpeter. Put the meat in this mixture, and let it remain until the pickle becomes bloody; remove the beef, and boil the pickle until clear. When perfectly cold, return to the beef

PICKLE FOR HAM OR BEEF.

To one hundred pounds of meat take seven pounds of coarse salt, four pounds of brown sugar, two ounces of saltpeter one half ounce of soda, and four gallons of water. Boil and skim the mixture; when cold pour it upon the meat, which should have a weight placed on it to keep it down.

TO KEEP EGGS.

In order to keep well, they must be perfectly fresh when packed. Take a stone pot which will hold from two to three gallons; pack the eggs close, sharp end down; take one pint of unslaked lime, one pint of salt; dissolve in sufficient water to cover the eggs. When cold, pour over. Be sure the eggs do not float. They will keep all the year.

ANOTHER WAY TO KEEP EGGS.

Have a cloth bag that will hold about one dozen eggs; immerse them in boiling milk for any time less than half a minute, and you can keep the eggs as long as you please.

ESSENCE OF GINGER.

Beat in a mortar three fourths of a pound of race ginger; put in a jar, and pour over it one quart of best alcohol. Allow it to stand three weeks; then strain and bottle.

VANILLA EXTRACT.

Five vanilla-beans cut up and two bruised; pour over these one half pint of alcohol. Allow it to steep till the strength is extracted, and bottle.

TO MAKE CREAM.

Mix two tea-spoonfuls of flour, the well-beaten yelks of two eggs, one tea-spoonful of sugar; pour on gradually one pint of boiling milk, stirring constantly to prevent lumps. A small bit of butter is sometimes added. For coffee, beat the white of an egg to a froth; pour the coffee gradually, that it may not curdle.

TO REMOVE MILDEW.

Wet the garment; soap *well;* scrape common chalk on the place until a thick paste is formed; expose to the hot sun.

ANOTHER WAY TO REMOVE MILDEW.

Take two ounces of chloride of lime; pour on it one quart of hot water; then add three quarts of cold water. Steep the linen in this for twelve hours, when every spot will be removed.

ANOTHER WAY TO REMOVE MILDEW.

Darby's Prophylactic Fluid is equally efficacious in removing mildew and some kinds of fruits-tains.

TO RENEW ALPACA.

Black alpacas may be restored to their first beauty by using a thimbleful of borax dissolved in a pint of warm water, and put on with a nail-brush.

TO TAKE OUT GREASE.

One table-spoonful of alcohol and a tea-spoonful of hartshorn.

TO REMOVE STAINS FROM SILK, LINEN, OR COTTON.

Four table-spoonfuls of spirits of ammonia, four of alcohol, and one of salt; shake the whole well in a bottle, and apply with a sponge or tooth-brush. This will remove ink, paint, fruit or acid stains.

ANOTHER WAY TO REMOVE STAINS.

Chloroform will remove paint from a garment, and often restore the original color.

ANOTHER WAY TO REMOVE STAINS.

Wine or fruit stains may be easily removed from table linen by spreading it tightly over a bucket, before soap or cold water is applied, and pouring upon the stained portion a stream of *boiling* water from a kettle. Repeat the operation if necessary.

FOR REMOVING GREASE, STAINS, ETC.

Two ounces castile soap, four ounces aqua ammonia, two drams sal soda, three drams spirits of wine, three drams chloroform. Cut the soap fine, and dissolve with the sal soda in one pint of water; then add another pint of cold water and the other ingredients.

TO WASH COLORED RIBBONS OR CRAVATS.

Make a strong suds of *cold* water and *toilet* soap; wash the ribbons thoroughly until clean; rinse in clean soap-suds. Sometimes it is necessary to rinse several times, *always* in suds When partially dry, iron carefully between cloths, taking care to have the ribbon perfectly smooth. If carefully done, the ribbon will look as good as new.

TO SET COLORS IN CALICO.

To a gallon of very warm (not boiling) brine in a bucket add half a cup of spirits of turpentine. Put in the dress, and see that it is well covered with the mixture; let it soak half an hour or more. If convenient, dry it before washing. Most colors are made permanent by it.

To set blue or green, a little alum should be added to the above mixture.

HOW TO CLEAN BLANKETS.

Put two large table-spoonfuls of borax and a pint of soft soap into a tub of cold water. When dissolved, put in a pair of blankets, and let them remain over night. The next day, rub them out, and rinse in two waters. Hang up to dry *without wringing*. This recipe will also apply to the washing of all kinds of flannel and woolen goods; also of lace curtains. Use *cold* water invariably.

FOR CLEANSING WOOLENS.

One fourth of a pound of white castile soap, one fourth of a pound of ammonia (three ounces), one ounce of ether, one once of spirits of wine. Cut the soap in small pieces, and heat in one quart of soft water until dissolved; then add four quarts of water and the other ingredients. Bottle, and keep well corked.

TO KEEP FLANNEL FROM SHRINKING.

Wash and rinse in *cold* water, and hang in the cold, dry

air. The garment will not shrink or thicken up, but will continue soft and thin to the last. *Never* use *warm* water.

POMATUM.

One heaping table-spoonful of lard, melted; two of castor-oil; two square inches of white wax. Perfume with bergamot while cooling, and stir until cool.

A GOOD TOOTH-WASH

Dissolve two ounces of borax in three pints of boiling water, and before it is cold add one or two tea-spoonfuls of camphor, and bottle for use. A table-spoonful mixed with an equal quantity of tepid water, and applied daily with a soft brush, purifies the teeth, prevents formation of tartar, and induces a healthy action of the gums.

TO REMOVE FRECKLES.

Fifteen grains of borax, one ounce of lemon-juice, one dram of rock-candy. Mix all together, shaking occasionally till dissolved.

TO REMOVE TAN AND SUNBURN.

Six drams of powdered borax, three fourths of an ounce of pure glycerine, twelve ounces of rose-water; mix, and use daily as a cosmetic.

ANOTHER WAY TO REMOVE TAN AND SUNBURN.

The irritation from sunburn may be allayed by washing with a solution of carbonate of soda and water.

HOW TO SAVE YOUR SHOE-SOLES.

Melt together tallow and common rosin in the proportion of two parts of the former to one of the latter, and apply the preparation *hot* to the soles of the boots or shoes,—as much of it as the leather will absorb.

TO STIFFEN COLLARS.

A little gum arabic and common soda added to starch gives extreme stiffness and gloss to shirt-bosoms and collars.

DURABLE STOVE-BLACKING.

By adding a tea-spoonful of pulverized alum to half a package of stove-polish, wet with a little water, much time and labor will be saved. It should be applied when the stove is nearly cold, and rubbed with a dry brush until it is dry and shiny.

TO CLEAN A BROWNED PORCELAIN KETTLE.

Boil peeled Irish potatoes in it. The porcelain will be rendered nearly as white as when new.

TO POLISH FLAT-IRONS.

If they are rough or smoky, lay a little fine salt on a board and rum them well. It will smooth the irons, and keep them from sticking.

EGG STAINS FROM SILVER.

To remove stains on spoons, caused by using them with boiled eggs, take a little common salt, moisten between the thumb and finger, and briskly rub the stain, which will soon disappear.

FOR CLEANING KNIVES.

Rub the knife with sliced Irish potato dipped in knife-brick, and ordinary stains will be easily removed.

TO CLEAN MARBLE.

Take two parts of common soda, one part of pumice-stone, and one part of finely-powdered chalk; sift through a sieve, and mix with water; then rub it well over the marble. After a few minutes, wash the marble with cold water.

SWEEPING.

Wet the broom about once a week in boiling soap-suds; it will last longer and sweep better. Sprinkle a handful of salt on the carpet while sweeping, and it will lessen the dust as well as brighten the colors. Moistened cornmeal sprinkled on the carpet while sweeping will have the same effect; also tea-leaves

A GOOD PASTE.

Make a paste of flour; boil as you would starch, only for a longer time, so that it will be quite thick and well cooked. To a pint of paste add, while boiling, a table-spoonful of pulverized alum.

SEALING FOR BOTTLES.

Nineteen ounces of resin, one ounce of bees-wax. Color with Venetian red.

WHITEWASH.

Take a clean, tight barrel, and slake one bushel of lime by covering it with hot water. After it is slaked, add cold water enough to make it of the consistency of cream, or thick whitewash. Then dissolve in water one pound of sulphate of zinc (white vitriol), and add to the lime and water, with one quart of fine salt; stir wefl until the ingredients are well mixed. This wash is pure white. If a cream-colored wash is desired, add half a pound of yellow ocher.

BRILLIANT WHITEWASH.

Take half a bushel of unslaked lime; slake with boiling water, covering it during the process to keep in the steam. Strain through a fine sieve or strainer, and add a peck of salt previously well dissolved in warm water, three pounds of ground rice boiled to a thin paste, and stirred in boiling hot, half a pound of powdered Spanish whiting, and a pound of clean glue which has been previously dissolved by soaking it well and then hanging it over a slow fire in a small kettle within a larger one filled with water. Add five gallons of hot water to the mixture; stir well, and let it stand a few days covered from the dust. It should be put on quite hot; for this purpose, it may be kept in a kettle on a portable furnace. It is said that a pint of this mixture will cover a square yard of the outside of a house, if properly applied. Brushes more or less small may be used, according to the neatness of the work required. It answers as well as oil-paint for wood, brick, or stone, and is cheaper. It retains its brilliance for years, and is superior to all other whitewashes, for inside or outside walls. Coloring-matter may be put in, and the wash made of any shade you like. Spanish brown stirred in will make it red-pink, more or less deep according to the quantity. A delicate tinge of this is very pretty for inside walls. Finely pulverized common clay well mixed with Spanish brown makes a reddish stone-color. Yellow ocher makes a yellow wash; but chrome yellow goes further, and makes a çolor generally esteemed prettier. Green must *not* be used; the lime destroys the color, and it tends to make the whitewash crack and peel off. If you desire to clean a smoked wall and make it white, squeeze indigo plentifully through a bag into the water you use, before it is stirred into the whole mixture. If a larger quantity than five gallons is required, the same proportions should be observed.

TO DESTROY BED-BUGS.

Take one ounce of quicksilver; beat up in the white of one egg; apply with a feather. Be careful not to let it touch your finger-rings, or anything metallic, as the quicksilver will adhere to it.

Another method of exterminating these repulsive insects is to take grease melted out of salt pork, and apply with a feather to every place where they can hide. Some persons use salt-water to wash the bedstead, and sprinkle salt in the cracks.

TO DESTROY RED ANTS.

Take half a pound of flour of brimstone and four ounces of potash; put them over the fire until united; then beat to a powder. Infuse a little of the powder in water, and wherever you sprinkle it the ants will die or fly the place.

COCKROACH DESTROYER.

Finely-powdered borax sprinkled freely in the crevices, or wherever the roaches are found, will exterminate them. Continue for a few weeks, repeating the sprinkling every few days. It will not fail.

COLIC IN HORSES.

Give one table-spoonful of chloroform in one pint of gruel.

REMEDY FOR BOTTS IN HORSES.

Make a strong decoction of tansy leaves in hot water. Drench the horse with about a quart of this. In about three hours follow with a dose of castor-oil—a small tea-cupful.

REMEDY FOR SICK TURKEY.

When young turkeys seem sick or drooping, give each one a small pill of tar, and after this a teaspoonful of brandy or whisky.

TONIC FOR CHICKENS.

The "Douglas Mixture" is a good constant tonic, and is made thus: One pound of sulphate of iron, two ounces of sulphuric acid, one gallon of water; mix, and dissolve. Dose: One to two tea-spoonfuls to a pint of drinking-water for chickens.

WOUNDS IN CATTLE.

These are quickly cured by washing several times a day with the yelks of eggs and spirits of turpentine.

TO OBTAIN A LARGE YIELD OF MILK.

Give your cow three times a day water slightly warm and slightly salted, in which bran has been stirred at the rate of one quart to two gallons of water. You will find that your cow will gain twenty-five per cent immediately, and will become so fond of the diet as to refuse to drink clear water unless very thirsty; but this mess she will drink at almost any time, and ask for more. The amount of this drink given is an ordinary water-bucketful at each time—morning, noon, and night.

TO TAKE OUT VARNISH, TAR, AND PAINT.

Spirits of turpentine, benzine, or butter, washing out afterward with butter.

To extract resin and turpentine stains, use best alcohol.

TO CLEAN OIL-PAINTINGS.

The following is taken from the *New York Tribune*, which in turn copied it from *The Atlantic*. It can be recommended, as it has been tried with most gratifying results:

Pettenkofer, of Munich, discovered the process, and was awarded by the king of Bavaria with a gift of one hundred thousand francs.

Wash the picture gently, if it is dirty on the surface, with water and a sponge, and wipe quite dry with a soft cloth. Then take a wad of cotton-wool in each hand, one wet with spirits of turpentine, and one dry, and gently rub the surface a bit at a time with the wet cotton, and dry it with the other, changing the cotton as often as it gets dirty. Then get a a box (made of wood for large pictures; card-board will answer for very small ones,) a little larger than the stretching-frame, and about three inches and a half deep. On the bottom, inside, place a layer of cotton batting or coarse blotting-paper half an inch thick or less, and fasten it down with tacks or cross strings, so that it will remain in place when the box is inverted. Lay the picture on the floor or a table, face upward Saturate the cotton or paper with strong alcohol, making it quite wet, but not so as to drip; and then turn the box upside down over the picture. Being a little larger than the picture each way, the box will not touch it, but will rest with its edges on the table or floor. The fumes of the alcohol will dissolve the varnish, penetrate the old coats of it, and clarify the whole.

After the first quarter of an hour, it is well to raise the box a little, and make sure that the paper or cotton does not touch the picture, and that the alcohol is not dripping or running down. The box is to be replaced, and left for about an hour. When it is lifted off again, if the surface be as soft and even and the varnish as clear as when just applied, the operation is finished. If parts are still rough or clouded, the spirits should be renewed, and the box put on again for half an hour, or an hour more, and then the picture may be left to dry, like any newly-varnished one. It may be stood up while drying, as less likely to collect dust.

FURNITURE POLISH.

One pint spirits of turpentine, half pint of sweet-oil, three table-spoonfuls of vinegar, two table-spoonfuls of flour.

COKER'S FURNITURE POLISH.

Twenty one ounces of alcohol, one ounce of oxalic acid, two ounces of gum shellac, fourteen ounces of linseed-oil, two ounces of white resin, two ounces of gum benzine. Dissolve the gums and acids in the alcohol, and let it remain twenty-four hours; then add the linseed-oil.

TO REMOVE WHITE SPOTS FROM FURNITURE.

A hot shovel held over varnished furniture will take out the white spots.

TO CRYSTALLIZE GRASSES.

Take one pound of the best alum, pound it quite fine, and dissolve it in a quart of clear water; but do not let it boil. Take a deep jar or pitcher, and suspend the grasses in it by a string from a stick laid across the top. When the solution is milk-warm, pour it over the grasses, cover it up, and let it stand for twenty-four hours. Then take them out carefully, and let them hang until perfectly dry.

For blue crystals, use a saturated solution of sulphate of copperas in hot water. For yellow crystals, use the yellow prussiate of potash; for ruby, the red prussiate of potash.

ERASIVE SOAP.

Two ounces of aqua ammonia, one ounce of white shaving-soap, one tea-spoonful of saltpeter, one quart of soft water. This recipe is worth ten dollars annually to any family that will try it. The cost is trifling.

GOOD HARD SOAP.

Pour twelve quarts of soft water boiling upon five pounds of unslaked lime; then dissolve five pounds of washing-soda in twelve quarts of boiling water. Mix the above together, and let it stand from twelve to twenty-four hours for chemical action. Now pour off all the clear liquid, being careful not to disturb the sediment. Add to this three and a half pounds of clear grease and three or four pounds of resin. Boil this compound one hour, and pour off to cool; then cut into bars.

SOFT SOAP.

To one pound of concentrated lye add three gallons of soft water. Let it stand ten or twelve hours; then boil a few minutes. Add three pounds of clear grease; boil until the mass is transparent, and all the grease has disappeared

Now add twelve gallons of soft water, boil a few minutes, and the soap will be ready for use. When cold it should be a perfect jelly. If too thick, add water until of the consistency desired.

THE INDEX.